MID-ATLANTIC
BUDGET ANGLER

MID-ATLANTIC
BUDGET ANGLER

Fly-Fishing for Trout in
Delaware • Maryland
New Jersey • Pennsylvania
Virginia • West Virginia

Ann McIntosh

STACKPOLE
BOOKS

Published by
STACKPOLE BOOKS
5067 Ritter Road
Mechanicsburg, PA 17055

Printed in the United States of America

10 9 8 7 6 5 4 3 2 1

First edition

Cover photograph by Douglas Lees

Cover design by Caroline Stover

Maps by David Siegfried

Hatch chart by Al Caucci

Library of Congress Cataloging-in-Publication Data

McIntosh, Ann.
     Mid-Atlantic budget angler / Ann McIntosh.—1st ed.
        p.   cm.
     Includes bibliographical references and index.
     ISBN 0-8117-2851-X
     1. Trout fishing—Middle Atlantic States—Guidebooks. 2. Fly fishing—Middle Atlantic States—Guidebooks. 3. Middle Atlantic States—Guidebooks.
I. Title.
SH688.U6M387   1998
799.1'757'0975—dc21
                                                          97-37985
                                                              CIP

Contents

SECTION FOUR: MARYLAND

SECTION FIVE: VIRGINIA

SECTION SIX: WEST VIRGINIA

*To the owners of destination fly shops in the Mid-Atlantic region
and elsewhere—promoters of sportsmanship,
the cold-water environment,
and the trout.
May all anglers open their hearts and their wallets to them.*

Acknowledgments

First, my deepest appreciation goes to the guides and anglers who fished with me on these trout waters, sharing much information and taking time to review draft material. Second, without Trout Unlimited (TU), both the national office and local chapters, this book would not have been born. At Maryland Trout Unlimited (MDTU), I thank those who supported the initial efforts, including Jay Boynton, Tom Gamper, Jim Gracie, Scott McGill, Richard Shaad, Dave Warnock, and Suzanne Wolff. At national, I thank Charles Gauvin, Pete Rafle, and Ken Mendez for giving me the opportunity to publish *The Budget Angler* as a feature in *TROUT* magazine. Without my friends in my own and other local chapters, my knowledge of trout streams would be paltry indeed.

I will always be grateful to Jack Goellner, former director of the Johns Hopkins University Press, who explained copyright to me; to Nick Lyons, who encouraged me to keep writing a decade ago and who remains my standard for good writing about angling; and to Eric Peper, who, at a moment's notice, helped me out of the tangle of taxonomic typesetting (how to designate the common and scientific names of insects and flies). Doubtless mistakes and inconsistencies remain, but Peper's rationale helped immeasurably.

I thank the following individuals for their help, always graciously given, sometimes more than once. If I have omitted someone, as I'm sure I will, please forgive me.

For information about the Delaware River, Bruce Foster and Al Caucci were patient and supportive, and they've greatly increased my understanding of that complex fishery. Thanks to Jerry Wolland for his advice and enthusiasm. And thanks also to Bob Wills and Jim Serio, two of the best fly shop managers anywhere.

For help on the state of Delaware's modest trout streams, I thank Alex Sansosti for his candor and Judy Laurie for her humor. Kudos to Laura Madara and her colleagues at the Delaware Department of Natural Resources (DNR) for their education programs and doing their best with limited resources.

I would not have been able to portray the big picture in my home state of Maryland without the help of Robert Bachman and his colleagues in the Maryland DNR, Freshwater Fisheries Division: Robert Lunsford, Howard Stinefelt, Charles Gougeon, and Ken Pavol. Along with Jim Gracie, the indefatigable past president of MDTU, and members of TU's Mid-Atlantic Council, these DNR staff members painted the picture for the rest of us to enjoy.

Wally Vait and Stacey Smith at On the Fly in Hereford, Maryland, have been encouraging me in this enterprise for years. So has Joe Bruce at the Fisherman's Edge and all my saltwater fly-flinging guides: Norm Bartlett, Brady Bounds, Kevin Josenhans, and Bo Toepfer. Jim Gilford was most helpful on Big Hunting Creek, as was his son Rob, who owns the Rod Rack in Frederick. Timothy Feeser's help was invaluable in the Westminster area.

I owe much to my friend Douglas Lees, the Virginia angler, photographer, and fisherman who introduced me to the pleasures of Big Hunting Creek and whose experience on the Gunpowder added depth to that chapter. His enthusiasm for the challenge of the Letort Spring Run never dims, no matter how many fishless days he spends on his knees there!

In western Maryland, thanks to Alan Nolan and Harold Harsh of Spring Creek Outfitters in Oakland, who floated my brother and me down the North Branch of the Potomac River, and to Joe Metz, who helped me on the Savage River and other streams in western Maryland.

In New Jersey, Mark Dettmar and Bruce Turner of Delaware River Outfitters in Pennington were the first to come to my aid as I explored the state. Les Shannon, owner of Les Shannon's Fly Shop in Califon and longtime guru of the South Branch of the Raritan, was very helpful, as were Steve Varga, owner of Steve's Bait & Tackle, in Hopewell, and Kevin Wnuck.

Patricia L. Hamilton and Lisa Barno at the New Jersey Bureau of Freshwater Fisheries were tireless in explaining that agency's complex water classification system and trout regulations. Laurie and Hal Curtis and their children, Susanna, Liza, and Parker, made my New Jersey weekends worth looking forward to, regardless of what the trout were doing.

I not only "have a friend in Pennsylvania," as some of the state's license plates read, I have many, and most of them fish! For the Poconos chapter, I will thank my new friend, the other "mature angler," Pat Woodhead, first—she deserves it. But Bob Sentiwany and my friend at the Baltimore *Sun*, Dan Rodricks, also helped immeasurably. For the Allentown chapter, I thank Ed Vatza and his son Mike, Joe Kohler, and the Little Lehigh Fly Shop. Mary Kuss, the Havertown angler, instructor, co-founder of the Delaware Valley Womens Fly Fishing Association

(DVWFFA), and fly fisher *extraordinaire,* gets all the credit for the Philadelphia area streams, as well as for also helping me out in New Jersey and Potter County, Pennsylvania. She is also to be thanked for her infallible ability to cheer me up. I have fished the limestone creeks in southcentral Pennsylvania with many and talked about them with even more individuals. The following come to mind: Dennis Labare (a leader of the Falling Spring Branch restoration), Mark Sturtevant, Douglas Lees, Harrison O'Connor (for his writing about the Letort), and of course, Ed Shenk.

The two chapters about trout streams in central Pennsylvania could not have been written without the encouragement and advice of Allan Bright, the owner of Spruce Creek Outfitters. Allan played an immensely important role during the adolescence of my angling years—that period in my life when I came of age as a fly fisher and learned the value of wild trout, spent time solving problems alone on the water, learned how to match the hatch, enjoyed early-morning angling gossip en route to a Trico hatch, and downed cold beer and burgers at the Twin Oaks Tavern.

Thanks are also in order to Dave Rothrock, a wonderful guide, teacher, and fly tier; Jon Witwer of the Feathered Hook; every died-in-the-wool Pennsylvania angler I ever met at the Millheim Hotel; and Tucker and Jean Morris, who defined angling hospitality for the rest of us B&B owners.

The Pine Creek Valley would not be the angling haven it is without Tom and Deb Finkbiner of Slate Run Tackle and Wolfe's General Store. Farther north, Phil Baldacchino at Kettle Creek Tackle was helpful about that stream. And I shall always be grateful to Dick Hrebar, Duran Knapp, and Bill Haldamann for showing me Potter County.

In western Pennsylvania, Mike Laskowski at Oil Creek Outfitters became a new friend. After a couple seasons of promises, I finally joined Randy Buchanan and Len Lichvar on Yellow Creek, Potter Creek, and the Stonycreek River. I acknowledge them as the best informants of all, and I know we'll fish together often.

I fished in Virginia with Jim Finn, Vann Knighting, Robert Cramer, and Jason Woods, all terrific anglers, all generous with their expertise. The West Virginia chapters could not have been written without David Keene, Charles Heartwell, Jim Martin, John McCoy, Ray Menendez at the West Virginia DNR, Libbo Talbott, and David Thorne, all of whom kept me from losing my way in that state!

Very special thanks to Keith Comstock, proprietor of Cranberry Wilderness Outfitters, and to his colleague Jeromy Rose, the mayor of Richwood, who, if he gets his way, will place trout squarely at the front of the state's political future!

This book could not have been written without the contribution of earlier volumes by three Pennsylvania angling authors, Dwight Landis,

Charles Meck, and Michael Sajna. Their wonderful books on the state's trout streams were an inspiration and a resource throughout this venture.

And finally, words of gratitude to friends and family: Charles Calvarese, who took the time to proofread the material; Peter Duchin, for his Foreword; my brother Dick, who understood why I wanted to write this book; George W. S. Trow, for his constant encouragement and timely advice; and my mother, Grace E. Hower, who is listed last but is really foremost—she kept my garden weeded and in bloom while I completed my research on trout streams.

Foreword

During the cold, dreary winter months, we addicted fly fishermen and women who live in the northeastern part of the United States sometimes indulge in a practice that the late Red Smith called "fly fondling." We sneak down to our basements, open up our collection of fly boxes, and with many furtive glances over our shoulders, start touching, stroking, and rearranging the flies within. Many have never been tied on a leader, many are scruffy and ratty and evoke vivid memories, but each fly is deeply personal, identifiable, and somehow holds unlimited possibilities if cast at the right time in the right place. It's time to call one's fishing buddies or, if one is lucky enough, as I am, to have children who would rather fish than eat, time to start making plans for the opening of the trout season. That is where Ann McIntosh's wonderful book, *Mid-Atlantic Budget Angler*, comes in.

What a great resource this book is! My friend Ann is clearly certifiable on the subject of fishing—she is an addict who very probably has never spent a weekend at home during the fishing season. She has explored every inch of fishable water within a radius of 250 miles of her home in Monkton, Maryland, and written a very detailed and accurate book about it. She tells us where to stay, where to eat, and even suggests what flies to use. She gives us detailed maps of each area, yet somehow never loses sight of the hidden landscapes around her—the complicated and delicate relationships in every stream, and between each stream and the area surrounding it. Nor has she lost sight of the real reason many of us fish—not to catch and kill a fish, but to slow our lives down and become a sentient part of the water and its banks. We notice things we never would have at the normal pace of our lives, and we allow ourselves the luxury of quiet, unhurried observation.

She does not see fly-fishing for trout as competitive in any way—nor do I. I see it as a means of becoming closer to nature in a respectful, even spiritual way. The trout is truly a great fish, and this book will tell you where to find it. You'll be amazed at some of the prolific streams Ann has fished and written about—how close some are to ugly malls and noisy highways, and how some are in a near-wilderness state. But once you find your trout, do release it for the joy of the next fisherman—who might even be you upon your return. Thomas L. Peacock wrote in *The Wise Men of Gotham:*

> In a bowl to sea went wise men three
> On a brilliant night in June;
> They carried a net, and their hearts were set
> On fishing up the moon.

Ann's wonderful book will truly help you to "fish up the moon."

Peter Duchin
Washington, Connecticut
January 28, 1997

Statement

Members of Trout Unlimited's Maryland Chapter have long looked forward to Ann McIntosh's regular newsletter column, but it's only recently that a wider audience has been introduced to "The Budget Angler" through *TROUT* magazine, TU's national quarterly. Even so, in the short time it has graced the pages of *TROUT*, "The Budget Angler" has become easily the best-read column in the magazine. We regularly receive letters from Trout Unlimited members who eagerly await each installment and glowing reports from anglers who have used Ann's meticulous research to plan successful fishing trips to destinations from California to Vermont.

In *Mid-Atlantic Budget Angler*, Ann has done more than review the where, when, and what-size-tippet of the region's best angling spots. She's done it from the viewpoint of a true conservationist, with an eye toward making sure those marvelous streams are here for generations to come. I am proud to say that many of the streams profiled in this volume —notably Maryland's Gunpowder, Pennsylvania's Falling Spring and Letort, Virginia's Mossy Creek, among countless others—have been restored to health, and protected from future harm, to a large extent through the tireless efforts of Trout Unlimited volunteers and other conservation-minded anglers. As you explore the region's angling opportunities, I hope you will follow Ann's example: Fish hard, fish smart, and have fun, but when you're done, give something back to our irreplaceable cold-water fisheries.

Charles Gauvin
Trout Unlimited

Introduction

I've traveled more than 30,000 miles to fish the trout streams in this book, and they are all within 250 miles of my home. I have few family obligations, so I can take weekend excursions frequently. Sometimes I go to unfamiliar trout streams that I've heard about and am eager to explore. Other trips are return visits to favorite waters. Throughout, I remain amazed at the number and quality of our eastern trout fisheries—all located within a few hours of the Boston-Washington coastal megalopolis. On the whole, our trout are not as large or as plentiful as those in western waters, but I doubt there's a trout in Montana that can give me more pleasure than a sixteen-inch wild brown taken on Fishing Creek in central Pennsylvania. Moreover, our trout are less gullible.

Most of my angling education took place on the Barton and Willoughby Rivers in Vermont's Northeast Kingdom. I drove that territory far and wide, exploring streams and learning to fish them. For what I learned, I credit Clay (Landy) Bartlett, who gave me one brief but unforgettable lesson; Mike Chater, my first fishing mentor; Art Lee, whose book *Fishing Dry Flies for Trout on Rivers and Streams* I read in the evenings and tried to put into practice by day; and Diane Wondisford, my best fishing buddy, who gave me Art Lee's book.

Lots of people find it puzzling that I spend so much time away from home fishing streams they've never heard of. They are accustomed to fishing locally or to making excursions to well-known trout waters. I think they miss a lot.

I find the more I travel, the more I see close up—in county after county, for mile after mile—the fragile relationship between our trout streams and our environment. I have an idea that fishing the same kind of country we inhabit, casting on streams that resemble our home waters, provides a visceral understanding of environmental issues. I sympathize intellectually with threatened western rivers, but my heart sinks when I see the effects of acid mine drainage and floods in West Virginia or Pennsylvania.

Most of my journeys are made alone. "You're going fishing alone?" friends say. "That can't be much fun." I explain that all anglers fish alone —once on the water. I enjoy sharing the wheel or dinner conversation as much as anyone, but not at the expense of missing a fishing opportunity. I also like to get to know new people, and I do that better alone.

Many of the new friends I have made own destination fly shops. I've spent hours with them: fishing, eating, reveling, listening to stories and theories. They've tolerated me and provided me with enough flies and suggestions for a thousand years of angling in paradise.

So I abandon my dogs, my garden, and my household duties for weekend angling excursions. These trips give me pleasure as little else will ever do. I hope the reader will be able to use the fruits of my travels, for those that explore the trout resources of the mid-Atlantic will not be disappointed.

ABOUT THIS BOOK

I am not nor will I ever be a professional angler, an expert fly fisher, an entomologist, a tier of flies, a long-distance caster, or an angling instructor. I am an experienced angler with lots to learn, and I intend to remain an amateur in my pursuit of this sport.

Mid-Atlantic Budget Angler began as a series of short features in *Hatch & Match*, the Maryland chapter of Trout Unlimited (TU) newsletter. The response to the column was enthusiastic, and I was particularly pleased when readers saved it for reference. Many commented that they hadn't realized the number of good trout streams in the region. Others found "The Budget Angler" practical for its combination of angling and travel information.

This book is addressed to anglers at all levels of experience. It doesn't attempt to teach or provide technical information (other than some recommendations for which flies to use on the streams). It should help readers plan short fishing trips.

The book is divided into six sections, one for each state. Each section has an introductory overview of angling possibilities in the state. These introductions should be read before jumping from chapter to chapter, as often they illuminate state agency policies and regulations or provide general advice that will make your fishing experience more productive. For New Jersey and West Virginia, a master hatch chart is included in the introduction.

In the course of writing the book, I've met many members of local chapters of TU. There are hundreds more whom I did not meet, but the fruit of whose labors I enjoyed when fishing the trout streams mentioned in this book. They are tireless volunteers engaged in projects to protect and conserve the cold-water resources that our trout need to live. Any reader who wants to give something back to a valued trout stream should join and support his or her local chapter of TU.

BIASES

I will always prefer angling for wild fish rather than stocked trout. Not only do they provide a much greater challenge, but they are also evidence of quality water in a healthy environment.

One cannot fish for trout long without getting interested in cold-water management, stream reclamation, and preserving the habitat that supports our sport. Hence my bias.

I do not expect others to share this bias, and there are many stocked trout waters recommended in this book. I certainly could not have caught many wild trout when I began fishing twenty years ago, and I still have fun fishing for stockies every season. But when there's a choice, I'll take the wild stream.

By the term "wild trout," I mean trout that have been born and raised untended in a stream. If their parents came from hatcheries, but they were spawned in the wild, they are "wild trout."

I prefer to angle under special regulations. Often these are catch-and-release areas that protect fish populations. Whatever the specific rules, I've bought into the philosophy that fish should be returned to water if they can survive and give pleasure to future anglers.

HIRING A GUIDE

Despite the word "budget" in the title of this book, anyone who can afford to do so should hire a guide when first fishing new water—unless there is a local pal to show the way. Guides will get you to the best water quickly, and they will share information to help you on your own. Tackle shop owners know that the better they treat you, the more frequently you will return.

HATCH CHARTS AND LISTS OF FLIES

The lists of effective flies should be used only as guidelines to help prepare for a given trip. Insects emerge at somewhat different times each season, depending on the weather and a variety of other conditions. Contact destination fly shops before you tie up patterns for a trip.

In some instances, I've included a hatch chart with each chapter. In others, I've used one list for an entire state. My decision was based on the variations and complexity of hatches in a given area. Hatches for the sections of New Jersey and West Virginia described in this book are sufficiently similar that to create separate lists for each stream or chapter would be redundant.

Pennsylvania, on the other hand, is huge and has a multiplicity of hatches. So, for example, I've used Allan Bright's chart for Spruce Creek for the central part of the state. But in Potter County to the north, emergence times are sufficiently different to merit another list.

Al Caucci's "Hatch Chart for the Delaware River" contains a list of almost all of the mayflies, stoneflies, caddisflies, and terrestrials an angler will meet in the east. The times that individual species emerge will vary greatly, but the angler who wants to be ready for every occasion can use this comprehensive list as a basis for filling fly boxes.

Every fly angler will improve skills as he or she becomes more knowledgeable about the bugs that provide food for trout. Never pass up the opportunity to learn more about the entomology of a fishery. Nonetheless, I've used few scientific species and subspecies names (the Latin) in this book, as I suspect I would be in error in many instances and only contribute to ignorance. The Latin I do employ is becoming more and more commonly used by fly fishers.

SAFETY PRECAUTIONS

It is not difficult for trout anglers to be safe rather than sorry. But I see many fly fishers wading the water with little concern for their safety. A few safety measures will suffice.

• Always carry a wading staff, particularly if you are fishing new water.

• Always have felt soles on the bottom of whatever boots you wear wading.

• Wear chest waders and a wading belt anywhere you don't know the depth of the water. I've almost abandoned hip boots, so rare is it that I don't have to empty them as a result of taking that one extra step.

• Always wear a hat, or you may end up with your (or someone else's) fly in your head.

• If you're fishing out of sight or hearing of others, carry a whistle so you can signal for help in an emergency.

MANNERS

As more and more anglers fish trout streams, etiquette becomes increasingly important. On popular water, with increasing pressure, the trout are becoming very spooky and you can ruin another angler's stealthy approach.

• Never step into a pool that is being fished by another angler—unless invited to do so.

• Give other anglers *wide* berth. Pass them well away from the banks of streams they are fishing.

• Keep quiet when you are fishing.

• If another angler asks for advice or what fly you are using, help him or her. There is no good reason not to.

MAPS

The maps in this book will help you reach the streams described in the text. However, they are not substitutes for the detailed atlases published by DeLorme Mapping Company, local county maps, or U.S. Forest Service (USFS) maps. There are some access points and other details our scale is unable to include. Always check directions with tackle shops.

TACKLE SHOPS, LODGING, RESTAURANTS

All these businesses come and go. The information provided is accurate to the best of my knowledge at press time. Always check before you go. Be prepared for some establishments to have closed their doors and for new ones to have appeared. When possible, I've listed chambers of commerce that should be able to provide current information.

REGULATIONS

Remember that all angling regulations are subject to annual change, and licenses must be purchased and carried on all trout waters listed in this book. Use the regulations book provided with the license to check current regulations.

KEY TO PRICING CATEGORIES

I've used the following amounts to categorize the lodging and restaurants as inexpensive, moderate, or expensive.

Lodging: Where to Stay
Inexpensive: Single—less than $40; double—$60 and less
Moderate: Single—$40 to $65; double—$61 to $85
Expensive: Single—more than $65; double—$86 and more

Restaurants: Where to Eat
Inexpensive: Meal (breakfast, lunch, or dinner) less than $10
Moderate: Entrees at dinner between $10 and $20
Expensive: Entrees at dinner begin at $15

I have listed telephone numbers for many restaurants. In some cases, however, no number is given because the restaurant does not have a telephone or it is unnecessary to call for reservations.

Pennsylvania

OVERVIEW

The state of Pennsylvania has the largest number of miles of quality trout water in the mid-Atlantic region. It would take more than a lifetime to fish all its good trout streams. I've included a representative sample from several parts of the state, but there are many others that space limitations precluded.

I've often heard well-traveled anglers say that if you can catch wild trout on this state's superb but difficult streams, you can catch them anywhere in the country. The casting is often difficult. You may have to deliver a long, delicate cast directly upstream in narrow six-foot channels; or from your knees, throwing line over long grasses onto still spring water; or shoot a fly several feet beneath tree limbs that almost touch the water. On the better streams, there is significant pressure, resulting in educated fish.

The state's trout management program is complex and includes a number of different water classifications and regulations. The regulations are too complex to enumerate here. Suffice it to say that there seems to be one for every occasion, including "Heritage Trout Angling," "Trophy Trout Projects," and "Miscellaneous Waters—Special Regulations." The state has 1,049 miles of Class A wild trout water. These are streams that sustain native trout reproduction and are not stocked with any species. The biomass criterion for brown trout is thirty-six pounds per acre and twenty-seven pounds per acre for brook trout. Some, but not all, Class A waters are regulated as Catch-and-Release or have creel limits. Others need habitat improvement to fulfill their potential.

In 1996, a partnership developed to enhance wild trout streams. The Coldwater Heritage Partnership Program is a joint effort of Pennsylvania Trout (the fifty-four chapter state council of TU), national TU, the Pennsylvania Fish and Boat Commission, and the Pennsylvania Department of Conservation and Natural Resources. The goal of the program is to protect wild trout by undertaking habitat improvement on a watershed-wide basis, rather than stream by stream or section by section.

Though this systematic approach may seem obvious on its face, it is not. In the past, many stream improvement projects have been undertaken on a stream-section basis, mitigating problems in one area but not in others. With this partnership, restoration decisions will be made after examining problems throughout an entire watershed. Priority consideration for expenditures will be given to streams and watersheds that have the potential to sustain highly productive and naturally reproducing wild trout populations. Streams targeted to receive the more than $50,000 budgeted annually for the program must have the potential for in-stream trout reproduction.

Without question, Pennsylvania is the mecca of mid-Atlantic trout fishing. Its tremendous angling opportunities are an antidote to the envy I feel for those who make frequent extended trips to western waters. All of us in the region have a stake in protecting this state's trout resource.

I am indebted to Al Caucci, who granted me permission to reprint his *Hatch Charts for the West Branch Delaware River, East Branch and Main Stem*, found in chapter 1. Although based on the Delaware River, it includes every significant hatch in the mid-Atlantic region. Savvy anglers will realize that the chart can serve as a guide to hatches on most eastern trout streams included in this book. Just remember that, as the Delaware is on the northern limits of the region, the times at which the various hatches emerge will be affected accordingly.

STATEWIDE RESOURCES

Pennsylvania Fish Commission. 3532 Walnut Street, Harrisburg, Pennsylvania 17106-7000. (717) 657-4518.

Pennsylvania State Parks. 1-800-63-PARKS.

Pennsylvania Department of Environmental Resources. (814) 349-8778.

Pennsylvania Atlas and Gazetteer. DeLorme, P.O. Box 298, Freeport, Maine 04032. (207) 865-4171.

Armstrong, A. Joseph. *Trout Unlimited's Guide to Pennsylvania Limestone Streams*. Harrisburg, Pennsylvania: Stackpole Books, 1992.

Landis, Dwight. *Trout Streams of Pennsylvania: An Angler's Guide*. Revised. Bellefonte, Pennsylvania: Hempstead-Lyndell, 1991.

Meck, Charles A. *Pennsylvania Trout Streams and Their Hatches*. Revised edition. Woodstock, Vermont: Backcountry Publications, 1993.

Sajna, Michael. *Pennsylvania Trout & Salmon Fishing Guide*. Portland, Oregon: Frank Amato Publications, 1988.

Shenk, Ed. *Fly Rod Trouting*. Harrisburg, Pennsylvania: Stackpole Books, 1989.

Pennsylvania Fish and Boat Commission, Publications Section. P.O. Box 67000, Harrisburg, Pennsylvania 17106-7000. (717) 657-4518.

CHAPTER 1

Northeastern Pennsylvania I— The Upper Delaware River: Main Stem ("Big D") from Hancock to Long Eddy, the West Branch, and the East Branch

The East and West Branches of the Delaware River and the upper "Big D" provide the most challenging wild trout fishing in the East. The river is a big, wide, open field of water, bordered by stands of hardwood and evergreens, overgrown meadows, and marshes. A combination of factors makes the angling exceptionally challenging even for the most experienced fisherman.

Understanding the habitat and the hatches is almost as difficult as catching the fish. Throughout the watershed, there are some of the wildest, wariest trout in the country.

The Delaware ranges from fifty to a hundred feet wide on the East and West Branches to three hundred feet wide below Dark Eddy. The river nurtures an average of six hundred trout per mile (rainbows and browns) —a healthy count, but by no means the most numerous in the East.

What makes the watershed exceptional is the abundant rich supply of trout food—the upper Delaware boasts hatches of *every mayfly, caddis, and stonefly found in the eastern United States.* It has more subspecies than any other river in the region. This extensive smorgasbord influences the fish, making them very selective and difficult to fool.

On the Delaware, one must match the hatch *precisely* or leave fishless. With so many varieties of food from which to choose, trout often won't give attractors a glance. There are exceptions, but the best traditional patterns—Coachmen, Patriots, Ausable Wulffs, and so on—are usually snubbed on this water. It is also not unusual for Delaware trout to pass up one natural in favor of another.

THE UPPER "BIG D" FROM HANCOCK TO LONG EDDY
Fish roam so far and wide in the upper main stem that the primary means of locating trout is to look for riseforms. Guides row MacKenzie-style riverboats until they see signs of fish. Then they tell their clients to begin casting. Most of us mess up the initial cast and learn the Delaware lesson the hard way: There are no second chances. One must be able to

3

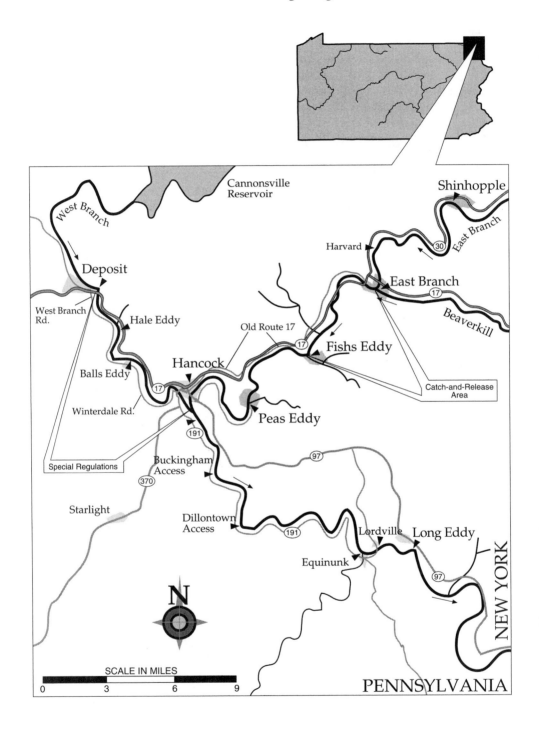

place the fly precisely, accurately, and delicately in a feeding lane to fool a wild Delaware trout.

The prize trout on the "Big D" is the wild rainbow. This species was accidentally introduced into the main stem more than a century ago. In the 1880s, Dan Cahill, a railroad brakeman and avid angler, was carrying young fish to stock in the coldest part of the river—the West Branch. But the train broke down at Calicoon, more than thirty river miles below his destination, and he had to release the fish.

These trout were transported from California's McCloud River, where a strain of warm-water tolerant rainbows had been developed. At the time, there were no reservoirs on the East and West Branches, and the Delaware was primarily a warm-water fishery. The river at Calicoon was noted for walleye and smallmouth bass fishing. But the rainbows surprised Cahill and his colleagues: Once released, they were able to tolerate the warm water and took hold. The strain proved a strong one, and we hunt their descendants today. By the time the dams were built and the cold water began to flow, the 'bows thrived, becoming more numerous than ever.

Brown trout, on the other hand, were not introduced to the Delaware until after the cold-water habitat was in place, after the Cannonsville and Pepacton Reservoirs were created in the mid-1950s. Therefore, brown trout did not develop a tolerance for water above 72 degrees Fahrenheit for more than a few days, having never had to adapt as Cahill's rainbows did. Thus, while brown trout tolerate higher water temperatures better than rainbows on most rivers, the reverse is true on the Delaware.

In addition to its rich bug life and wild trout, the Delaware boasts a number of very big fish. Fry and fingerlings grow up in deep swift water, quickly developing into fit muscular adults. Al Caucci, coauthor of *Hatches* and *Hatches II* and coproprietor of the Delaware River Club, says that he has fished all over the East and most of the West and has never had trout fight as hard as those in the Delaware, not even on the Missouri. These fish also have unusual stamina. Once past the surprise of being hooked, they seem oblivious to opposition at the other end of the line. It's common to have a sixteen-inch fish take you into the backing. Bruce Foster, my guide, timed me playing an eighteen-inch rainbow: It took twenty-five minutes to lead the fish to his net, and it sped off energetically when released.

Floating the "Big D" from Hancock to Long Eddy

The main stem of the Delaware starts at the confluence of the East and West Branches just above Hancock, New York, across the river from Starlight, Pennsylvania. Floating the Delaware from Hancock to Long Eddy is reminiscent of a western angling experience. On my first trip, I accompanied Bruce and the amiable Ed Hornung. We put the boat in at

11:00 A.M. at the Buckingham public access launch and took out at 9:30 P.M. in Long Eddy, a tiny hamlet ten miles downstream.

Although it was the Friday of Memorial Day weekend, the trip was a near-wilderness experience. Along these ten miles, the river runs within waving distance of only three isolated hamlets in the river plain. In places, I could see up- and downstream for a mile with nothing but uncut brush, hardwoods, evergreens, and water to obstruct my view. We saw only four other boats and an occasional lone angler fishing from the bank.

I hooked my first Delaware River rainbow two miles upstream of Long Eddy. I was wading off reedy marshes full of big golden stonefly nymphs. The trout took one of Bruce's sulphur emergers, as I recall. My memory is consumed by its first long run (perhaps fifty yards), and the run after that (maybe thirty yards), and the one after that, until—after nearly half an hour—I dragged the fish to net.

That first trip was a good but not overwhelming float experience, according to Delaware regulars. The only major disappointment was that Bruce had timed the float to put us on an exceptionally active pool for the sulphur hatch at dusk. We arrived on time, tied on our emergers, and sat back to wait for the hatch. We talked and waited, cast blindly and waited some more, sighed and had a glass of wine, still hopeful. The hatch never materialized. It had done so the preceding day and likely it would do so the next.

My next Delaware float was earlier in the season, scheduled for the Hendrickson hatch. This time my partner was Mary Kuss, an angling instructor from Philadelphia. Bruce had called a few days earlier to warn that the water was very high and cold. He suggested postponing the trip. Then he called the day before we were to leave, reporting that the fish were "taking the ladies"—the light Hendricksons. He had turned rocks and found lots of nymphs. He was optimistic about our trip, despite the high water.

While waiting to launch at Hancock, I saw a number of rising fish, apparently taking small blue-winged olives. It was a balmy overcast day, and I anticipated great fishing.

The scenery was as magnificent as on the preceding trip. I relaxed into the bow, setting my rod down while Bruce looked for working fish.

Mary was not as laid back. She had never floated the Delaware before and was eager to fish. After trying numerous caddis patterns (imitating the thousands of downwings coming off the water), she tied on a brown-and-black Woolly Bugger and drifted it through deep runs and riffles. Still nothing happened. We'd seen one rise all morning, and by the time we got within sixty feet of it, the fish had stopped feeding.

We were slipping down the middle of the river when Mary spotted a second rise. She drifted a Hendrickson emerger deftly over the trout and it took. Twenty minutes later, a sixteen-inch brown was in hand, posing for a picture. We thought a good time was developing.

But that day, the Hendrickson hatches never took off, and the fish continued to snub our caddis flies. None of the other boats had any luck either. Mary remembers the day fondly, calling the big brown her $135 fish (her part of the trip fee). There is no definitive explanation for such piscatorial behavior, but I'll settle for Al Caucci's. "I'll bet the water never reached 55 degrees today," he said, meaning the water temperature wasn't warm enough to trigger the Hendrickson hatches.

I remained in the area a couple more days waiting for the water to drop and warm. Cruising the pull-offs along the West Branch the next day, I interviewed seven anglers, none of whom had had any luck. Soon more rain and cold weather developed, and the season Caucci dubbed "the spring from hell" marched on into summer.

Two Notes about the "Big D"
At Equinunk, Equinunk Creek empties into the main stem. This twenty-five-foot-wide stream is a good alternative fishery in the spring when the water is too high to fish elsewhere. The village of Equinunk is worth a stop. There's a historical society, church, general store, and a few decrepit houses. Access is on SR4007 off Route 191.

While shad lie outside the scope of this book, I would be remiss not to mention the outstanding shad fishing on the upper Delaware from mid-April through May. There are a number of hot spots on the "Big D," and also on the East and West Branches. (The tackle shops listed below can provide detailed information.)

Regulations on the "Big D"
No-kill, Catch-and-Release angling with artificials and flies only is now permitted from October 1 through Opening Day of the next season (mid-April) on the main stem of the Delaware, beginning at the confluence of the East and West Branches just above Hancock, New York.

From Opening Day (mid-April) to September 30, one trout fourteen inches or longer may be kept per day.

Access: The "Big D" from Hancock to Long Eddy
On the New York side, there are a few pull-offs along Route 97 south of Hancock. On the Pennsylvania side, Route 191 runs along the river, and the Pennsylvania Fish Commission maintains several large access areas:
- 1.8 miles downstream of the Hancock Bridge.
- Buckingham access. (The stretch downstream from the boat put-in is known as Shangri-La. It's a good place to fish from the banks; there's a long stretch of accessible productive water.)

- Dillontown access.
- Equinunk (access for the wading angler, but not as easy to reach on foot).
- The Lordville Bridge (a very popular spot to wade).
- Long Eddy access.

There is private land along many of the banks of the Delaware. Please do not trespass. Ask permission and obey posted signs.

Hatch Matching on the Delaware

No other river east of the Mississippi has hatches as prolific as those of the Delaware. After asking various knowledgeable Delaware anglers to explain the basis of this rich environment and becoming overwhelmed with contradictory and inconsistent explanations, I asked Al Caucci for his help. He explained:

> Both the East and West Branches used to be rich bass streams with a high pH alkaline content. Now that the sources are icy cold bottom releases from both reservoirs, excellent bass water has been turned into a very rich trout system, especially in the West Branch and the main stem, which benefit from heavy cold releases from the Cannonsville Reservoir. If the supply of cold water were ever to be cut back or shut down, it would endanger the whole upper Delaware system.

The Delaware is home to well-fed, privileged trout that can afford to be picky. Their buffet is constantly replenished and always fresh. They take exactly what they want, where they want, when they want it. Delaware trout will spurn an entire family of bugs one day and eagerly feed on a subspecies the next.

There at least forty major emergences on the Delaware between February and November. Caucci and his colleagues have identified six subspecies of Hendricksons *(Ephemerella subvaria)*, and they provide patterns to imitate each.

The Delaware River Club professionals call the insects by their Latin names for purposes of accuracy and to differentiate among genera, species, subspecies, and common names or names of imitation patterns. This approach is not pretentious; it is the only scientifically accurate way to make clear which insect is being named.

In addition to mayflies, there are abundant stoneflies, caddis, and terrestrials. The Delaware defines the concepts "specific hatch" and "hatch matching." To fish this water, an angler must identify and attempt to match the stage of emergence of a particular insect as closely as possible.

There can be three or four species coming off the water simultaneously, and the fish may be interested only in a particular stage of one of them. Anglers should educate themselves about the different stages of insects and likely emergence times. The Delaware River Club Fly Shop carries imitations of all the major and minor hatches, including flies imitating the stages of each emergence (nymphs, emergers, duns, and spinners).

Despite the respect I have for the Delaware, it has some drawbacks. Catching these fish requires experience and skill. The neophyte, unless significantly more knowledgeable than I was when I began, will quickly feel frustrated, helpless, and stupid. Beginning anglers should seek help. Invest in a guide, take a lesson, or find an experienced Delaware angler to take you under his or her wing. There may be a lot of room for sloppy casting on this water, but you never know when your continued flailing may be putting fish down. Despite its size, the river demands stealth, respectful presentation, and knowledge of the hatch activity on a given day.

Fishing the Delaware—whether casting from a boat or from shore—is notoriously unpredictable. Until I consulted Al Caucci, I thought the fish were picky, finicky, and temperamental. For no reason *I* could discern, I'd seen fish ignore one natural and take another or gulp one bug for breakfast today and not again until supper tomorrow.

Caucci explains that *fish key onto the most vulnerable insects on the water,* taking the bugs that are easiest to catch. For instance, a particular hatch may materialize on a cool, overcast summer afternoon. Unable to dry their wings and take off as quickly as on hot days, flies stay on top of the water longer than usual, making them more vulnerable to the fish. The Delaware constantly demands this sort of technical observation and savvy fishing.

Because the most efficient way to find fish is to hunt for rising trout, guides generally prefer dry-fly angling to nymphing or using wet flies. (All admit that some very fine specimens have been taken on these as well.) Because there is a huge expanse of holding water and many lies, the fish do not congregate in any one place for very long. They cruise in pods and are difficult to locate from one day to the next. Nymphs and streamers can be cast for hours without ever being seen by a trout. By presenting an emerger or dry to a riseform, on the other hand, one is at least certain of a target. Anglers very familiar with the river know good places to cast subsurface, but they do this only when nothing is showing on top.

I once took a trout drifting a nymph through a fishy-looking riffle. I was using a tandem system with a beadhead Pheasant-tail nymph on the bottom and a Patriot as the top fly. Bruce Foster was at the oars, explaining in full voice the folly of nymphing on the Delaware. "You just can't tell if the fish are there, so why drift a nymph through the water? There's too much of it," Foster said. "You've got to wait till they show themselves

Al Caucci Hatch Charts for the West Branch Delaware River, East Branch and Main Stem

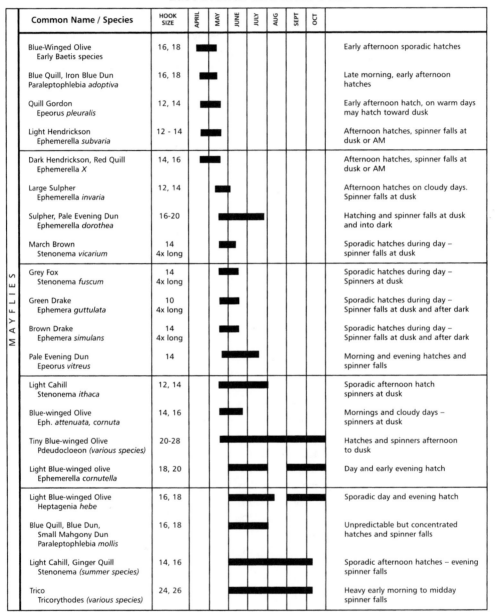

Common Name / Species	HOOK SIZE	APRIL	MAY	JUNE	JULY	AUG	SEPT	OCT	
Blue-Winged Olive Early Baetis species	16, 18								Early afternoon sporadic hatches
Blue Quill, Iron Blue Dun Paraleptophlebia *adoptiva*	16, 18								Late morning, early afternoon hatches
Quill Gordon Epeorus *pleuralis*	12, 14								Early afternoon hatch, on warm days may hatch toward dusk
Light Hendrickson Ephemerella *subvaria*	12 - 14								Afternoon hatches, spinner falls at dusk or AM
Dark Hendrickson, Red Quill Ephemerella *X*	14, 16								Afternoon hatches, spinner falls at dusk or AM
Large Sulpher Ephemerella *invaria*	12, 14								Afternoon hatches on cloudy days. Spinner falls at dusk
Sulpher, Pale Evening Dun Ephemerella *dorothea*	16-20								Hatching and spinner falls at dusk and into dark
March Brown Stenonema *vicarium*	14 4x long								Sporadic hatches during day – spinner falls at dusk
Grey Fox Stenonema *fuscum*	14 4x long								Sporadic hatches during day – Spinners at dusk
Green Drake Ephemera *guttulata*	10 4x long								Sporadic hatches during day – Spinner falls at dusk and after dark
Brown Drake Ephemera *simulans*	14 4x long								Sporadic hatches during day – Spinner falls at dusk and after dark
Pale Evening Dun Epeorus *vitreus*	14								Morning and evening hatches and spinner falls
Light Cahill Stenonema *ithaca*	12, 14								Sporadic afternoon hatch spinners at dusk
Blue-winged Olive Eph. *attenuata, cornuta*	14, 16								Mornings and cloudy days – spinners at dusk
Tiny Blue-winged Olive Pdeudocloeon *(various species)*	20-28								Hatches and spinners afternoon to dusk
Light Blue-winged olive Ephemerella *cornutella*	18, 20								Day and early evening hatch
Light Blue-winged Olive Heptagenia *hebe*	16, 18								Sporadic day and evening hatch
Blue Quill, Blue Dun, Small Mahgony Dun Paraleptophlebia *mollis*	16, 18								Unpredictable but concentrated hatches and spinner falls
Light Cahill, Ginger Quill Stenonema *(summer species)*	14, 16								Sporadic afternoon hatches – evening spinner falls
Trico Tricorythodes *(various species)*	24, 26								Heavy early morning to midday spinner falls

MAYFLIES

Al Caucci Hatch Charts for the West Branch Delaware River, East Branch and Main Stem

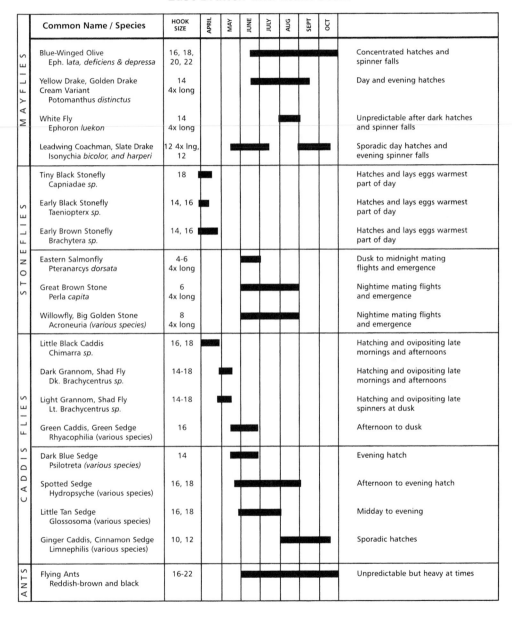

	Common Name / Species	HOOK SIZE	APRIL	MAY	JUNE	JULY	AUG	SEPT	OCT	
M A Y F L I E S	Blue-Winged Olive Eph. *lata, deficiens & depressa*	16, 18, 20, 22								Concentrated hatches and spinner falls
	Yellow Drake, Golden Drake Cream Variant Potomanthus *distinctus*	14 4x long								Day and evening hatches
	White Fly Ephoron *luekon*	14 4x long								Unpredictable after dark hatches and spinner falls
	Leadwing Coachman, Slate Drake Isonychia *bicolor, and harperi*	12 4x lng, 12								Sporadic day hatches and evening spinner falls
S T O N E F L I E S	Tiny Black Stonefly Capniadae *sp.*	18								Hatches and lays eggs warmest part of day
	Early Black Stonefly Taeniopterx *sp.*	14, 16								Hatches and lays eggs warmest part of day
	Early Brown Stonefly Brachytera *sp.*	14, 16								Hatches and lays eggs warmest part of day
	Eastern Salmonfly Pteranarcys *dorsata*	4-6 4x long								Dusk to midnight mating flights and emergence
	Great Brown Stone Perla *capita*	6 4x long								Nightime mating flights and emergence
	Willowfly, Big Golden Stone Acroneuria *(various species)*	8 4x long								Nightime mating flights and emergence
C A D D I S F L I E S	Little Black Caddis Chimarra *sp.*	16, 18								Hatching and ovipositing late mornings and afternoons
	Dark Grannom, Shad Fly Dk. Brachycentrus *sp.*	14-18								Hatching and ovipositing late mornings and afternoons
	Light Grannom, Shad Fly Lt. Brachycentrus *sp.*	14-18								Hatching and ovipositing late spinners at dusk
	Green Caddis, Green Sedge Rhyacophilia (various species)	16								Afternoon to dusk
	Dark Blue Sedge Psilotreta *(various species)*	14								Evening hatch
	Spotted Sedge Hydropsyche (various species)	16, 18								Afternoon to evening hatch
	Little Tan Sedge Glossosoma (various species)	16, 18								Midday to evening
	Ginger Caddis, Cinnamon Sedge Limnephilis (various species)	10, 12								Sporadic hatches
A N T S	Flying Ants Reddish-brown and black	16-22								Unpredictable but heavy at times

and then go after them." A bump returned my attention to my rod, and I reeled in a twelve-inch rainbow. Bruce never missed a beat. "See that," he said. "Nice little fish. Another thing: Don't get cocky and make rules about this river—it'll prove you wrong as soon as you do!"

Careful presentation is important on the Delaware. Although the top of the water is textured, it is also very clear and the fish are extremely wary—particularly about coming up for an imitation. Caucci developed the Compara-dun pattern to duplicate the naturals *in* the surface film rather than *on top of it.* The Compara-dun, Compara-emerger, and Compara-spinner look vulnerable like the natural.

Best Time to Fish the "Big D"

Water level and temperature are the two primary factors to consider when planning a trip to the Delaware. Caucci's rule of thumb: In the early part of the season (April), wait until the water recedes and its temperature is 50 to 55 degrees Fahrenheit for a few days. This will trigger good hatches and rising fish.

The timing of cold-water releases from the reservoirs is also important. Try to avoid periods of very high or very low water, and be mindful of summer droughts. There is a regulated flow of cold water from the bottom of Cannonsville Reservoir—three hundred cubic feet per second between June 15 and August 15—to help the trout withstand summer droughts. The New York State Department of Environmental Conservation also releases cold water any time the water reaches the low seventies and threatens trout survival.

When the first cold releases occur, the trout and the bugs seem stunned by the change. It takes several days for both to acclimate and return to normal hatching and feeding activity. By the time summer arrives, they are more used to frequent temperature changes and feed with greater regularity.

To avoid the disappointment and frustration of ending a Delaware River trip empty-handed, I recommend a three-day minimum stay—one of the days devoted to a float. Jerry Wolland, Caucci's partner, emphasizes, "You just don't come up here and catch good fish in one day. You have to spend a lot of time waiting for the magnificent moments." And do not approach this water anticipating catching lots of fish. A day that brings three or four fish between sixteen and twenty inches is something to be proud of here. Unless there is uncommonly bad weather or a severe drought, three days will provide sufficient chances for one or two outstanding experiences.

Which hatch or hatches anglers should select is largely a matter of personal preference. The green and brown drakes are phenomenal, and despite the hatch's popularity, there's plenty of water to absorb angling pressure. Bruce Foster says that if forced to choose his personal preference, it would probably be the early-season Hendricksons and the brown drakes later on.

Though I cannot resist a spring weekend on the Delaware, my wiser self prefers the fall fishing (September and October). The weather is more reliable, and the water temperatures are stable.

Moreover, there are fewer anglers. Cold-water releases keep the West Branch and the main stem fishing well throughout most summers. Insect activity continues unabated.

Equipment for the Delaware

It's a good idea to carry an $8 \, 1/2$- or 9-foot rod (5/6-weight line) rigged with a weight-forward floating line and an extra reel spooled with a 6- or 7-weight sinking-tip line. In summer at midday, when there are few hatches or rising trout, the sinking tip will make it easier to get streamers, stoneflies, and big nymphs down to trout on the bottom.

THE WEST BRANCH

The West Branch has not been stocked by the state since 1994. The record trout taken on a fly is a thirty-three-inch brown caught in 1996. It probably fattened up in the Cannonsville Reservoir and slipped out into the river.

The most fun I've had on the West Branch was fishing Jimmy Charron's alewife streamer on the special regulations section near Deposit, New York. It was early on a drizzly September morning, and my friend Diane Wondisford and I were fishing together. We saw fish smashing something big, near—but not on—the top of the water. We couldn't figure out what it was. It certainly wasn't any of the bugs we saw hatching. But the fish kept on devouring it. We were puzzled and frustrated, because these were big fish and not at all cautious.

When it began to rain hard, we left the water to visit local fly shops. At the Delaware River Club, Jerry Wolland listened to our tale.

"Stop! Stop!" Jerry said, holding up a silencing finger. "I've got just what you need. I've got it right here." He handed us Charron's alewife pattern. "Do you know what that is? No, of course you don't. It's an alewife; there are hundreds of them washing out of the bottom of the dam, floating dead on top. The trout just love 'em. Fish it on top now."

The next morning, Diane and I went back to Deposit and tied on our alewives. After we figured out how to present them in a drag-free drift, we took three nice (fourteen inches or longer) trout each. It was one of those rare and wonderful moments on the Delaware, in touch with the fish and landing the big ones! Since that time, I always take alewives in my arsenal when going to unfamiliar tailwaters.

When to Fish the West Branch

The prime season on the West Branch is from April 15 through August. September and October can be the best months of all, especially in years when releases from the Cannonsville Reservoir are consistent and there has been no major drought.

In addition to the special regulations section at Deposit, I enjoy fishing the river along West Branch Road from Balls Eddy to Hale Eddy. Except where pull-offs are near the roads, I haven't experienced much fishing pressure—even on holiday weekends—and I find it easy enough to walk fifteen minutes and be alone on the water. This is a very scenic area, and there is no stretch of unproductive water.

The West Branch and upper Delaware can be very difficult to fish in years where there has been little snowfall or spring rain. Dick Jogodnick, an experienced Delaware angler, reported one May that the upper Delaware was very hard to fish. He found the water very low, the fish in hiding, and a lack of flies on the water. Under these conditions, he suggests fishing near Hale Eddy (park near the bridge that is out, walk upstream along railroad tracks, then drop down to the river). Or try the Deposit Catch-and-Release area.

West Branch Regulations

From the Pennsylvania–New York border downstream to its confluence with the East Branch, artificial lures or flies only are permitted on the West Branch from October 1 to Opening Day of trout season. All trout hooked must be released immediately. From Opening Day (mid-April) through September 30, two trout twelve inches or longer may be kept per day.

West Branch Access

Most of the land along West Branch Road from Balls Eddy to Hale Eddy is public. There are pull-offs and parking areas along the road. Take Pennsylvania Route 191 west of the Hancock Bridge and travel upriver along Winterdale Road (the first road north on the west side of the bridge). The road runs along the west side of the West Branch to Balls Eddy. Then continue on West Branch Road, a dirt road that follows the river beyond Hale Eddy. There are numerous pull-offs along the way.

The Delaware River Club owns two miles of streambank along the Delaware beginning two miles upstream of the junction of the East and West Branches. Guests and school attendees have access to the river.

Direct private access is also possible for guests at the West Branch Angler. I've stayed in one of the log cabins on the banks of the river and caught fish just beyond the front porch, although the angling was better two hundred yards downstream.

To access the river from the Deposit side, take a right after the bridge near the paper mill, drive along the river a few hundred yards, and park in the lot designated for anglers. Fish upstream or down. This is where I had my alewife experience.

THE EAST BRANCH
The East Branch fishes best from early April through mid-June and again from mid-September through late October. (It also provides excellent sport for shad from mid-April to mid-May.) The releases from the Pepacton Reservoir are not regulated, but the water comes out of the bottom at an average temperature of 42 degrees Fahrenheit. The lower East Branch can get too warm for trout by mid-June.

Brown and rainbow trout are stocked in the East Branch. There are numerous brook trout in the upper reaches (from Shinhopple to Downsville), and wild and holdover browns coexist with their stocked brethren.

The East Branch gains cover and looks more attractive and fishy as one drives up the river along old Route 17. Above the town of East Branch (near the mouth of the Beaverkill), it changes from flat open water to smaller reaches overhung with hardwoods and hemlocks.

According to Larry Duckwall, a noted Catskill fly tier and angler, water quality in the East Branch is good. There is a healthy pH level, and although there are long stretches without cover, there is enough shade to help keep water temperatures down. Nonetheless, the East Branch is not at its best in midsummer.

Like the rest of the watershed, the East Branch has rich hatches. All the standard early-season mayflies come off here. Duckwall's personal preference is the Hendrickson *(Ephemerella subvaria)* emergence in spring, closely followed by hatches of insects imitated by Quill Gordons, March Browns, and little blue dun patterns. Before the early-season hatches commence, hatches of little black and little brown stoneflies appear on sunny days in February.

Al Carpenter, Sr., owner of Al's Wild Trout Ltd. at Shinhopple, imparts a wealth of information about the upper East Branch. He emphasizes the numbers of wild brook trout in the river, advising anglers to fish for them from the village of Corbett upstream to the Pepacton Dam. The record East Branch brook trout was twenty inches long, taken above Shinhopple in 1996. In April 1992, a ten-pound, twenty-nine-inch brown was taken in the same area.

I have explored the East Branch more extensively by car than by water. During the limited time I had to fish there, East Branch angling was thwarted by high-water conditions. Nonetheless, I was intrigued by the water—slick as a big spring creek through long reaches in the upper section.

On one of the days I was unable to wade the East Branch, I took the opportunity to explore. I drove out of Hancock on Old Route 17 and turned onto a dirt road, following a small wooden arrow sign that read, "Smokehouse." My objective was to stay close to the water and identify access areas. The road soon narrowed to a rutted track. Low-hanging evergreens scraped my windshield. I could barely see the deep-green pools of the East Branch.

After several wrong and confused turns, I came to the smokehouse. Under the hemlocks, a faded blue sedan sat on cinder blocks and a repainted, dull black Buick rested nearby. A sorrel cur yapped on a chain while a larger black dog growled in the bush. Over the big dog's back, I could see dimples of rising trout on the green pools.

The smoker emerged from the smokehouse, wiping his hands on a dirty apron. "Can I help . . . ? Shut *up*, Abigail." He combed his beard with his fingers. The hound slunk behind his knees. "What can I do for you?" "I hope I am not . . . I would like to see what you sell," I said, barely able to take my eyes from the rising fish. I could not ask permission to fish, for I had already spotted three Posted—No Trespassing signs on the homestead.

The smoker, Ray Turner, led me into a small front office. I tasted smoked eel and smoked trout and collected mail order forms. We chatted about the nasty weather and high water until he returned to his oven. I took home smoked eels, trout, and turkey. I've since discovered the Smoke House (Delaware River Delicacies) has a reputation far wider than the remote little plant suggests. It's definitely worth a detour.

East Branch Regulations

Anglers are required to have a New York State license to fish the East Branch. Catch-and-Release regulations apply, and artificial lures, flies, and single barbless hooks only may be used from the bridge at the town of East Branch downstream to the Fishs Eddy Bridge (below the mouth of the Beaverkill) from October 1 to the end of November. (Note: These regulations may soon change.) The stretch from Corbett Bridge upstream to the Pepacton Dam is closed September 30 to protect spawning activity. From April 1 to September 30, one trout twelve to fourteen inches in length may be kept per day.

East Branch Access

Take Old Route 17 northeast out of Hancock. The East Branch runs parallel to the road. You can cross land to the water anywhere that is not posted:

• Near the junction of Old Route 17 and new Route 17, northeast of Hancock. Watch out for very strong currents here in the early part of the season.

• At the village of East Branch. Wade the river or put a boat over the bank.

- At the hamlet of Harvard.
- At Shinhopple.

IF YOU GO . . .
From New York City, take Route 17 west toward Binghamton to Hancock, New York. Take exit 87A or 87 to Hancock. This is a two-and-a-half-hour trip.

From Philadelphia, it is about three hours to Hancock. Take the Northeast Extension of the Pennsylvania Turnpike to Route 81 north above Scranton, then take Route 374 (exit 64). Take Route 674 east to Route 171 north to the bridge crossing the Delaware into Hancock, New York.

From the Baltimore-Washington area, the trip takes four and a half to five and a half-hours, depending on the starting point. Take I-83 north to Harrisburg, then I-81 to Wilkes-Barre and Scranton. Pick up Route 9, a bypass around Scranton, and return to I-81. Continue north on I-81 to Route 374. Take Route 374 east to Route 171 north to Route 370 east to Route 191 across the bridge from Hancock. Alternate route: Take I-95 to Route 476 (Blue Route) in Philadelphia to the Northeast Extension of the Pennsylvania Turnpike to Route 81 north at Scranton (see above).

From Pittsburgh and points west, take I-80 east to I-81 north and follow directions from Scranton (see above).

Tackle Shops and Guides
Al Caucci's Delaware River Club Fly Shop. Starlight, Pennsylvania. Two miles of private access to the Delaware River. Fly shop, nationally famous fly-fishing schools, guides, private campground, hunting (including bow hunting for white-tailed deer, turkey, and black bear). 1-800-6-MAYFLY.

Gray Ghost Guides & Flies. Hancock, New York. Jim Sirio, proprietor. (607) 637-3474.

Al's Wild Trout Ltd. Shinhopple, New York, on the East Branch. Tackle, flies. Al Carpenter, Sr., knows the East Branch well. Stop here for good conversation and advice. (607) 363-7135.

Delaware River Fly & Tackle. Hancock, Pennsylvania. This shop is on the Pennsylvania side of the Hancock Bridge on Route 191. It is owned by West Branch Angler. (607) 635-5983.

Bruce Foster. Hancock, New York, and Grasonville, Maryland. Foster is one of the most successful guides on the upper Delaware. A native of Kent Island, Maryland, Bruce also guides up and down the East Coast for salt- and freshwater species. (410) 827-6933.

Indian Springs Camp. Lordville, Pennsylvania. Lee Hartman, proprietor and guide. This establishment is several miles downstream from Hancock, near the Lordville Bridge and some of the best fishing on the

Big D. Hartman is a respected upper Delaware angler. One-on-one lessons, guide service (floating or wading). (215) 679-5022.

Mr. Moose (aka Roger Stewart). Starlight, Pennsylvania. Float trips. Mr. Moose is the eternal optimist, a bearded jovial fellow. Don't underestimate his knowledge of the river. Available April and May only. (717) 635-5971.

Pat Schuler. Float trip guide, Starlight, Pennsylvania. Co-owner of the Starlight Lodge (see below), Pat floats the river himself or finds other guides to accommodate his guests. (717) 798-2350.

West Branch Angler. Deposit, New York. Full-service tackle shop and guide service. Trips on the Beaverkill and Willowemoc as well as the Delaware. Excellent fly selection. (607) 467-5525 or (607) 467-2215.

If you plan to float the river, guides advise bringing the following gear in addition to tackle: cold drinks and lunch (in a cooler), polarized sunglasses, wide-brim hat, heavy and lightweight shirts, flashlight, rain jacket, sunblock, and insect repellent.

Where to Stay

Capra Inn. Hancock, New York. Recently renovated motel. Simple, clean, and convenient. Inexpensive. (607) 637-1600.

Delaware River Club. Starlight, Pennsylvania. Cabins with kitchenettes; lodge with single and double rooms. Motel suites with one and two rooms. Moderate. 1-800-6-MAYFLY.

Indian Springs Camp. Lordville, Pennsylvania. Lee Hartman, proprietor and guide. Well-equipped cabins near the Lordville Bridge. Lodging rates based on fishing packages. Moderate. (215) 679-5022.

Inn at Starlight Lake. Starlight, Pennsylvania. A year-round Modified American Plan (MAP) traditional Pocono country inn serving breakfast and dinner. Fourteen rooms; ten cottages. Tennis, biking, hiking, and convenient to trout fishing. A nice place to take family or nonangling spouses, and a good place for dinner after a long day on the river. Moderately expensive. 1-800-248-2519 or (717) 798-2519.

Smith Colonial Motel. Hancock, New York. Two miles south of Hancock, New York on Route 97. Inexpensive. (607) 637-2989.

Starlight Lodge. Starlight, Pennsylvania. Beth and Pat Schuler operate this B&B. The large log cabin house has four attractively appointed guest rooms with private baths. Superb food and hospitality. Moderate. (717) 798-2350.

Step-A-Way B&B. Long Eddy, New York. Off Route 97. Two-story Victorian farmhouse. Inexpensive. Attractive house and a cabin. Good getaway with hunting, hiking, biking nearby. (914) 887-4078.

West Branch Angler and Sportsmen's Resort. Deposit, New York. On the west bank of the West Branch between Hancock and Deposit. Lodge, cabins, breakfast, dinner served Thursday, Friday, and Saturday. Cabins have air conditioning, cable TV. Moderate to expensive. (607) 467-5525. (See also tackle shops, above.)

White Pillars Inn B&B. Deposit, New York. Convenient to the special regulations section of the West Branch downstream from Deposit. Moderate. (607) 467-4191.

Camping

Delaware River Club. Year-round campsites. Water hookups and other facilities. 1-800-6-MAYFLY.

Oxbow Campsites. East Branch, New York. On the East Branch. (607) 363-7141.

Terry's Campsite. East Branch, New York. (607) 363-2536.

West Branch Anglers. Deposit, New York. (607) 467-5525.

Where to Eat

Circle Diner. Front Street, Hancock, New York. The best breakfast spot in town. Open 6:00 A.M. to 10:00 P.M. daily.

Cookies' Steak & Seafood. Cadosia, New York, just outside Hancock. Very good food. Try the veal à la Al Caucci. Moderate. (607) 637-4404.

Delaware Inn. Hancock, New York. Bar and restaurant. Good place for late supper—serves until 10:00 P.M. Inexpensive to moderate. (607) 637-2749.

Inn at Starlight Lake. Starlight, Pennsylvania. A refined dining experience in a casual and cozy atmosphere. Moderate to expensive. Reservations advised. (717) 798-2519.

La Salette. Hancock, New York. A good Italian restaurant situated on a hill overlooking Hancock and the Delaware. Moderate. (607) 637-2505.

Olde Cotter Restaurant. Hancock, New York. Italian American. Moderate. (607) 637-3387.

Delaware River Delicacies. Smoke House Delicacies. Smoked products: trout, turkey, eel, grouse, chicken. Don't miss this unusual attraction on Green Flats Road off Old Route 17 northeast of Hancock. Ask locally for exact directions. (607) 637-4443.

Resources

Pennsylvania Atlas and Gazetteer. DeLorme Mapping Co., P.O. Box 298, Freeport, Maine 04032. (207) 865-4171.

Panola, John. *Fishing the Delaware River with John Panola.* Madison, New Jersey: Outdoors USA Inc., 1993.

Deposit, New York, Chamber of Commerce. (607) 467-3214.

Hancock, New York, Chamber of Commerce. (607) 637-4756.

Pocono Mountain Vacation Bureau. 1-800-762-6667.

Pennsylvania Fish Commission State Headquarters. 3232 Walnut Street, Harrisburg, Pennsylvania 17106-7000. (717) 657-4551.

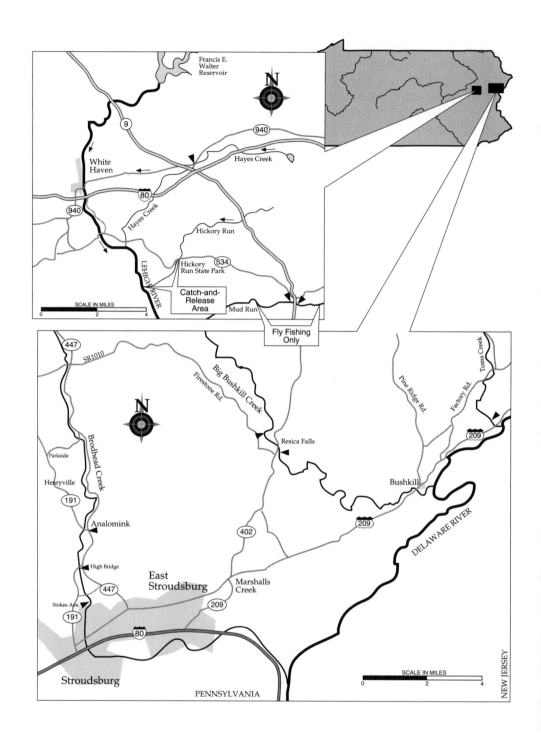

CHAPTER 2

Northeastern Pennsylvania II— The Poconos: Brodhead Creek, Big Bushkill Creek, the Pohopoco, Toms Creek, McMichaels Creek, Hickory Run, Hayes Creek (Black Creek), Mud Run, and Nescopeck Creek

The Pocono region gave rise to some of the earliest legends of fly fishing in America. Brodhead Creek, the best known of area streams, enticed many celebrated anglers to its waters, including James Leisenring, remembered for the "Leisenring lift" presentation of soft-hackle flies. The oldest trout-fishing hotel in America, the Henryville House, was established in 1835, and private fishing clubs have been responsible for maintaining the quality of several Pocono streams.

The last quarter century has not been kind to Pocono trout waters. Housing development has resulted in clear-cutting, leaving long unshaded reaches of fresh water that used to hold trout year-round, but that now warm in the summer. Floods, such as the one in 1955 resulting from Hurricane Diane, have devastated the area and led to unwise channelization of water. Until the Baltimore *Sun* columnist Dan Rodricks told me about the Pohopoco, his most recent wild trout stream discovery, I discounted the area, driving through to more productive water. Fishing Pocono streams, Rodricks converted from a spin fisherman to a fly angler. Now he advises any angler on vacation or honeymooning in the area to pack a fishing rod. It was Dan who introduced me to Pat Woodhead, another recent convert to the sport.

Pat, who describes herself as a mature angler, had no sooner learned to fly-fish than she got involved in conservation issues and was elected president of the Brodhead chapter of TU. We met one morning outside her garage in Stroudsburg to begin a two-day tour of Pocono trout water. Before my car door was closed, she had spotted the jury-rigging that stored my rods beneath the roof of my Toyota RAV4. "Let me show you how I did it," she said, hauling up the back of her new minivan. A long blonde wooden box ran the length of the floor from the tailgate to the steering column. She rolled the top back through handmade grooves, revealing a beautifully crafted interior housing for rods. "I never have to break down a 9-foot rod when I travel from stream to stream," she said.

As we drove around Monroe and Pike Counties, Pat explained that the whole region has a growing number of people who want to enjoy the natural beauty of the area, but with this increase in population comes potential for stream pollution and other environmental problems. Sewage treatment plants, quarries, and industry all threaten streams in the area. Pat and other individual members of local conservation organizations are the constant watchdogs of the rich stream heritage of the region.

BRODHEAD CREEK

This stream was decimated by flooding as a result of Hurricane Diane in 1955. As a flood prevention measure, the Army Corps of Engineers trenched the stream and built a huge berm along the channel near Stroudsburg. Remarkably, although there is almost no cover over the water, stocked fish hold there throughout the summer, supported by the heavily oxygenated water. One morning, Pat and I stood on top of the dike, watching two trout rise intermittently to caddisflies.

Along Route 191, Brodhead TU, working with Jim Hartzler (a fisheries biologist) and Don Baylor (the chairman of conservation for Brodhead TU and an aquatic resources consultant), has made major strides in restoring the natural meander of the stream. More than 250 tons of rock have been put in five hundred yards of water to create holding water, channels, and other in-stream habitat.

The Brodhead, which varies in width from twenty-five to seventy-five feet, is stocked from one mile above the Delaware River at the I-80 bridge upstream to the bridge on SR1002 just above Analomink. It has good footing and fishy runs and riffles, and its open water makes casting a delight. There is nothing wild or challenging about angling on today's Brodhead, but there remains satisfaction in catching good trout on historic water.

Access

• Take I-80 west to Stroudsburg exit 50 (Broad Street). Cross over bridge to light. Turn right on Main Street and cross interborough bridge. Bear left on 209 north, turn left on Starbird Street, then make another left on Washington Street to Rosen's Furniture. Park behind the building and walk over the berm to the creek. Or take I-80 east to Stroudsburg exit 49 (Park Avenue). Turn left on Park Avenue to Main Street, then turn right. Bear left on 209 north, turn left on Starbird Street, then another left on Washington Street to Rosen's Furniture. Park behind building and walk over berm to creek.

• Behind the Moose Lodge on Stokes Mill Road off Route 191 (Fifth Street) north of Stroudsburg.

• Pull-offs along Stokes Mill Road up to the bridge on Stokes Avenue. Walk to the water anywhere that is not posted.

• At the High Bridge, where 5th Street (Route 191) intersects Route 447. This is where the TU chapter has done major stream improvements. Look up- or downstream from the bridge to see the structure. On the Route 191 side of the creek, drive down the first dirt road to parking.

• Cross High Bridge and park just beyond Department of Transportation on left. Access the water from the railroad tracks.

• Analomink Bar, Routes 447/191 north. Park behind the bar. I witnessed a prolific hatch of tricos here about 10:00 one mid-September morning. The stream also has a well-deserved reputation for an outstanding Hendrickson hatch in the early season. The bar used to be an anglers' lodge, the Hotel Rapids, until the 1950s. It was owned by sportsman Charles Rethoret, whose fly rod now belongs to the Brodhead chapter of TU. Fish downstream from here or up through the pocket water to the Red Rock swimming hole. The Red Rock marks the upper end of the public water.

BIG BUSHKILL CREEK

This is one of the cleanest, prettiest streams in the Poconos. But because it is also very accessible, it receives lots of angling pressure. The stream falls through massive ledge rock and widens out into pools, riffles, and runs. The stream is noted for a heavy hatch of blue quills *(Paraleptophlebia)* during the third week of April, when there should also be Hendricksons on the water. The creek warms early in the summer—don't count on fishing it after Memorial Day. But the Bushkill is active again in the fall, producing good caddis hatches.

There is a six-mile Fly-Fishing-Only, Delayed-Harvest stretch at Resica Falls Boy Scout Reservation. The camp rents cabins early in the season. The Delaware Valley Women's Fly Fishing Association often hosts an early-season outing here.

Access

Take Business Route 209 north from Stroudsburg to Marshalls Creek. Take a left on Route 402 and go six miles to Resica Falls.

• Scout Camp. Take the road to the camp office at the bridge on Route 402. The scouts request a $20 donation for fishing in the reservation. Drive past the office down to the fishermen's parking area.

• Firestone Road. Exit Scout Camp, turn left on Route 402, and turn right on Firestone Road (about two blocks). Proceed one mile to the fire gate parking area. Walk about one-third mile down to Little Falls.

THE POHOPOCO

The wild trout water of the upper Pohopoco (not on map) is Dan Rodricks's favorite Pocono trout stream. He fishes it regularly throughout the year and is always certain to be there for the sulphur and Light Cahill hatches. Although the water above the Beltzville Reservoir is not stocked, the reach between the dam and the Lehigh River is.

I visited the stream for the first time with Pat Woodhead in September. As we pulled off just beyond a small bridge over wild trout water, we met a young angler with a light spinning rod. It was his first time fishing the stream, and he had just hooked and released two eleven-inch wild brown trout, two brookies, and a rainbow. He introduced himself as Jeff Eyster and showed us the little gold spoon that he had made. He assured us he would return to the Pohopoco soon!

The following day I had a similar experience. I used caddis imitations and a slate drake to land two brook and one brown trout. The stream is only about twenty-five feet wide as it flows through wetlands above the reservoir. The banks are lined with alders and other fly-catching bushes until the stream flows into a deep hemlock gorge.

Pohopoco wild trout require some effort to catch. A stealthy approach is necessary. Step into the water carefully, wade very slowly, avoid all wake, and cast directly upstream—angling from side to side—to entice fish. Exert sufficient caution and the fish will not be alerted, but you'll be surprised at their spunk.

Regulations
The eight-mile stretch of the Pohopoco, from SR3013 (Merwinsberg) to SR0209 (Kresgeville), holds wild brown trout and is regulated as Class A wild trout water. It is no longer stocked, and all fish must be released. Below the Beltzville Dam, the water is heavily stocked for 3.4 miles, and there are wild and holdover browns present as well. This tailwater remains cool all year, and it is hoped that the Pennsylvania Fish Commission will soon consider managing it as a Class A stream.

Access
• To reach the wild stretch, take Route 209 southwest to Kresgeville. Turn right on Route 534 and take an almost immediate left onto Beltsville Drive, then left on Koch Road. Park at Koch Road bridge.

• To reach the tailwater section below the reservoir, continue on Route 209 to the junction of Routes 476/9 and 209 at Beltzville. The Pocono Gateway Tackle Shop is on the stream. Walk behind the shop, slide down a steep bank, and you're on the water.

• To fish directly below the dam, take Beltzville Road, turn right at the Platz Restaurant to Old Mill Road, and take Old Mill Road to the bottom of the dam.

TOMS CREEK
Toms is a small wild trout stream with a population of brown trout about seven inches long. It can be found at the Toms Creek Picnic Area five miles north of the town of Bushkill on Route 209 north. The lower part of

the stream is in the Delaware Water Gap National Recreation Area. This is a very pretty spot, popular with hikers and picnickers as well as fishermen.

McMICHAELS CREEK
This famous Pocono stream (not on map) is mentioned here only for historical reference. It is accessible only through private land southwest of Stroudsburg, and landowner permission is required to fish it.

HICKORY RUN
Hickory Run State Park is about thirty miles west of Stroudsburg, near the Northeast Extension of the Pennsylvania Turnpike. The park has a campground, store, beach, and picnic area, as well as snowmobile, hiking, and cross-country ski trails.

Bob Sentiwany, proprietor of the A. A. Pro Shop, not far from the park, selected Hickory Run as the best option for me to fish one September afternoon. It is a small wild trout stream that flows through Hickory Run State Park to the Lehigh River.

On the lower one and one half miles, Catch-and-Release, artificial-lures-and-flies-only regulations apply, and the water is not stocked. Bob has taken wild browns up to nineteen inches here. I had no such luck, however, drawing a blank afternoon. There had been a sudden downturn in temperature, and I thought the fish might be instinctively lying low, acclimating to the change.

The stream is only about twelve feet wide, flowing over rocks that look butterscotch through the tannic water. There is canopy for much of its length, so although it may get low in summer, the stream remains cool. Sentiwany likes to fish Hickory Run in February, when there is a prolific hatch of little black stoneflies.

Access
Take Route 209 to Kresgeville, then turn onto Route 534 north to Hickory Run State Park. Drive to the park office, where a map of the park is available. It's a short hike to the stream from the office.

HAYES CREEK (BLACK CREEK)
This twenty-five-foot-wide crystal-clear stream in Hickory Run State Park holds native brook and brown trout and has been called the second-best small stream in the state by Pennsylvania Fish Commission biologist Steve Kepler. It is not stocked, remains cool in the summer, and has prolific hatches throughout the year. This stream will provide anglers with total privacy, as it is seldom fished. No one who minds using small flies (#20 and smaller) on a narrow stream should consider fishing it. Stealth is essential to catch trout here.

Access
Continue north of the park office on Route 534 about three miles. Park at the bridge on Route 534.

MUD RUN
Sentiwany describes Mud Run as "big water for a small stream." He showed me a videotape made in a remote area of the stream that looks more like the steep falls and deep plunge pools of the Andes than the Poconos.

Mud Run holds water most of the year as it flows beneath a thick canopy of mountain laurel and wild rhododendron. It is one of the most scenic streams in northeastern Pennsylvania. There are deep pools more than twenty feet long that give up good fish.

Mud Run has been stocked only recently and only in its uppermost reaches. It also holds wild brown and brook trout and, like Hayes Creek, can be fished throughout the year.

Regulations and Access
There is a two-and-a-half-mile stretch of Fly-Fishing-Only water in the park on either side of Route 476/9.
* Route 534 at the Route 476/9 exit (Northeast Extension) east or west of the overpass. Marked trails lead to the water.
* Route 534 east of overpass. Park at the gate near a sign for group camping and walk in half a mile to the water.

NESCOPECK CREEK
The Nescopeck Creek (not on map) is located in one of the least developed state parks in Pennsylvania, Nescopeck State Park in Luzerne County, south of Wilkes-Barre. I have not fished the Nescopeck, but anglers have highly recommended the Delayed-Harvest, Artificial-Lures-Only section in this 3,000-acre park surrounded by state game lands. The section extends 2.4 miles from its upstream boundary at State Game Lands marker #187 downstream to a cable across the stream.

Access
From White Haven (exit 40 off I-80) take Route 437 toward State Game Lands #187, where the Nescopeck crosses Route 437. It also crosses Route 309 west of White Haven.

HATCHES, FLIES, AND BEST TIMES TO FISH
Generally, the Poconos fish best early in the season, from mid-April through June. Where there is sufficient water, the fall is also productive. Summer fishing should be approached on a stream-by-stream basis. All

Pocono streams have very good hatches of *Stenonema* (Gray Fox, Light Cahill) species.

Spring (mid-April to mid-May)
Gray Fox (#14), Quill Gordon (#12–#14), Blue Quill (#18), Hendrickson (#12–#14), caddis (Spotted Sedge #14), Blue-Winged Olive (#16–#20), grannom (#14).
May: green caddis (#18–#20), Blue-Winged Olive (#16–#20), tan caddis (#14), March Brown (#12), sulphur (#16).

Summer (June through August)
Slate drake (*Isonychia*, #12–#14), Light Cahill (#14), Blue-Winged Olives (#16–#18), March Brown (#12), Yellow Sally (stonefly #14–#16).

IF YOU GO . . .
From Baltimore or Washington, take I-83 north to Harrisburg, then I-81 toward Allentown. Before Allentown, take I-78 to the Pennsylvania Turnpike Northeast Extension (Route 476/9) to Exit 34 and Route 209. This route will put you almost on the Pohopoco at Beltzville.

To reach Stroudsburg, continue on Route 209 north. For a more direct route to Stroudsburg, continue on Route 476/9 to I-80; take I-80 east to Pocono exits (exits 44–53). The trip should take three to four hours.

From the west (Pittsburgh), take Pennsylvania Turnpike I-76 or I-80 east to Route 476/9 (Northeast Extension) and follow the directions above.

From the north (New York, northern New Jersey), take I-80 to Pocono exits and Route 209 south. Follow directions above.

Because it is a traditional vacation destination, there is much for nonanglers to do in the Poconos. There is golfing, skiing, horseback riding, canoeing, whitewater rafting, hiking, and mountain climbing.

Tackle Shops and Guides
   A. A. Pro Shop. Blakeslee Corners. Bob Sentiwany, proprietor. Large inventory of tackle and flies to support a large mail-order business; schools; guide service. Sentiwany has access to almost two miles of private water on the Brodhead and a tributary that provides good fishing for wild trout throughout the year. (717) 643-8000.

   Dunkleberger's Tackle. Stroudsburg. Orvis dealer. Tackle, guides. (717) 421-7950.

   Pocono Gateway Sporting Outfitters. 1501 Interchange Road, Lehighton. On the banks of the Pohopoco near Route 209 and Pennsylvania Turnpike Northeast Extension (Route 476/9). (610) 377-3441.

   Windsor Fly Shop. Stroudsburg. Flies and tackle. (717) 424-0938.

Where to Stay

Budget Motel. East Stroudsburg, exit 51 off I-80. AAA. Nice, but no breakfast. J. R.'s Green Scene restaurant on site. Moderate. (717) 424-5451.

Pocono Plaza Hotel. Stroudsburg, near the Main Street exit. Central atrium with swimming pool. Restaurant. Moderate. (717) 424-1930.

Pocono Inn (Best Western Motel). Stroudsburg. Chop House restaurant and bar on first floor. Moderate. (717) 588-6602.

Pocono View Motel. Route 209, Sciota. Moderate. (717) 992-4167.

Shannon Inn and Pub. East Stroudsburg/Marshalls Creek. Exit 52 off I-80. Irish pub on premises. Moderate to expensive. 1-800-424-8052.

Super 8 Motel. East Stroudsburg. Exit 51 off I-80. AAA. Moderate. (717) 424-7411.

Camping

River Beach Campsites on the Delaware River. 1-800-FLOAT-KC.
Hickory Run State Park. (717) 443-9991.
Delaware Water Gap KOA. Off Route 209 north near Stroudsburg.

Where to Eat

Beaver House. Route 611 north/Ninth Street, Stroudsburg, near Stroud Mall. (717) 421-1020.

The Dutchman. Route 209, two miles north of Marshalls Creek. Homemade soups and baked goods. Steak, ribs, seafood. Moderate. (717) 223-8100.

J. R.'s Green Scene. In the Budget Motel at Exit 51 off I-80. East Stroudsburg. Moderate. (717) 424-5451.

King Arthur Room. Sciota. Four miles south of Stroudsburg on Business Route 209. Very popular local spot. Moderate. (717) 992-4969.

Petrizzo's. Next to the Fernwood Resort on Route 209 North. East Stroudsburg. Moderate. (717) 588-6414.

Stone Bar Inn. Snydersville, on Business Route 209 five miles south of Stroudsburg. Moderate to expensive. (717) 992-6634.

Sunset Diner. Kresgeville. Reliable. Inexpensive. No reservations.

Resources

Pocono Mountains Vacation Bureau. Information and brochures on resorts and activities throughout the region. 1-800-762-6667 or (717) 421-5791.

Chamber of Commerce. 556 Main Street, Stroudsburg. (717) 421-4433.
Bushkill Falls State Park. (717) 588-6682.

CHAPTER 3

Eastern Pennsylvania— Allentown/Bethlehem Area: The Little Lehigh, Cedar, Monocacy, and Saucon Creeks

THE LITTLE LEHIGH: A MODEL FOR URBAN WILD TROUT MANAGEMENT

If you're seeking relief from the winter doldrums and don't mind looking for trout while snow is on the ground, if you like to fish from the banks in sneakers, and if you like angling near comfortable lodging and good food, a winter weekend near Little Lehigh Creek may be a good idea. The stream courses through a greenway several hundred yards wide that transects Allentown. This buffer zone is carefully landscaped and serves as a citywide park.

The Little Lehigh is a testimonial that there can be effective steward-ship of a wild trout fishery in an urban setting. The water withstands tremendous year-round angling pressure; some regulars wet a line morn-ing and evening every fishable day of the year. A partnership between the City of Allentown, Trout Creek Fish and Game, Pioneer Fish and Game, and the Little Lehigh Fish and Game Protective Association maintains the stream throughout the park.

The Little Lehigh Chapter of TU and members of the Little Lehigh Fly Fishers put thirty gabions in the one mile of Catch-and-Release water, creating lies for the fish. The water is about fifty feet wide, consisting of riffles and long pools. Willows overhang the banks, and cool springs keep the water from freezing or exceeding 68 degrees Fahrenheit in prolonged summer heat waves. Except during blizzards or severe thunderstorms, you will see anglers on this stretch even on the coldest days.

The special regulations section of the Little Lehigh has *the densest pop-ulation of trout of all Pennsylvania streams* (412 kilograms per hectare). Many of the fish are wild browns, eleven to fourteen inches long. The Little Lehigh's closest competitors in Pennsylvania for density of fish popula-tion are Falling Spring Run (372 kg/ha), Spring Creek at Fisherman's Par-adise (261 kg/ha), and Fishing Creek in Clinton County (246 kg/ha).

Wild fish inhabit the stretch from the bridge over Fish Hatchery Road downstream to just above the Oxford Drive bridge, although many hatch-ery fish escape into the Catch-and-Release area. The water below the cov-ered bridge is stocked.

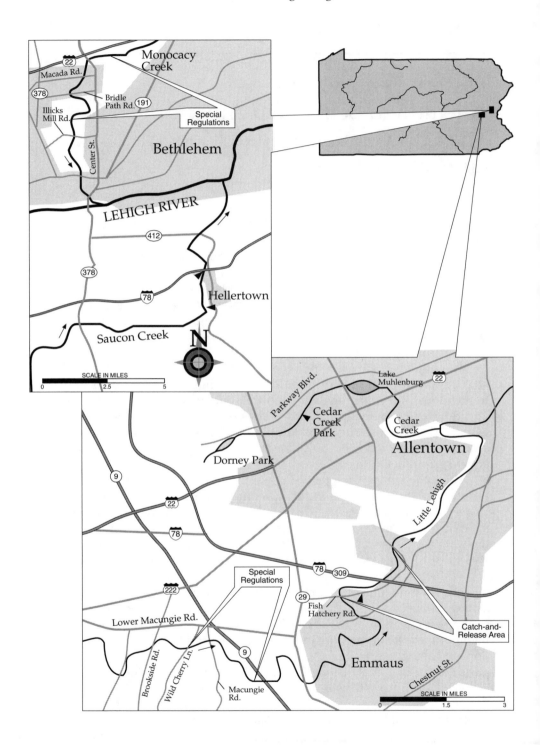

The Little Lehigh is easy to find and difficult to fish. These trout probably receive the greatest constant pressure from *experienced* anglers of any stream in the state. (Even the Yellow Breeches fish get a rest in the winter.) The fish are educated by local anglers, many of whom fish three hundred days a year or more.

The most plentiful insects are tiny midges (#22 and smaller), which come off the water all year long. It's often difficult to detect why or to what the fish are rising. Unless there is a major emergence in progress, the fish seem to take at random, without discernible pattern or reasons. This can result in hours of frustrating fishing. But when you hook one, you are ready to celebrate.

Mike Vatza, an avid young sportsman who has caught the fly-fishing bug from his father, Ed, spurns the idea that Little Lehigh trout respond only to midges. He regularly takes large fish on Woolly Buggers, small Clouser Deep Minnows, crayfish, and frog patterns. He chucks a big attractor into the water next to the bank, gives a couple of seductive twitches of his rod, and bang—fish on! So don't be too precious or listen too closely to the experts when you fish the Little Lehigh. Hedge your bets and take long leaders 9 to 12 feet and light tippets (6X–8X) with you as a precaution, but always be ready to try something different.

Joe Kohler, an accomplished Little Lehigh regular, recommends fishing for big wild browns both below the Police Academy and in the Robin Hood area from April 15 on. He likes the challenge of these fish and feels they get less pressure than their cousins upstream.

Regulations
Heritage Trout Angling regulations apply for one mile, from the Fish Hatchery Road bridge downstream to the 24th Street bridge. Artificial flies and fly tackle, single barbless hooks only may be used. All fish must be released. There is no wading in the stream along this stretch. From the wooden bridge at the fly shop downstream, wading is allowed.

From Lauderslager's Mill Dam upstream to township road T508, Delayed-Harvest, Fly-Fishing-Only regulations apply. Between June 15 and Labor Day, three trout nine inches or longer may be kept per day.

Access
• To reach the fly shop and Catch-and-Release area from I-78, take exit 17 for Cedar Crest Boulevard south (Route 29) and proceed half a mile to a stoplight. Turn left onto Fish Hatchery Road. Proceed .7 mile to a sign on the left for the Little Lehigh Fly Shop. Make a sharp left. The shop and parking lot are at the bottom of the hill.

• The Little Lehigh is also accessible from Lower Macungie Road. From the fly shop, return to Route 29, turn left (south), drive to the second light, and take a right on Lower Macungie Road. Then take the second left onto Wild Cherry Lane. This stretch is regulated as a Delayed-Harvest, Fly-Fishing-Only section. Be careful to note posted property. Wild browns are mixed with stocked fish. Many Little Lehigh diehards prefer this stretch when the downstream section is crowded.

Hatches, Flies, and Best Times to Fish
I like to fish the Little Lehigh whenever the weather is bad and I can find nowhere else to go that has wild fish and is within a half-day drive. Bad weather can mean either summer heat—when the Little Lehigh can have great Trico hatches—or, more likely, the winter doldrums, when access to other trout streams is difficult, if not impossible. This stream fishes well and is difficult all year long.

Winter
Midges (all year), Al's Rat.

Spring: March to April
Blue-Winged Olive (#20), Blue Quill (#18), Iron Blue Dun (#16–#18).
   May to June: caddis (Spotted Sedge #16), sulphur dun (#16), Cream Cahill (#14) (June–July).

Summer (late June to September)
Cream Cahill (#14), Tricos (#24), slate drake (#16), black caddis (#18–#20), *Hexagenia limbata* (late August).

CEDAR CREEK
Cedar Creek is classified as a Class A wild trout stream by the state. It provides two miles of cool limestone stream bordered by willows as it runs through the city greenway. To reach the Cedar, take Route 29 north, then make a right on Parkway Boulevard. Cedar Creek will be on the right. Park at the Park and Recreation Bureau lot. I was very surprised and delighted by this peaceful meadowlike stream and the nice fish it produced.
   Cedar is smaller than the Little Lehigh—about twenty-five feet wide as it runs through the greenway. The regulated wild trout water is from the Ott Street bridge just above Muhlenberg Lake up to its headwaters. It is stocked in the very short stretch from the Ott Street bridge to the lake and below the lake to its confluence with the Little Lehigh.
   Cedar is well known for its Trico hatch and spinner fall from July 1 to October, but attention should also be paid at dusk in May and June, when good hatches of sulphurs (#16), Light Cahills (#14), and tan caddis (#16) appear. In April, there is a good hatch of #20 blue-winged olives.

MONOCACY CREEK

The Monocacy is surrounded by the prettiest land of all the trout waters described in this chapter. Though it also runs through developed land, the houses are situated well away from the stream, often invisible behind vegetation. Averaging forty feet in width, the Monocacy offers anglers more than nine miles of trout water. Fish are a mix of wild and stocked browns lying in deep holes, riffles, and long pools throughout the creek. Wading is essential, as it is often impossible to fish from the banks. Emergences on the Monocacy are much the same as on Cedar Creek.

Access

To reach the Monocacy, take Route 29 (Cedar Crest Boulevard) north to Route 22 east toward Bethlehem. Exit Route 22 at Route 512, and turn left onto Route 512 (Center Street, Bethlehem). There are three access points to the Monocacy off Center Street.

• Turn right on Macada Road (first light). Park at the stream and access along the railroad tracks. This section is a wild trout area governed by Trophy Trout regulations.

• Take a right on Bridle Path Road. Park at the pull-off just past the stream at the foot of the drive to Monocacy Manor, and access the stream along the railroad tracks. This is also in the Trophy Trout section.

• Turn right on Illicks Mill Road and fish the open water in the park. There is a large parking lot to the left as you cross the stream. Park here and access the open water in the nature conservancy.

SAUCON CREEK

Saucon is a little-known tributary of the Lehigh that converges with the river on the Bethlehem Steel Company property in Hellertown. Fishing the Saucon sometimes feels like fishing in a wasteland where you wander among old tin cans on the banks of a stream that more resembles the River Styx than a trout stream. Nonetheless, in this down-trodden neighborhood of Hellertown, there are fertile trout waters that few people fish. Ed Vatza, a rod collector and angler, has fished the Saucon weekly for a number of years. He realizes that the surroundings may put off visiting anglers, but he doesn't mind. The lack of pressure allows him to return several times a week from April through October to hunt healthy wild brown trout. If you are in the area, a half day on the Saucon is well worth it.

Access

To get to the wild trout portion of the stream, take I-78 and exit at Route 412 (Hellertown/Bethlehem). If you exit from I-78 eastbound, turn right at Route 412, and go left at the next light.

- Go through the underpass and pull off under the interstate bridges.
- Take Route 412 to the light at High Street. Go right on High Street, cross the wooden bridge over the railroad, and drive beyond the bridge over the stream. There are pull-offs on either side. The wild trout area extends both up- and downstream.

IF YOU GO . . .

From Washington, Allentown is about two hundred miles. Take I-83 past Harrisburg to Route I-81 to Route 78 to Allentown exits.

From Philadelphia, Allentown is a seventy-minute drive via the Northeast Extension of the Pennsylvania Turnpike. Exits 16, 17, and 18 will lead you to the establishments listed below. Be sure to book well in advance in the summer, as many tourists visit Dorney Park and the Wild Water Kingdom.

Tackle Shops and Guides

Little Lehigh Fly Shop. Allentown, on the banks of the Little Lehigh. On Fish Hatchery Road off Route 29 south of Route 222. Stream report updated daily. This is *the* place to buy midges for the Little Lehigh and elsewhere. Make sure to purchase Al's Rat midge pupa imitation. (610) 797-5599.

Pro-Am Fishing Shop. 5916 Tilghman Street, Allentown. (610) 395-0885.

Nester's Rod and Bow. 2510 MacArthur Boulevard, Whitehall. Route 22 east and exit north on MacArthur Boulevard. (610) 433-6051.

Where to Stay

Comfort Suites. Exit 16 off I-78 to Route 222 (Hamilton Boulevard). Expensive. (610) 437-9100.

Days Inn. 2622 Lehigh Street, Allentown. Exit 18 off I-78. Inexpensive. (610) 797-1234.

Holiday Inn Express. Allentown. Route 222 (Hamilton Boulevard). Moderate. (610) 435-7880.

Holiday Inn. Bethlehem. Center Street (Route 512) off Route 22 east. Expensive. AAA special rates available. (610) 866-5800.

Hotel Bethlehem. Main Street, Bethlehem. Expensive. Pioneer Restaurant. (610) 867-3711.

Howard Johnson's Motel. 3220 Hamilton Boulevard, Allentown. Exit 16 off I-78, Route 222 (Hamilton Boulevard). Moderate. 1-800-446-4656.

Where to Eat

Ambassador Restaurant. 3750 Hamilton Boulevard, Allentown, just west of Comfort Suites. Continental and Mediterranean cuisine. Moderate. (610) 432-2025.

Brass Rail. 3015 Lehigh Street, Allentown. A favorite of local anglers. Seafood, steaks, cocktails. Inexpensive. No reservations.

The Farmhouse. 1449 Chestnut Street, Emmaus. A charming inn, cozy and very good food. Casual. Expensive. (610) 967-6225.

King George Inn. At the junction of Route 29 and Route 222. Good atmosphere, varied menu. Moderate. (610) 435-1723.

O'Hara's. In the Comfort Suites in Allentown. American food and cocktails. Serves late. Moderate. No reservations.

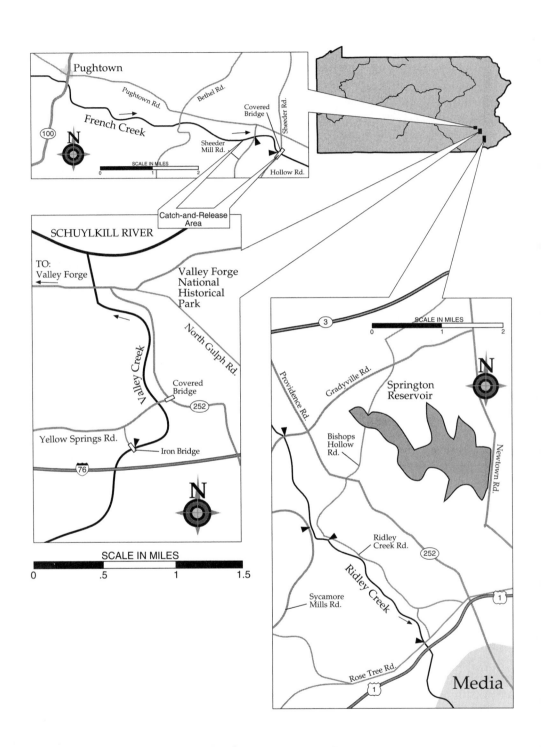

Pughtown

Pughtown Rd.

Bethel Rd.

French Creek

Covered Bridge

Sheeder Rd.

100

N

Sheeder Mill Rd.

SCALE IN MILES
0   1   2

Hollow Rd.

Catch-and-Release Area

SCHUYLKILL RIVER

TO: Valley Forge

Valley Forge National Historical Park

North Gulph Rd.

Valley Creek

Covered Bridge

252

Yellow Springs Rd.

76

Iron Bridge

N

SCALE IN MILES
0   .5   1   1.5

3

SCALE IN MILES
0   1   2

Providence Rd.

Gradyville Rd.

Springton Reservoir

N

Bishops Hollow Rd.

Newtown Rd.

Ridley Creek Rd.

252

Ridley Creek

Sycamore Mills Rd.

1

Rose Tree Rd.

1

Media

CHAPTER 4

Southeastern Pennsylvania— Philadelphia Area: Ridley, French, and Valley Creeks

To fish in Delaware and Chester Counties is to angle in history. On the way to any of these trout streams, you are never far from historic sites such as Valley Forge, Chadds Ford, or the Brandywine Battlefield. Also nearby are cultural sites like the Brandywine Museum, the Franklin Mint, Longwood Gardens, and—just beyond the Delaware line—Winterthur, the Du Pont residence, garden, and museum. Covered bridges are scattered throughout the area, and many Revolutionary War–era limestone buildings have been restored and are now in use as banks, gift shops, and residences.

These historic sites and trout streams all exist in the midst of suburban sprawl and shopping malls. Visitors frequently stumble upon a greenway or shaded stream where one would expect a traffic light or housing development. It speaks well for conservation efforts that sufficiently high water quality can be maintained despite this degree of habitat disruption. Residents of the area have taken an active role in maintaining local streams and ensuring that trout can be caught in Chester County on a year-round basis.

RIDLEY CREEK

Ridley Creek is one of the suburban trout streams closest to Philadelphia. It is a very pretty, twenty-foot-wide stocked freestone stream in Ridley Creek State Park, off Baltimore Pike (Route 1) just west of Media.

Mary Kuss, the angling instructor and cofounder of the Delaware Valley Women's Fly Fishing Association, took me to Ridley one October. There was still plenty of water in the stream because there had been no drought the preceding summer.

We drove to the park offices, next to a limestone bridge at the junction of Ridley Creek Road, Bishop Hollow Road, and Chapel Hill Road. The leaves were turning but were not yet a nuisance to our flies. There were lots of hikers and dogs, but no one else was fishing, and we had the entire Fly-Fishing-Only stretch to ourselves.

We fished above and below the bridge. We each caught trout, but Mary was more successful, using Green Weenies and Woolly Bombers. As I recall, I grew fixated blind-casting dries to trout I was certain were lying just beneath the surface under a huge sycamore.

Ridley Creek is protected by the 650 forested acres of Tyler Arboretum and 2,600 acres of Ridley Creek State Park. These wooded areas act as buffers, greatly reducing the amount of runoff from local development. There is sufficient cover and deadfall to keep the stream cool and the trout hidden. If I lived in the area, I'd fish Ridley early in the year, practicing rusty casting skills before going farther afield to more challenging water.

Access
To get to Ridley from Philadelphia, take Route 1 south to Route 252. At bottom of ramp, turn right onto Route 252 north, then turn left at first traffic light onto Rose Tree Road. Go half a block, then turn right onto Sycamore Mills Road; follow that to its intersection with Ridley Creek Road. Continue straight ahead to Fly-Fishing-Only stretch.
   • Rose Tree Road at Ridley Creek Road. This intersection is southeast of the park, downstream of the Fly-Fishing-Only stretch. Lots of cover makes casting a challenge. Wade in the water, and avoid posted land.
   • Sycamore Mills access—the Fly-Fishing-Only section—at the junction of Ridley Creek Road and Chapel Hill Road.
   • Gradyville Road where it crosses Ridley Creek Road, in Ridley Creek State Park.
   • At the Colonial Plantation in Ridley Creek State Park. Park in the lot and walk down to the stream. Ridley is at its widest (twenty-five feet) and most shallow here. This is some of the prettiest water on the stream, but it is a favorite spot for bait anglers, and it warms up quickly in the summer.

Regulations
The Delayed-Harvest, Fly-Fishing-Only stretch is from the Sycamore Mills Dam .6 mile downstream to the mouth of Dismal Run. Put-and-take regulations apply to the rest of the stream.

Hatches, Flies, and Best Times to Fish
Winter (December to March)
Midges (Ridley seldom freezes), light brown caddis (#22), Blue-Winged Olives (#14–22), early black stonefly (#18–#14) (February).

Spring
April to May: grannom (#16), black caddis (#14–#16), and green caddis (#14–#16), *Paraleps* (Blue Quill #14–#16), and sporadic hatches of bugs

imitated by Quill Gordon, Hendrickson, Red Quill, March Brown, and Gray Fox (#14–#16) patterns.

May to June: sulphurs (#14–#16), slate drakes (#12–#14), Light Cahills (#12–#16), inchworms (Green Weenies), flying black ants.

Summer (June to August)
Tan or gray caddis imitations (#14–#16), cream-colored cranefly imitations (#16), Tricos (July to November).

Fall (September to November)
Slate drake patterns (#12), Blue-Winged Olives (#18–#20), Gray or Olive Microcaddis (#22).

Mary Kuss advises anglers *never* to be without a Green Weenie, a Black Woolly Bomber, and a beadhead Gold-Ribbed Hare's Ear (#14) on Ridley.

FRENCH CREEK
French Creek is located in western Chester County near Phoenixville. The largest water described in this chapter, it is a thirty- to forty-foot-wide freestone stream that meanders through farms and horse country. The stream is well stocked (for fifteen miles from St. Peters to Kimberton), often fished, and very pretty. Wading and casting are easy. The canopy is high, and there are numerous runs and riffles and fishy-looking water.

Mary Kuss and I fished from the Sheeder Mill covered bridge up to a bend in the stream that meets the road. Mary was again outfishing me using Green Weenies and Woolly Buggers and Bombers; I can't remember what I was using—probably the same patterns with less skill! We saw a few other anglers but were able to get away from them.

Access
• To get to French Creek from Philadelphia, take I-76 (the Schuylkill Expressway) to I-276 (the Pennsylvania Turnpike). Go west on I-276 to the Downingtown exit (Route 100). Take Route 100 north (Pottstown Pike) to Pughtown. Then take a right on Pughtown Road.

• To reach the upper end of the regulated water, take a right on Sheeder Mill Road. The road name is not marked, but there is a sign for Sheeder Mill Farm. The road will lead you through the farm to an iron bridge over the creek. The regulated water extends upstream a couple hundred yards above the bridge.

• To reach the lower end of the Delayed-Harvest, Fly-Fishing-Only stretch, turn right on Hollow Road off Pughtown Road and park on the left, just past the covered bridge.

Hatches, Flies, and Best Times to Fish
The hatches listed for Ridley Creek will do well on French Creek. The stream is noted for early (March and April) tan, brown, black, and olive caddis. Standard mayflies appear throughout the spring, but the water warms considerably in summer, resulting in little in-stream reproduction.

VALLEY CREEK
Valley Creek is a limestone spring creek with a good population of PCB-ridden streambred trout. This Class A water was polluted by Conrail in the mid-1980s and became a wild trout stream by accident. The Fish Commission stopped stocking the water after the PCB contamination. Two years later, wild trout were found in the stream. Brown trout have been happily reproducing there ever since.

Mary Kuss aptly describes Valley as freestone in character but limestone in chemistry. Cool springs feed it from the headwaters west of Route 29 downstream to its mouth. Alternating between fast runs and pools, and shaded by hardwoods, Valley is only about twenty feet wide and receives a lot of pressure.

The most productive reaches of Valley are in Valley Forge National Historical Park. Along Valley Forge Road (Route 252), most of the casting is done from the banks in order to remain undetected by the fish. There is little vegetation in the water here, and the canopy is very high.

The Valley Forge chapter of TU maintains streambank stabilization projects on an annual basis. Whenever there is a sudden thaw or heavy rain, flood conditions soon occur, and large chunks of the bank collapse into the water. The riffles and pools are soon filled with sediment. The chapter has done much to protect the trout and keep the water productive for anglers.

I fished the upper stretch—from the iron bridge to the Pennsylvania Turnpike—with Mary Kuss late one fall afternoon. We each caught small browns on beadhead Pheasant-tail nymphs.

Although our catch was small, I heard accounts of trout more than fifteen inches long caught in Valley. The upstream reach is a peaceful section to fish, and the traffic sounds surprisingly distant. The water can be waded easily, and there is plenty of room to cast. As I approached the turnpike overpass, I was greeted by a small doe having her evening drink. Local anglers say that Valley gets better the farther upstream it is fished.

Access
Access to Valley Creek can be found in Valley Forge National Historical Park, between the Pennsylvania Turnpike (I-276) and the Schuylkill River.
  • There are several pull-offs on Route 252 (Valley Forge Road) south of Route 23.

• To reach the upper section, turn right over the white covered bridge just off Route 252 south of Route 23. Take the first left (a dirt road) just past the large stone house (Maxwell's Headquarters in the Revolutionary War), and the road will end at an iron bridge over the stream. Fish upstream to and above the turnpike overpass, or downstream toward Maxwell's Headquarters and the covered bridge.

Hatches, Flies, and Best Times to Fish
Valley Creek can be fished all year long. The first time I went was after a major snowstorm in late February. Numerous anglers lined the banks, fishing with midges and large subsurface patterns.

Good hatches and flies to use on Valley Creek include olive caddis imitations (#16), Blue-Winged Olives (#16–#22), and craneflies (#20) in April; green caddis (#16), sulphurs (#16), and Light Cahills (#14) in May; and Tricos (#24) from early July until the first hard frost. In the fall, an olive caddis appears in the afternoon.

IF YOU GO . . .
From Philadelphia, take Route 1 (Baltimore Pike) south to Route 252 and Media. Follow directions under Ridley Creek Access (above). The shortest way to French Creek from Philadelphia is via I-276 (the Pennsylvania Turnpike). Take it west to the Route 100 exit, and follow local directions (above). Valley Creek can also be reached by following I-276 west to the Valley Forge exit. Follow Route 202 south to Route 252 and turn right (north) onto Valley Forge Road (Route 252). Follow local directions (above).

Tackle Shops and Guides
Brandywine Outfitters. Exton. Excellent selection of rods and all other fly-fishing equipment and flies. (610) 594-8008.

Chip's Bait and Tackle. 325 East Gay Street, West Chester. (610) 696-FISH.

Eyler's Fly'n Tackle. Bryn Mawr. Tom and Alice Forwood, proprietors. Rods, clothing, flies, tackle. (610) 527-3388.

French Creek Outfitters. 1414 South Hanover Street (Route 100), Pottstown (2 miles south of Route 422). (610) 326-6740.

Gray's Outfitters. Near Valley Forge. (610) 630-0988.

The Sporting Gentleman. 306 East Baltimore Pike, Media. Barry Staats, proprietor. Orvis dealer. Full-service fishing shop. (610) 565-6140.

Where to Stay
Coventry Forge Inn and Guest House. Coventry. Route 23, one and one-half miles west of Route 100. Expensive. (610) 469-6222.

French Creek Inn. Route 734 near Route 23, Phoenixville. Plain and simple. Moderate. (610) 935-3838.

McIntosh Motor Inn. Media. Moderate. (610) 565-5800.

Motel 6. King of Prussia. Moderate. A Denny's next door. (610) 265-7200.

The Media Inn. Media. Restaurant on premises. Moderate. (610) 566-6500.

Where to Eat

No one will starve in this area, as there are numerous restaurants of all varieties and prices. Here are a few of the better ones—none of them cheap.

Coventry Forge Inn. Coventry. Route 23, one and one-half miles west of Route 100. Expensive. (610) 469-6222.

Flowing Springs Inn. Near Spring City. Route 100, seven miles north of the Pennsylvania Turnpike. Moderate to expensive. (610) 469-0899.

Kimberton Inn. Phoenixville. One mile down Kimberton Road off Route 113. Very good local reputation. Expensive. (610) 933-8148.

Rosetree Inn. Route 252 north of Media. Excellent food and service. Expensive. (610) 891-1905.

The Royal Scot. Phoenixville. Pub lunch. Extensive dinner menu. Moderate. (610) 983-3073.

Seven Stars Inn. Near Phoenixville at the junction of Route 23 and Hoffecker Road. Steaks, chicken, fish platters. Moderate. (610) 495-5205.

Resources

Dame Juliana League. Bob Molzahn, president, 210 Nottingham Dr., Spring City, PA 19475. (610) 469-6365.

Delco-Manning Chapter of TU (Ridley Creek). P.O. Box 183, Media, Pennsylvania 19063.

Valley Forge TU. P.O. Box 1356, West Chester, Pennsylvania 19380. Carl Heine, president. (610) 363-7238.

Valley Creek Keepers of the Stream. Information: Neil Waters (610) 754-9817, or administration (610) 524-9692.

CHAPTER 5

Southcentral Pennsylvania's Limestone Creeks: The Letort Spring Run, Falling Spring Branch, and the Yellow Breeches

Within two and a half hours of Baltimore or Washington—and about the same time from Philadelphia—an angler can fish for wild trout on two of Pennsylvania's best limestone spring creeks: the Letort Spring Run and Falling Spring Branch. You can leave the city after work, fish the Letort or the Yellow Breeches in the evening, and finish the day with a good meal at the Boiling Springs Tavern or the Allenberry Resort. Early the next morning, get on the Letort before other anglers spook the fish. Approach cautiously and fish the hatch or standard Letort patterns such as cress bugs and shrimp. Once the sun is high and the action slows, drive down I-81 to Falling Spring Branch. Fish through the day, and return to the Yellow Breeches for the evening hatch and late spinner fall. The Breeches will repair any injury to your ego incurred by uncooperative fish on the first two wild trout streams.

THE LETORT SPRING RUN

The Letort is a historic limestone spring creek originating at a spring south of Carlisle and flowing northeast to the Conodoguinet. The Letort was home waters to Charles Fox and Vincent Marinaro, two of America's most renowned trout fishers. Both observed the feeding patterns of wild brown trout in the Letort and authored books that resulted in lasting innovations in modern fly fishing.

The Letort is the most difficult stream I've ever fished. I've spent hours on my knees on its soggy streambanks trying to place a dry fly or nymph delicately two feet in front of a Letort trout. When I don't line them or spook them, they usually ignore my offerings.

I first went to the Letort in midsummer during a hot, dry spell when other streams were not fishing well. Because it is spring fed, the Letort runs cool all year long. I attempted to fish the Trico hatch, my first experience with these minuscule flies. That was like taking a class in advanced calculus without ever having learned math. I was hopeless and clueless and came away fishless. Later that day I tried terrestrials—crickets and beetles—with little more luck.

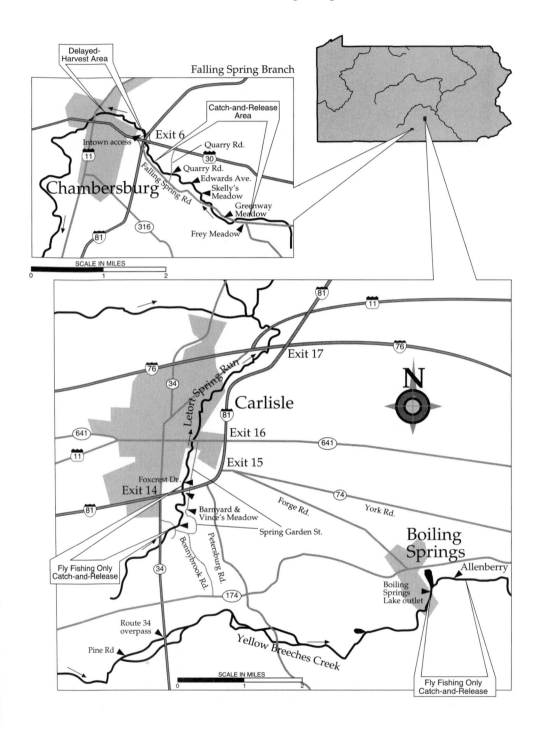

DOUGLAS LEES

Letort Spring Run

Over the years my angling skills and knowledge grew, and I returned to the stream annually, usually in the summer, but I still could not catch fish. Then one year I went in March. I fished streamers and caught three fish downstream from Charles Fox's meadow. I was using a Clouser Redd Foxee Minnow (#12). I drove home thinking I'd finally broken the spell. But when I returned in July, I was skunked again. That's when I promised myself I had to take action to beat the jinx.

Tom Gamper, an angling friend, and I teamed up and booked Ed Shenk as our guide for a day on the stream late in June. Shenk, an internationally recognized angler and author who has fished since he was two years old, is one of the few remaining Letort angling legends. His best fish on the Letort was a twenty-seven-and-one-half-inch brown. He puts in thirty or forty hours on the stream every week. I figured if I couldn't catch fish, I could at least watch him do so and learn how.

At 8:00 A.M. we were approaching the water cautiously near the I-81 overpass when Ed spotted a family of mink—a mama and five little ones—on the far bank. Ed cupped a forefinger and thumb around his mouth and imitated the chirping sound of an injured rabbit or field mouse. All the mink turned around, slipped into the water, and swam single file across the current to within a few yards of Shenk. The mama mink stopped cautiously at the water's edge, but two of the young came up and sniffed Ed's boots, looked up into his puckish face, and then scurried under a nearby bush. The mink must be a good omen, we all felt.

We started the day with crickets cast to fish across several of the braided currents that constitute the flow of the Letort. Tom and I both overshot casts and lined fish. Ed then had us lengthen 6X tippets to thirty inches. When the crickets didn't work, we switched to Pheasant-tail nymphs. There were fish showing, apparently feeding, but not accepting our offerings. After an hour or so, we had both refined our casts, but for some reason the trout still wouldn't take. How fortunate to be with an expert, I thought. This is just the kind of experience I was used to on the Letort, and now I could discover how to change my luck.

We hiked up the meadow, taking turns casting to dimpling trout that ignored our flies. Shenk remained patient, telling us that one of these feeding fish was bound to take what we offered. He told us anecdotes about the pools we fished. He showed us where Charles Fox built his spawning beds and where, twenty-five years ago, he himself planted small willow switches that have become big enough to shade the water. He showed us the rosebush near the lie of a legendary trout. The feeding trout continued to elude us, and soon Shenk's pleasant memories couldn't cover his frustration. He began to swear at the fish and mumble about anglers who walk too close to the water.

Just before lunch we picked out a sandy-colored Letort brown feeding more actively than others. "If this one doesn't take, we'll throw rocks at him!" Ed hissed. In order, I offered a cricket, a beetle, Al's Rat, Ed's Hopper, a Patriot Emerger (to Shenk's horror), an olive caddis pupa, an inchworm, and a cress bug—Shenk's sure-thing fly. No takers. Tom cast more of the same, adding to the series a #24 black midge that had turned an earlier fish's head. But there were still no takers. Shenk said the day was not going well.

I suggested we try a smaller tippet—7X or 8X. But Shenk explained that he prefers to avoid these ultralight options, feeling there is a high likelihood of a large Letort trout breaking off. His seine revealed bugs too small to imitate. The fish should prefer our larger offerings, he said, because it takes less energy to get much more food. By this time, we were casting with sufficient care and delicacy not to put fish down, so we couldn't entirely blame ourselves.

We invited Shenk to try his skills. He fetched his favorite, short, 6-foot Letort rod. His technique is to cast large sculpin to fish hiding in pockets undercut in the streambanks. He puts out very little line and flips three feet of leader into the water right next to the streambank. Punched hard, the big imitation gets through the vegetation and plunks down on the water where the fish can hear and see it. Often, a big brown comes out to grab the Shenk sculpin and the fight is on. But not on our day!

None of us landed a fish in eight hours. I missed two, as did Tom. On the drive home, Tom and I figured Ed would have taken a couple—if he had used his short rod earlier in the day.

Nonetheless, I've seldom had a better time *not* catching fish. Shenk is an excellent teacher with a great sense of humor. I missed a nice fish after getting a take by sending a cricket on a long drag-free drift. The expletives spewed from my lips. Lack of line control was the problem, we agreed, but knowing the reason didn't make me feel any better. When I apologized for my language, Ed said, "Oh you're entitled to that and much, much more—anything else you can think of to call him, say it!"

I asked Shenk how the Letort of today compares with earlier times. He says there is no question that the stream has deteriorated. Between development, runoff, and toxic spill from cress farms, he doesn't believe the water will ever again be the pristine stream of the 1950s. Moreover, the angling pressure increases annually. I had wondered about this, because the trout are so difficult to catch. Shenk believes the stream is so famous that people feel they must come here to fish. Fishermen, particularly novices, don't understand the need to walk well back from the water and tread lightly to minimize vibrations through the ground. He prefers to be the first on a given section of stream, feeling that once put down, it takes hours for Letort trout to feed again.

Shenk says nine out of ten fish landed on the Letort are hooked on the first cast. These fish spook so easily that one must put the fly drag-free two feet in front of them with only the tippet visible. Birds, primarily herons, are a big threat to Letort fish, as are anglers. Always walk as far from the banks as possible. As you approach the water, stoop or crawl till you spot fish. False casting will put them down instantly, so you will have to get line out over land or pull it out by hand. Any way you can, make the first cast count.

Regulations

Catch-and-Release, Fly-Fishing-Only for one and one half miles—from three hundred yards above the bridge on Township Route 481 downstream to the Reading railroad bridge at the southern edge of Letort Spring Park.

Access

To reach the Catch-and-Release renowned barnyard and meadow reaches, take exit 15 off I-81 north and turn left onto Route 74 north, heading toward Carlisle. Go to the first light and turn left onto Giant Lane, then take a right on Samuels Drive and a left onto Spring Garden Street.

Approaching from the north, take I-81 south to exit 16. Bear right onto Route 641 west and continue to the second traffic light. Turn left onto Spring Garden Street.

- Take Foxcrest Drive off Spring Garden Street (the fifth right turn) to the dead end. Park at Pumping Station.
- Park near the I-81 overpass and walk down to the water.
- Continue south on Spring Garden Street until you see a gate on the right and a picnic pavilion at the bottom of a field. This is Vince Marinaro's meadow, complete with a monument.
- Continue on Spring Garden Street several more miles to Bonny Brook Road, turn right, cross the stream, park at the pull-off next to a wooden bridge or in the parking lot at the next bridge (at the quarry).

Access to the Lower Letort

There are four other roads in Carlisle that lead to the stocked sections of the Letort. Take exit 14 off I-81 and turn onto Route 34 north (Hanover Street), heading toward Carlisle. Go north through town and continue on Hanover Street past the Harvon Motel and the U.S. Army War College. To reach the stream, turn right from Hanover Street (now Route 11) onto Post Road (just past the War College), Harmony Hall Road, Shady Lane, or South Middlesex Drive. (There's good Trico fishing at a bridge just beyond shops at Colonial Peddlers on Shady Lane.)

Hatches, Flies, and Best Times to Fish

Because it runs cool throughout the year, the Letort can be fished at any time. The Letort has few mayfly hatches; however, in April and May, blue-winged olives *(Baetis)* will emerge.

Herb and Cathy Weigel at Cold Spring Anglers like the sulphur hatch, when Letort trout are slightly less wary and will take drys more readily than at other times.

Phil Marion, a fly fisher from Delaware, fishes the Letort about forty-five days a year. He admits to being a dry-fly snob. He fishes CDC Blue-Winged Olive *(cornuta)* patterns in spring and in November and December, midges in winter, and terrestrials in summer. He told me of one Letort experience when he and a fishing buddy took no fish one day and returned the next to land fifteen fish each on terrestrials!

Personally, I go when I'm up to the challenge, and some years, despite the fact that I live nearby, I don't venture to the Letort at all. Shenk advises fishing in the very early morning and at dusk, when the angler is less visible. He says winter fishing is the toughest.

In spring or in high-water conditions, large black or white Shenk Sculpins and Clouser Redd Foxee Minnows are highly effective. Tricos in July and August provide the classic Letort experience. Standard spring creek patterns such as scuds, shrimp, and cress bugs always work. Terrestrials (ants, grasshoppers, beetles, inchworms, jassids) should be tried in the summer.

FALLING SPRING BRANCH

This stream is currently experiencing a well-earned comeback after many years of deterioration. The Falling Spring Greenway has completed major stream restoration projects and has purchased two meadows through which the stream runs. As a result of habitat improvement, the waters promise to resume their once-legendary status in the annals of wild trout fisheries.

The Falling Spring Greenway, Inc., is a not-for-profit volunteer organization dedicated to the conservation of Falling Spring Branch. In addition to stream habitat improvement, the organization has purchased land along Falling Spring that otherwise would have been developed. In 1994 and 1995, more than nine acres, including almost a half mile of wild rainbow trout nursery water, was purchased. The land was placed in the public domain to be conserved in perpetuity by the Pennsylvania Fish and Boat Commission.

Falling Spring is a wild trout stream that is as challenging during surface feeding activity as the Letort, although its surroundings are much more pleasing. The water runs through pastures and swampy meadows fed by springs throughout its length. The best approach is long downstream casts, especially on very smooth water.

The fish are spooky, but wading is unnecessary, as anglers can walk the banks throughout most of the regulated water. Casting is easy, as there are very few bushes to hang up your backcast—if you keep it high over the streamside grasses. The novice can have a good time here, but because of lack of cover, it is easy to line your target.

Regulations

Catch-and-Release, Fly-Fishing-Only regulations apply for 2.4 miles, from T544 downstream to a wire fence crossing the Geisel Funeral Home property near I-81. Delayed-Harvest regulations apply in town for 1.1 miles from Walker Road downstream to Fifth Avenue.

Access

Take Falling Springs Road right at Shoney's past the I-81 underpass. There are five places to park along the stream off Falling Springs Road. To reach the Delayed-Harvest stretch in downtown Chambersburg, go west on Route 30 into town and access by turning right on any street between Walker Road and Fifth Avenue.

- Quarry Road. (Park across bridge in the lot with farm machinery.)
- Edwards Avenue.
- Skelly's meadow. After the elementary school, go left into a farm, proceeding *very* slowly over the cattle grates, and park near the fallen sycamore tree.

- Greenway meadow. Pass Skelly's lane, cross the bridge over the stream, park in the designated parking area at Spring View Drive and Falling Spring Road. This meadow, upper section, can also be accessed off Garman Road, to the left off Falling Springs Road.
- Frey meadow. Access the upper stretch by Briar Lane, to the left off Falling Springs Road after Spring View Drive. The Briar Lane bridge marks the end of the Special Regulation Heritage Trout water.

Hatches, Flies, and Best Times to Fish

Falling Spring Branch can be fished all year. I like it on warm days in late winter or early spring when there is snow on the ground. In winter or early in the season, the trout are more forgiving and the careful beginner can take trout and be proud to have done so. Stealth and accurate casting remain mandatory, however. Woolly Buggers, sculpins, cress bugs, and scud patterns are always effective.

Sulphurs start mid-May and peak around Memorial Day, finishing by July 4. The blue-winged olives emerge in April, and a second-generation hatch appears in October and November. Midday during the summer months, try terrestrials, as well as Pheasant-tail nymphs, cress bugs, shrimp, and scud patterns. The once famous Tricos are coming back slowly. The trikes begin in mid-July and continue into the fall.

THE YELLOW BREECHES CREEK

The moderately experienced angler who leaves the Letort or Falling Spring frustrated can fish the Yellow Breeches and take nice big brown trout. Although these fish are not as challenging as the wild trout on the two limestoners, they are fun to catch. The Yellow Breeches is about thirty to forty feet wide at the Boiling Springs–Allenberry Resort stretch. It is very easy to wade, and casting is not a problem—unless you hook a bat, which I did late one evening during a spinner fall! The Yellow Breeches does get muddy quite quickly after a thunderstorm; however, as it begins to clear, I've caught big trout on black Woolly Buggers.

The Yellow Breeches is one of the most popular trout streams in the mid-Atlantic. I have never been able to figure exactly why so many anglers like to fish here. Perhaps it is the convenience of the Allenberry Resort, an affordable place to stay and eat located right on the creek. Or perhaps it is the accessibility of the water and its proximity to northern Virginia, Baltimore, Washington, and Harrisburg. Whatever the reason, you will have plenty of company on the Breeches. But I've found most of the anglers friendly and pleased to let you know what patterns are working for them—if and when your own are not.

The whitefly hatch that appears on the Yellow Breeches at dusk in mid-August must be seen to be believed. The water is blanketed with duns and then spinners, and there seem to be as many anglers as flies!

This hatch is an excuse for partying with local and visiting anglers. Don't go to the Breeches for the whitefly hatch unless you like even more company than usual on the stream.

Regulations
Catch-and-Release, artificial lures or flies only are permitted from the outflow of Boiling Springs Lake downstream through the Allenberry Resort property.

Access
- To reach Boiling Springs, take I-81 north to exit 15; turn right onto Route 74 south and follow for about four miles to Route 174 west; take 174 west a few miles to Bucher Hill Road at Boiling Springs village, about a half mile beyond Allenberry. Just past Highland House B&B, turn left into the parking lot next to the stream.
- Go into the Allenberry Resort just east of Boiling Springs and follow the signs for the Fisherman's Parking Lot.

Hatches, Flies, and Best Times to Fish
The Yellow Breeches can be fished twelve months of the year. During the winter, large streamers (Woolly Buggers, Matukas, and so on) will work. In March, little black stoneflies appear, and by April caddis will emerge. In early May, March Browns and Quill Gordons emerge, and there is an excellent sulphur hatch later in the month. Tricos and terrestrials can be counted on throughout the summer. The famous whitefly appears in mid-August.

In the fall, blue-winged olives hatch and Tricos continue until the first heavy frost. Slate drakes and caddisflies will also produce fish.

IF YOU GO . . .
From Washington to Carlisle, it is about 130 miles via I-83 to the Pennsylvania Turnpike (I-76) west to Carlisle exit (Route 11). Washington to Chambersburg is about 60 miles via I-795 to Route 97 north to Route 30 west to Chambersburg. Chambersburg to Carlisle is 40 miles on I-81.

Tackle Shops and Guides
Cold Spring Angler's. Carlisle. Complete fly shop and guide service. (717) 245-2646.

Thomas E. Baltz. Guide. Boiling Springs. Baltz knows the area well. Also guides for bass on the Susquehanna and Juniata. (717) 486-7438.

Falling Spring Outfitters. Scotland, near Chambersburg and Falling Spring. Mark Sturtevant, proprietor. (717) 263-7811.

Ed Shenk. Master guide. Carlisle. *Do not miss the opportunity to fish with this Letort legend!* (717) 243-2679.

Yellow Breeches Outfitters. Boiling Springs. Complete tackle shop. (717) 258-6752.

Where to Stay

Allenberry Resort on the Yellow Breeches. Route 174 at Boiling Springs. Monday through Thursday, show a TU membership card for special rates. Moderate. (717) 258-3211.

The Highland House. Boiling Springs. Also on the Yellow Breeches. Moderate. (717) 258-3744.

Ragged Edge B&B. Near Falling Spring. Moderate. (717) 261-1195.

Falling Spring Inn B&B. Chambersburg. Limestone farmhouse two hundred feet from the stream. Moderate. (717) 767-3654. Nearly every major motel chain has a facility at the intersection of I-81 and the Pennsylvania Turnpike (I-76) in Carlisle. There are also many motels at the Chambersburg exit off I-81.

Where to Eat

Allenberry Resort. Boiling Springs. Large dining room and cozy, casual bar. Moderate. (717) 258-3211.

Boiling Springs Tavern. Boiling Springs. Fine chef, excellent food. Moderate to expensive. (717) 258-3614.

The Copper Kettle. Route 30, Chambersburg. Excellent prime rib. Moderate. (717) 264-3109.

The Depot. Clark Summit. Oak and fern decor. Moderate. (717) 587-1533.

Resources

Chambersburg Chamber of Commerce. (717) 264-7101.

Falling Spring Greenway, Inc. P.O. Box 961, Chambersburg, Pennsylvania 17201. For additional information, call Dennis J. LaBare, (410) 922-7476.

CHAPTER 6

Central Pennsylvania I: Spruce Creek, the Little Juniata River, and Spring Creek

I pulled up to Allan Bright's Spruce Creek Outfitters in the village of Spruce Creek, Pennsylvania, for the first time late on a Friday afternoon in August. The thermometer read 85 degrees Fahrenheit on the shop's front porch. Midsummer is not a propitious time to begin fishing central Pennsylvania streams, but I had heard that the area was a mecca for trout fishermen, and I came north from Maryland to escape the humidity and explore new waters.

As a neophyte in the area, I asked Allan where I should go. It was dry and the streams were low in Centre and Huntingdon Counties. "You got the *Pennsylvania Atlas?*" I did. Allan marked stretches on the rivers and streams I should explore, specific to the pull-offs, with stick-on notes that read, "Life's a bitch and then you die." Then he set me up with some flies—little blue duns, beetles, ants, and a few midges—and told me to come back later and let him know how I made out.

Though I did not catch many trout that first trip, I now return three or four times a year, and I have yet to find an area within four hours of Baltimore, Washington, Pittsburgh, and Philadelphia with as many productive wild trout streams as the central Pennsylvania waters listed below. Visiting the area in May, June, or September, my biggest problem is deciding which stream to fish! In the summer, the Trico and terrestrial fishing can be outstanding.

Most of the fish in public wild trout waters in central Pennsylvania range between eleven and fourteen inches, but Spruce Creek, Penns Creek, the Little Juniata River, and Fishing Creek all net fortunate anglers fish from eighteen to twenty inches every season. Our eastern wild browns are noted more for their ability to discern the difference between naturals and imitations (as well as their inclination to hold in unreachable lies) than for their size. Accuracy, drift-free presentation and stealth are essential after early June. Long delicate tippets (10 to 12 feet, 6X to 8X) are *de rigueur.* As those who fish these waters know, if you can catch fish in central Pennsylvania, you are ready to fish almost anywhere else in the country.

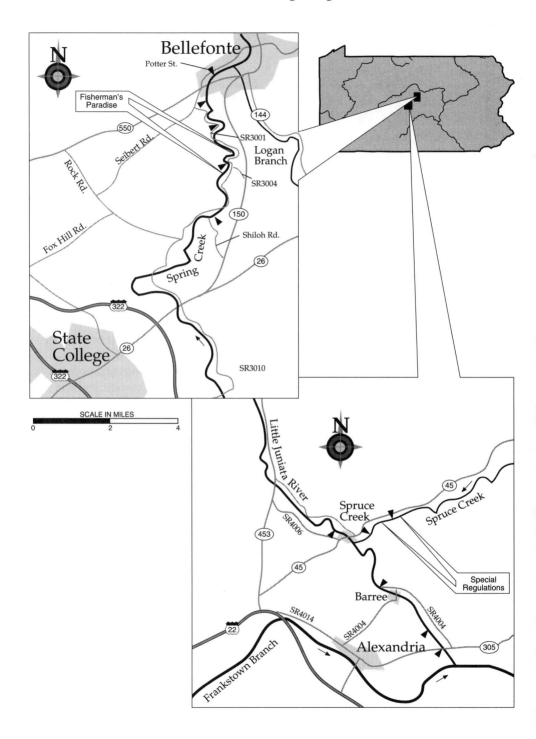

Except for Fishing Creek in Clinton County, all the streams described here lie along either Route 45 (Penns Valley) or Route 192 (Brush Valley). Both roads pass traditional Amish and Mennonite farms and include some of the prettiest agricultural land in the East. Whether you approach central Pennsylvania from the east or the west, it is possible to fish some of the streams in a single weekend, and all of them in four or five days. My happiest fishing vacations have been ten-day trips when I plotted a course that included all these waters.

SPRUCE CREEK

Despite its reputation, Spruce Creek offers few stretches of *public* wild trout water. The section made famous by former President Carter is a stocked, privately owned stretch, as are several others from which most reports of the Spruce Creek lunkers originate. Spruce Creek does hold a few very large wild trout, but the ones your angling friends are likely to have caught and photographed are usually stockies. The exceptions are fish taken on the Colerain Club private water, where the brown trout are all wild. A few fingerling Kamloops rainbows have been put in here and have grown remarkably large and strong.

Spruce Creek has magnificent hatches of mayflies, as well as good caddis and stonefly activity. The water is twenty-five to thirty feet wide and just deep enough to require chest waders in the deepest pools. Wading is not a problem, but casting can be. There are several reaches where the water narrows considerably, and one must be able to cast straight ahead upstream through an alley between alder bushes.

I also have ongoing contests with a willow tree and two mean evergreens on three of the public water's best pools: Their lower branches are as intent on taking my flies as I imagine the fish would be, could I but cast them accurately enough to find out.

The most productive stretch of public, Catch-and-Release wild trout water is maintained by Penn State. It lies less than one mile east of Spruce Creek village. Park in the weedy field on the right side of road where you see a big wooden sign dedicated to George Harvey. Walk downstream seventy-five yards to where the water divides and fish up- or downstream. As you move upstream, the southern (right) branch is the easiest to fish.

Regulations

Catch-and-Release regulations apply on the Penn State water from about .6 mile above the village of Spruce Creek to .5 mile upstream to a wire across the stream that marks private property.

Access
- The Penn State water is .6 miles east of Spruce Creek. Look for a weedy field on the south side of the road. Park there and fish up- or downstream.
- A second, shorter open stretch lies on the east side of Spruce Creek village. Sign in with John at the white cottage just across the bridge over the stream.

Hatches, Flies, and Best Times to Fish
Except for the little black and gray midges that appear in late March, Spruce Creek hatches don't emerge in earnest until the appearance of the Blue Quills and Hendricksons in April and early May. Spruce Creek fishes well from April through October. The following hatch information was provided by Allan Bright at Spruce Creek Outfitters for Spruce Creek and the Juniata River.

March
Black midge (#20–#22), gray midge (#20–#22), black stonefly (#14–#16).

Spring (April to May)
Blue Quill (#18), blue dun (#20), Blue-Winged Olive (#18–#20), Hendrickson (#14), Red Quill (#16), grannom (#12–#14), black caddis (#16), green caddis (#14).

Late spring (May to June)
Blue Quill (#18–#20), blue dun (#20), sulphur (#14–#16), March Brown (#12–#14), Gray Fox (#12–#14), green drake (#10), slate drake (#12–#14), Blue-Winged Olive (#14), Ginger Quill (#12–#14), Light Cahill (#12–#14), green caddis (#14–#16), yellow cranefly (#16–#20).

Summer (June to July)
Yellow drake (*Potamanthus distinctus*, #12), Blue-Winged Olive (#14–#20), blue dun (#20), sulphur (#16–#18), slate drake (#10), Cream Cahill (#14–#16), tan and cream caddis (#16–#18).

Midsummer (July to August)
Trico (#22–#24), little blue dun (#20), little white mayfly (#28), slate drake (#14), cream caddis (#16–#18). On the Juniata, the third week of August, the whitefly (*E. leukon*, #14–#18).

THE LITTLE JUNIATA RIVER
The river originates upstream of Altoona, merges with the main stem south of Alexandria, and empties into the Susquehanna River at Duncan-

non, just north of Harrisburg. The hatch information above will work for the Juniata. The river fishes well late into the fall.

At the bridge in Spruce Creek, the Juniata is about a hundred feet wide and three to five feet deep during an average May or June. It is not a difficult river to wade at this junction, although chest waders and felt soles are a must. The river is stocked with fingerling trout, many of which grow to sixteen inches or more and put up very good fight. There is productive holding water throughout the Little Juniata above Spruce Creek.

Below the mouth of Spruce Creek, the riverbanks are posted by a private fishing club enterprise. Because the Juniata is a navigable river, the public is allowed access to the streambed throughout its length. However, the gradient becomes steeper and larger rocks create imposing pocket water as the Juniata descends into the gorge area. It's the kind of stretch where walking in the water is a nuisance, and one would prefer to use the streambanks and get in the water nearer the good lies.

The best August whitefly fishing I've ever had was based on Charlie Meck's recommendation to go into the Little Juniata above the railroad bridge where Route 305 crosses the river east of Alexandria. Turn left (north) up the dirt road just west of the bridge and park when you see the railroad bridge. If the whitefly is there, you'll see other fishermen. Prominent among them will be Meck, strolling the stream, commenting, and instructing friends and strangers alike.

Access
- At Spruce Creek Outfitters in the village of Spruce Creek.
- Roads on both sides of the river upstream from Spruce Creek.
- The gorge section. Go to Alexandria and follow the signs to Barree. Cross the railroad tracks in Barree, and take a left at a dead end. This will lead to another dead end and parking lot. For the best fishing, walk upstream one mile.

SPRING CREEK
This limestoner has always been a well-known fishery; however, it gained publicity recently when the state purchased a section closed to anglers and threatened by developers. It is now conserved as public, Catch-and-Release water, and it is not stocked.

Like Valley Creek near Philadelphia, Spring Creek became a wild trout stream somewhat accidentally. It used to be stocked; however, in the 1950s the state stopped putting in fish because pollution in the water made them unsafe to eat. The result was that in a few years, Spring Creek boasted a fine population of wild brown trout.

The stream has a reputation for producing large fish, and I've seen some caught there. I like Spring Creek for two other reasons: its excellent

Trico hatch and the fact that it is a successful public reclamation project. The purchase of property along SR3001 is a showcase for the Fish Commission and its partners that helped preserve this magnificent trout water.

Regulations
Catch-and-Release, Fly-Fishing-Only regulations apply from the bridge on SR3010 at Oak Hall to the mouth of the stream and also on the Fisherman's Paradise stretch near Bellefonte.

Access
Spring Creek is twenty-two miles east of Spruce Creek between State College and Bellefonte. Take Route 26 east out of State College, and make a left on Route 150.
  • Fisherman's Paradise. Take a left off Route 150 onto SR3004 and another left on SR3001 (Spring Creek Road) to parking and special regulations.
  • From Fisherman's Paradise to Route 550. Much of this stretch, which used to be closed, has been purchased by the Pennsylvania Fish Commission and is now open to fly anglers. Follow directions to Fisherman's Paradise, but take a *right* on SR3001. There is parking along SR3001.
  • Bellefonte. Take SR3001 and cross Route 550 onto Potter Street. There are several places to pull off along Potter Street.

Hatches, Flies, and Best Times to Fish
Cold limestone springs keep the water fishable year-round. Spring Creek does not have a lot of mayfly hatches, especially not traditional early-season bugs like the Hendrickson, Quill Gordon, March Brown, or green drake. It does have an excellent sulphur hatch from mid-May to mid-June, as well as blue-winged olives (April to May, #20), Blue Quills (May, #18), Cahills (June #14–#16), and caddis (grannom, tan, and olive #16–#18). Charles Meck advises anglers to carry a size 24 gray midge pattern to match a hatch that occurs throughout the winter.

Get to this stream by 7:00 A.M. from mid-July into September and you'll experience one of the best Trico hatches in the state. In summer, Blue Quills, sulphurs, and olives may appear, and the terrestrial fishing is excellent.

IF YOU GO . . .
From Washington, the trip is about four and one-half hours. Take the Capital Beltway to I-270 to Frederick, Maryland, then I-70 west from Frederick to Breezewood, Pennsylvania. At Breezewood, go east on the Pennsylva-

nia Turnpike to exit 13. Then take Route 522 north to Mount Union, go west on Route 22 to Route 453 at Water Street. Turn right on Route 453, then right on Route 45 to Spruce Creek.

From Philadelphia, it's about four hours to Spruce Creek. Take the Pennsylvania Turnpike west to I-83 north (just east of Harrisburg) to Routes 22/322 to Lewistown. Continue on Route 322 to State College, or go east on Route 45 at Boalsburg to reach Millheim, or west on Route 45 to Spruce Creek.

From Pittsburgh, the drive takes under three hours. Take Route 22 east past Altoona to Water Street. At Water Street, go left on Route 453, then right on Route 45 to Spruce Creek.

US Airways and other carriers run commuter flights from major metropolitan areas into University Park Airport at State College.

Tackle Shops and Guides

Spruce Creek Outfitters. Spruce Creek. Allan Bright, proprietor. Flies, tackle, guides, information. Allan has exclusive guiding rights to a private stretch of wild trout water on Spruce Creek. It's an unusual opportunity to fish private water for big wild browns and Kamloops rainbows. He also has access to private lodgings, which may be available for rental. (814) 632-3071.

Fisherman's Paradise. 2603 East College Avenue, State College (just off Route 26). Complete fly-fishing outfitter: rods, guides, flies, etc. (814) 234-4189.

Where to Stay

Spruce Creek B&B. Spruce Creek. Dean Nelson, proprietor. Attractive old Victorian house in Spruce Creek village. Suites accommodating up to four people. Moderate. (814) 632-3777.

Cedar Hill Farm B&B. Spruce Creek. Opposite Penn State's water on Spruce Creek. Inexpensive. (814) 632-8319.

John Carper's Bed and Beer B&B. Spruce Creek. Two two-bedroom suites with kitchenettes in a building next to the Spruce Creek Tavern. Continental breakfast, TV, AC. Inexpensive. (814) 632-3287.

Hearthwood House. Alexandria. Ten minutes south of Spruce Creek. Hospitable to anglers. Inexpensive. (814) 669-4386.

Camping

Penn Roosevelt Campground. Near State College. (814) 667-1800.
Poe Paddy Campground. Penns Creek. (717) 667-3622.
Poe Valley Campground. Penns Creek. (814) 349-8778.

Where to Eat

Spruce Creek Tavern. Spruce Creek. A favorite local hangout. The "small" order of french fries is a large waiter's tray heaped with deep fries! Inexpensive.

Old Oak Tavern. Pine Grove Mills, near State College. Route 45. Good food. Moderate. (814) 238-5898.

Sports Bar. Alexandria, fifteen minutes from Spruce Creek. Convenient for very late dinner after June spinner falls or the August white fly hatch on the Juniata. No reservations. Inexpensive to moderate.

CHAPTER 7

Central Pennsylvania II: Penns Creek, Elk Creek, Pine Creek (Centre County), Fishing Creek (Clinton County), and White Deer Creek

PENNS CREEK

Penns Creek is one of the largest, longest, best-known trout streams in the state, and its trout habitat always seems to be at risk. TU and other conservation groups maintain a constant vigil on interests that would rob Penns of its good-quality water and diminish its stature as a trout fishery. The Con-Stone Company recently threatened a mine that would severely degrade the watershed. The Penns Valley Conservation Association, an alliance of conservation-minded organizations and individuals, has lobbied to have Penns' status upgraded to "exceptional value," a designation that precludes tampering with cold-water resources. The matter remains unresolved.

Penns is about a hundred feet wide, beginning below Coburn through the Catch-and-Release area near Weikert. There are many deep holding pools and productive riffles. The bottom is not difficult to negotiate, but chest waders and felt-soled boots are recommended. Because the river is so wide, casting on Penns is a joy.

My best fish on Penns have been taken during the green drake and sulphur hatches. I like to fish from late afternoon until well after dark, often casting to fish I can hear but not see. There are excellent spinner falls, and nighttime visibility is comparatively good.

The green drake hatch on Penns is legendary. Many angling buddies gather for this emergence on an annual basis. It usually occurs between May 27 and June 14. Make a trip the first weekend in June and you are *almost* guaranteed big green drakes! The bar at the Millheim Hotel is a repository of serious Pennsylvania anglers from all corners of the state.

Regulations

In 1995, the Pennsylvania Fish and Boat Commission imposed new regulations on Penns Creek. For seven miles, from its confluence with Elk Creek in Coburn downstream to the Catch-and-Release area, there is a two-fish-per-day, fourteen-inch-minimum-size creel limit from Opening Day through Labor Day. Between those dates, all fish must be released.

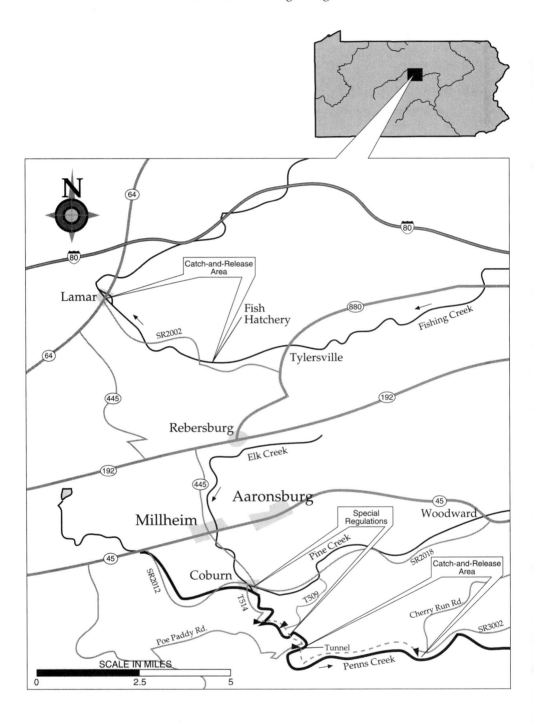

In the Catch-and-Release area, at the Poe Paddy campground, 3.9 miles from Swift Run downstream to the R. J. Soper property line, artificial lures or flies only are allowed, and all fish hooked must be released.

Access
• From Spring Mills to Coburn, along SR2012. Most of this water is slow and deep. It warms quickly in the late spring.

• In Coburn, along T514, and at parking lot at the end of T514 below Coburn, where the pedestrian bridge crosses the river.

• At Ingleby. Take SR2018 out of Coburn toward Woodward. Turn right on T509, Ingleby Road. Follow the rough dirt road past some cabins to the water. This puts you in the middle of the Trophy Trout section. The Catch-and-Release (artificial-lures-only) stretch is 3.9 miles from Swift Run downstream to below Cherry Run.

• Upper end of Catch-and-Release area. From Coburn, take Siglerville-Millheim Pike (a dirt road) over Big Poe Mountain. Make a left on Poe Valley Road, past Poe Valley State Park to Poe Paddy Campground. Continue through the campground and follow the road past cabins. Park, walk across the railroad bridge, through a tunnel, and onto a railroad bed that follows Penns down into the Catch-and-Release area.

• Lower end of Catch-and-Release area. Take SR3002 (not on map) 2.7 miles east of Weikert. Then take SR3002 1.3 miles to a parking area.

Hatches, Flies, and Best Times to Fish
The best time to fish Penns is between Opening Day and July 1. The water warms up in all but the most forgiving of summers, and trout anglers shift to nearby limestone streams or waters with more canopy.

The Spruce Creek hatch information in chapter 6 will serve anglers on Penns. Allan Bright says that hatches on Penns, especially the green drake hatch, usually occur about a week later than emergences on Spruce Creek. His information is based on forty years' angling experience in central Pennsylvania.

Other outstanding hatches on Penns include the grannom (end of April), March Browns, sulphurs, blue-winged olives (mid-May through June), Cahills in June, and the whitefly (below Weikert) from mid-August into September.

ELK CREEK
Elk Creek is a midsize (twenty feet wide) limestone creek that flows through Millheim to join Penns at Coburn. This has always been a very special stream for me. I had the privilege of fishing the narrows section above Millheim with Allan Bright and landing one of the most beautiful sixteen-inch wild brown trout I've ever seen. It was also one of the most difficult to catch: I had to place my fly, a #18 black ant, directly under

some hemlock boughs that touched the water. I caught the fish in about eighteen inches of water.

Until Bright showed me differently, I couldn't believe this stretch of Elk actually held trout. It is shallow and very clear, and you have to look very closely to detect fish. Some days, you'd swear there are no trout in the water. However, casting dry flies to rising fish on Elk is as good and as challenging as trout fishing gets!

To my dismay, the narrows section has since been posted, and one must join an angling association to fish it. This is a sad development for people like me and many other local anglers who drove off poachers, picked up trash, maintained the stream, and cherished its fish.

The water is still open downstream through Millheim. Between Millheim and Coburn, the stream is less accessible, but if you ask permission, landowners will usually let you fish.

Regulations and Access

Elk is not stocked. General trout-fishing regulations apply. The stream can be accessed in Millheim at Park Street (ask permission from the property owner on the northwest corner of the stream at the bridge), downstream where it runs along Water Street in Millheim, and in Coburn, behind the high school.

The best time to fish Elk is anytime you see a hatch, and hatches are plentiful! I find it very difficult to interest fish when there are no bugs in sight. Watch for hatches of Blue Quills and blue-winged olives in the spring and fall. Terrestrial fishing is also excellent, and the stream has good emergences of sulphurs and green drakes.

PINE CREEK (CENTRE COUNTY)

This Pine is not the big creek that flows through the Pine Creek Valley north of Williamsport. This one is a small limestone stream that empties into Elk, just before Elk enters Penns at Coburn. It comes into its own late in the spring in time for the sulphur hatch. Pine also provides excellent terrestrial fishing midsummer, and it produces well late into the fall.

Much of the water flows slow and deep and is tricky to wade without giving away your presence and disturbing the fish. The best stretch to wade is along SR2018 between Coburn and Broad Road (not on map). You can park on the shoulder and enter the water at the bridges or wherever land is not posted.

General trout regulations apply on Pine Creek, and its hatches are much like those on Elk and Penns.

FISHING CREEK (CLINTON COUNTY)

This is a trophy trout stream, holding at least three times as many fish now as it did when stocking ceased in the 1980s. There are a substantial number of trout more than sixteen inches long. I've landed a couple of them after dark, during the sulphur spinner fall in mid-June.

Fishing Creek offers seven miles of wild trout water, most of it accessible to the angler. The deep-green water is overhung with hemlocks and fed by small freestone tributaries and limestone springs. It's one of the buggiest streams I've ever fished.

There is nothing easy about angling on Fishing Creek. The water gets a fair amount of pressure (more and more in recent years), and the fish provide a graduate school education. They are careful, choosy, and spooky. Once hooked, they put up a long, substantial battle. I remember an eighteen-inch brown that took a sparsely tied Pale Evening Dun after dark one night in June. He fought me for fifteen minutes, putting down every other fish in the large pool as he thrashed around.

Fishing Creek is a good stream for nymphs. I've had days where a Green Weenie produced surprising numbers of large fish, and other days when I couldn't get a nibble. Pheasant-tail and small beadhead patterns also do well here.

Regulations
The Trophy Trout section extends five miles between the Lamar and the Tylersville Fish Hatcheries. Only artificial lures and flies may be used. Between Opening Day and Labor Day, two trout at least fourteen inches long may be kept daily. At other times, all fish must be released.

Access
There are numerous pull-offs on SR2002 between Tylersville and Lamar. A walk-in behind the Seig Conference Center gets you to less pressured water, but I've had some of my best luck fishing the beautiful pools next to the road in the cottage section.

Take Route 45 to Route 445 north in Millheim. Take Route 445 to Route 192, make a right on Route 192 (east) to Rebersburg, and take a left on Route 880. At the stop sign in Tylersville, make a left onto SR2002, pass the hatchery, cross a bridge, and you will be in the narrows section.

Hatches, Flies, and Best Times to Fish
The Fishing Creek green drake hatch begins about the same time as the Penns Creek hatch and may last a few days longer. Fishing Creek is also known for its winter (February and March) hatch of small blue-winged olives as well as for the midges that can always be found there.

Other major hatches include Blue Quill, Quill Gordon, Hendricksons, black caddis (mid-April); sulphurs, green drakes, Cahills (mid-May to June); blue-winged olives, green caddis, slate drakes, terrestrials (early June to late July). In July, Tricos show up downstream of Mackeyville.

WHITE DEER CREEK

White Deer Creek is a freestone stream located just south of I-80 in Bald Eagle State Forest (see DeLorme's *Pennsylvania Atlas and Gazetteer*, pp. 49–50). The stream is heavily wooded and remains cool when other freestoners are too low and warm to fish. It is an excellent dry-fly stream. Often trout will rise to an attractor pattern when no bugs are emerging.

Although White Deer is stocked, the fish are not easy to catch, and there are plenty of wild browns. About twenty feet wide, White Deer has good footing. Casting can be challenging, as there are lots of overhanging trees and deadfalls. As soon as the water level drops in the spring, White Deer can get shallow and require a stealthy approach. It remains clear except after substantial storms. I've found it clean when other waters were off-color. It has good hatches. The hatch information in chapter 6 covers any flies you will need on White Deer.

Regulations

There is a Delayed-Harvest, Fly-Fishing-Only stretch 3.1 miles from Cooper Mill Road upstream to the Union-Centre County line.

Access

Take Route 445 north off Route 45 in Millheim to Route 192. Take Route 192 east to R. B. Winter State Park. Take McCall Dam Road into the park to White Deer Road. Turn right on White Deer Road. There are pull-offs along the road. For the first mile or two, you may not be able to see the water, but walk down one hundred yards and you will be on the stream.

IF YOU GO . . .

The trip from Washington to State College or Millheim takes about four and one-half hours. Take the capital beltway to I-270 to Frederick, Maryland, then I-70 west from Frederick to Breezewood, Pennsylvania. At Breezewood, go east on the Pennsylvania Turnpike to exit 13. At the exit, take Route 522 north to Mount Union and Lewistown, then west on Route 322 to State College. Go right (east) on Route 45 south of State College to Millheim.

From Philadelphia, take the Pennsylvania Turnpike west to I-83 north (just east of Harrisburg) to Routes 22/322 to Lewistown. Continue on Route 322 to State College, or take Route 45 south of State College to Millheim.

From Pittsburgh, the trip to State College is a little less than four hours. Take Route 22 east past Altoona to Water Street. At Water Street, go left on Route 453, then right on Route 45 to Spruce Creek. Continue east on Route 45 to Boalsburg, and take Route 322 north to State College. Or continue on Route 45 to Millheim.

US Airways and other carriers run commuter flights from major metropolitan areas into University Park Airport at State College.

Tackle Shops and Guides

Spruce Creek Outfitters. Spruce Creek. Allan Bright, proprietor. Flies, tackle, guides, information. (814) 632-3071.

Fisherman's Paradise. 2603 East College Avenue, State College, (just off Route 26). Complete fly-fishing outfitter: rods, guides, flies, everything you could possibly need. (814) 234-4189.

The Feathered Hook. On Penn's Creek in Coburn. John Witwer, proprietor. Destination fly shop and guide service. (814) 349-8757.

Penns Creek Fly Shop. Selinsgrove. Not very near Penns Creek, but a good shop. (717) 743-5008.

Where to Stay

Autoport. State College. Pool and restaurant. Inexpensive. (814) 237-7666.

Centre Mills B&B. Millheim. Limestone farmhouse on upper Elk Creek. Private fishing on Elk for guests. Moderate. (814) 349-8000.

Feathered Hook B&B. Coburn, on Penn's Creek. Inexpensive. (814) 349-8757.

Lead Horse B&B. Spring Mills, near State College. Lynn Ralston, proprietor. In a historic landmark—a three-story Victorian house. Moderate. (814) 422-8783.

Millheim Hotel. Route 45, Millheim. An amiable, old-fashioned hotel. No private baths. Inexpensive. Be sure to ask about the weekend B&B package. (814) 349-5994.

Many hotel and motel chains are represented in State College.

Camping

Hemlock Acres Camping Area. Coburn. (814) 349-5955.

Twin Oaks Campground. Bellefonte. (814) 355-9820.

Penn Roosevelt Campground. Near State College. (814) 667-1800.

Poe Paddy Campground. Penns Creek. (717) 667-3622.

Poe Valley Campground. Penns Creek. (814) 349-8778.

Where to Eat

The Hummingbird Room. Just west of Millheim. Excellent food. BYOB. Expensive. (814) 349-8225.

Millheim Hotel. Millheim. Very good, reasonably priced food all day long. Decent wine list. Entrees and lighter fare. Moderate. (814) 349-5994.

Old Oak Tavern. Route 45, Pine Grove Mills, near State College. Good food. Moderate. (814) 238-5898.

State College, the home of Pennsylvania State University, has many good restaurants. Check local listings.

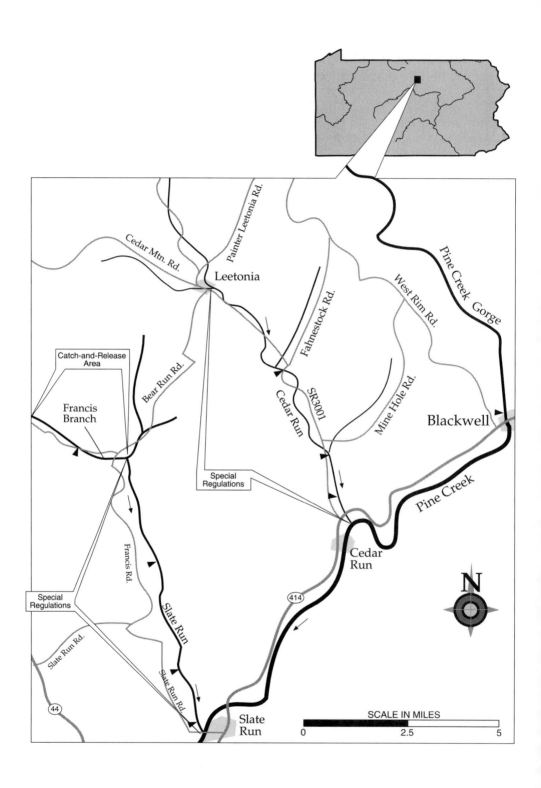

Catch-and-Release
Area

Francis
Branch

Cedar Mtn. Rd.

Painter Leetonia Rd.

Leetonia

Fahnestock Rd.

West Rim Rd.

Pine Creek Gorge

Bear Run Rd.

Cedar Run

SR3001

Mine Hole Rd.

Blackwell

Special
Regulations

Francis Rd.

Special
Regulations

Slate Run Rd.

Slate Run

Pine Creek

Cedar
Run

414

44

Slate Run Rd.

Slate
Run

N

SCALE IN MILES

0   2.5   5

Northcentral Pennsylvania I— The Pine Creek Valley: Pine Creek, Slate Run, Francis Branch, Cedar Run, Little Pine Creek, and Young Womans Creek

The Pine Creek Valley is one of the most dramatic scenic areas in all of Pennsylvania. It is the beloved getaway of many Keystone State hunters and anglers, many of whom park campers year-round along the river. With few exceptions, residents are unsophisticated and lifestyle-basic. Stir-crazy urban anglers look forward to spring weekends here. They seek out the streams in this area to find the instant sensation of wilderness and rural atmosphere.

On the drive north from Interstate 80 and Williamsport or Jersey Shore, Pennsylvania, on Route 44, the countryside suddenly changes from gentle rolling farmland to forested uplands and mountains. Pine Creek helps define the change: Between Waterville and its mouth at the West Branch of the Susquehanna, where the water is about two hundred feet wide, Pine Creek is a warm-water fishery. From Waterville upstream to Blackwell, Pine is a wide swath of grosgrain water, flanked by gentle slopes rising on either side of the river valley. The river is an endless series of fishy-looking riffles, runs, and pools. Overhanging trees, however, are sparse, and the lack of shade results in big water that warms quickly in the early summer.

Above Blackwell, Pine makes a ninety-degree swing to the north through the Pine Creek Gorge, known as Pennsylvania's Grand Canyon. Ledgerock and trees rise abruptly several hundred feet above the water, and there are no bridges here. Canoers and kayakers love the section, and anglers find the water at the foot of steep paths. Above the gorge, the water ranges from twenty-five to thirty-five feet wide, and the gradient is not steep.

Pine Creek and its tributaries provide anglers with a huge variety of water, ranging from Pine Creek (where it is about 150 feet wide near Slate Run) to Francis Branch (a steep mountain stream tributary of Slate that can be jumped over at most points after spring runoff). All the water in the area fishes best in the spring. The fall season is also beautiful, and if there has been adequate rainfall through the summer, the streams will fish then.

For many Pennsylvania trout fishermen, a trip to the Pine Creek Valley is an annual tradition. Anglers usually travel for the Hendrickson, Quill Gordon, March Brown, or green drake hatches in late April and May. There is a spirit of camaraderie among fishermen who congregate at the local watering holes such as the Hotel Manor, the Blackwell, and the Cedar Run Inn. Everyone wants to know what fly or lure is working best, and most knowledge is freely shared.

PINE CREEK
Pine Creek originates in Potter County and flows more than seventy-five miles to its mouth on the West Branch of the Susquehanna River. The river for most of its length is big, wide water and contains both stocked and wild trout. It warms considerably by mid-June, so plan a trip early if you want to fish the big water at its most productive time. Moreover, the most famous hatches on Pine Creek and its tributaries are the green and brown drakes in late May and early June—another reason to make early reservations for spring fishing.

The big undifferentiated water of Pine Creek is also an excellent wet-fly fishery. If you like fishing droppers, this is one place you can do so without tangling a leader of multiple flies.

Regulations and Access
General trout regulations apply on Pine Creek. There are pull-offs along Route 414 from Waterville to Blackwell. At Slate Run and Cedar Run (Pettecote Junction Campground), there are large parking areas. The lower gorge section above Blackwell can be very productive in early May. Blackwell is located on Route 414, twenty-six miles east of Route 44.

SLATE RUN
The upper section of Slate Run has been designated a Heritage Trout angling area: Fly-Fishing-Only, Catch-and-Release. The protected section is the half mile from the Tioga County line upstream to the confluence of the Cushman's and Francis Branches, both of which are good, smaller wild trout streams. Slate Run has the steepest gradient of all the streams in this chapter. If you don't like a steep hike and a fair amount of boulder hopping, Slate Run is not for you. However, the water flows and the scenery are magnificent, and, though the footing is tricky, the streambed is not particularly slippery.

Regulations and Access
Fly-Fishing-Only, Catch-and-Release from the mouth of Francis Branch to the mouth of Slate Run on Pine Creek. There are several pull-offs along

Slate Run Road from which you can drop down to the stream. Slate Run Road runs north off of Route 414 in the village of Slate Run, which is located on Route 414 seventeen miles east of Route 44.

FRANCIS BRANCH

This is a wild trout tributary of Slate Run. It is often suggested as an alternative to Slate, especially when the latter is too high and swift to fish. Francis Branch Road runs along the water north from its mouth on Slate Run. Unfortunately, runoff from this road can muddy Francis Branch during heavy rainfall. From its mouth to Kramer Hollow, Francis Branch is governed by Catch-and-Release, Fly-Fishing-Only regulations.

CEDAR RUN

Cedar Run is one of my favorite Pennsylvania trout streams. I love the waterscape: hemlocks shading a stream that is easy to wade and punctuated with limestone outcroppings. Mossy banks and pine needles make Cedar Run an ideal picnic spot. Cedar is not very deep, however, so as soon as the water gets low, its trout become as spooky as any I've ever approached. I thought it was my own ineptitude until Dave Rothrock took my brother Dick and me there, and we all had the same experience. In periods of low water, prepare to cast on your knees, and you'll have to be able to roll out forty feet of line terminating in 7X tippet!

Regulations and Access

Cedar Run has more than seven miles of designated Trophy Trout water. Only artificial lures or flies may be used from the mouth of Buck Run downstream to the mouth of Cedar Run. The minimum-size trout that may be kept is fourteen inches, and the daily creel limit is two trout.

A dirt road runs along the stream from its mouth at Cedar Run to Leetonia. Like Slate Run, there are a number of places to park along the way. The village of Cedar Run is located on Route 414, twenty-one miles east of its junction with Route 44.

LITTLE PINE CREEK

Little Pine empties into Pine at Waterville (see DeLorme's *Pennsylvania Atlas and Gazetteer,* p. 49). It is about forty feet wide and is a stocked trout stream with little of the distinction that marks Cedar and Slate Runs. The hatches here are similar to those on Pine Creek. Little Pine warms up by mid-June.

Little Pine is governed by Delayed-Harvest, artificial-lures-and-flies-only regulations for one mile from the confluence of Carson Run downstream to the confluence of Schoolhouse Hollow.

YOUNG WOMANS CREEK

This is an excellent early-season stream teeming with wild trout in the nine- to twelve-inch category. Young Womans gets less pressure than other local streams, perhaps because it is not in the Pine Creek Valley. However, it is only a scenic thirty minutes from Slate Run.

Young Womans is a small to medium-sized stream, easy to access and to wade. Trout up to sixteen inches can be found in the special-regulations reaches. The grade of the stream is much gentler than that of Cedar or Slate Runs. It has excellent water quality and prolific mayfly and stonefly hatches. It is also well shaded, and the water remains cool through most summers.

Regulations

Selective harvest: artificial lures and flies only on the Right Branch of Young Womans Creek for five and one-half miles from the state forest property line upstream to Beechwood Trail. Fishery open year-round. Minimum size is twelve inches for brown trout and nine inches for all other trout; two-trout daily limit from Opening Day until Labor Day; Catch-and-Release the remainder of the year.

Access

From Waterville, stay on Route 44 (after Route 414 branches off to Slate Run). After about a twenty-minute drive from Waterville, you'll come to Benson Road. Take a left on Benson Road and go one-quarter mile to a fork; bear right and follow this road that runs along Young Womans to a steel bridge at Bull Run. This bridge is located approximately in the middle of the special regulations section. There is good fishing upstream or downstream.

Hatches, Flies, and Best Times to Fish

I like the Pine Creek Valley in late spring (May) and early fall (late September and October). In spring, high water may dictate where you fish; if Pine is too high or too warm, the folks at Slate Run Tackle will suggest you go "up on the runs." Pine does warm up quickly and cannot be counted on after June 15. Cedar and Slate Runs will remain cool throughout all but the hottest, driest summers, but they can begin to be very low by the end of June.

Early season (March)

Early black stonefly, early brown stonefly, Blue-Winged Olives.

Spring (mid-April to mid-May)

Grannom (dark brown sizes #14 and larger), Quill Gordons (#14), and Hendricksons (#14). The biggest caddis hatch on Pine Creek is the green egg-sac caddisfly (#16), which normally occurs during the third week of May. An olive beadhead caddis pupa pattern also works well at this time of year.

The first important hatch of the season and also the most consistent is the *Paraleptophlebia* (Blue Quill #18), which occurs on all the streams in the Pine Creek Valley beginning in late April or early May and continuing into late October.

Other important hatches are the March Browns (mid-May to June, #10), sulphurs (late May, #16), the aforementioned green and brown drakes late (May, #10), Light Cahills (early June, #14), and slate drakes (mid-June, #12). All streams have a moderate Trico hatch in July, but the water may be too low to fish by that time.

IF YOU GO . . .
From Baltimore or Washington, take I-83 north to Harrisburg. Pick up Route 11/15 north from Harrisburg, driving on the west side of the Susquehanna River. At Allenwood (four miles north of the junction of Route 15 and I-81), turn left on Route 44. Continue on Route 44 past Jersey Shore, join Route 220/44 west for two miles and exit, continuing on Route 44 to its junction with Route 414. Turn right on Route 414 toward Slate Run, Cedar Run, and Blackwell.

Tackle Shops and Guides
   Slate Run Tackle and Wolfe's General Store. Slate Run. Located at junction of Pine Creek and Slate Run on Route 414. This full-service Orvis dealer has an enormous inventory of equipment plus well-tied local flies. The store is also a wonderful takeout shop for pastries, sandwiches, wheel cheese, and hand-dipped ice cream. Fly-fishing schools and guides available. Store owners Tom and Debbie Finkbiner publish the best angling newsletter in the East and have also produced an excellent map of Slate and Cedar Runs as well as a local hatch chart. (717) 753-8551.
   Pine Creek Outfitters. Route 6 in the village of Ansonia, eleven miles west of Wellsboro. Outfitters for rafting, canoeing, hiking, bicycling, as well as a source of fishing advice. Best advice on floating the canyon; owners Chuck and Susan Dillon will mark best fishing spots on complimentary waterproof map of canyon area. (717) 724-3003.

Where to Stay
   Cedar Run Inn. Located just of Route 414 in charming village of Cedar Run, upstream from Slate Run. Moderate. (717) 353-6241.
   The Manor. Slate Run. A renowned angling establishment with somewhat Spartan accommodations. Restaurant and bar. Inexpensive. (717) 753-8414.

There are many B&Bs and motels near Wellsboro on Route 6. Inquire through Pine Creek Outfitters or through Slate Run Tackle.

The area is known for its "big woods" feeling. If you like camping, do so on this trip.

Camping

Campgrounds in Pennsylvania's Grand Canyon:

Twin Streams Campground. Morris. Twelve miles south of Wellsboro. (717) 353-7251.

Happy Acres Campground. Waterville. (717) 753-8221.

Little Pine Campground. Near Waterville. (717) 753-6000.

Blackwell Access Area. Blackwell. On Route 414 south of Pine Creek bridge at Blackwell. Parking, facilities. For information, contact the district forester in Wellsboro. (717) 724-2868.

Pettecote Junction Campground. Cedar Run, on the banks of Pine Creek, near inflow of Cedar Run. Fully equipped. (717) 353-7183.

Where to Eat

Cedar Run Inn. Cedar Run. This establishment has the only really excellent food and good wine list in the area. There is nothing like it in the Pine Creek Valley. Moderate. (717) 353-6241.

Slate Run Tackle and Wolfe's General Store. The best takeout breakfast and lunches in the area. Also, wonderful pastries. Inexpensive. (717) 753-8551.

The places listed below serve basic American bar food. You won't go hungry, but you won't miss it when you leave. None require reservations.

Manor Hotel. Slate Run. Basic American dishes. Bar. Inexpensive. (717) 753-8414.

Blackwell Hotel. Blackwell. Burgers and similar fare. Inexpensive. (717) 353-7435.

Penn Hotel. Morris, at the intersection of Routes 414 and 287. Inexpensive. (717) 353-6881.

Resources

Slate Run Tackle Map, Slate Run. This tackle shop has produced a large-scale map of the valley. It includes all the major streams and their tributaries and makes finding local roads and access points a pleasure.

CHAPTER 9

Northcentral Pennsylvania II— Potter County: The Upper Allegheny River, Oswayo Creek, Cross Fork, Yochum Run, Lyman Run, the East Fork of the Sinnemahoning Creek, and Kettle Creek

If I had all the time in the world and only one Pennsylvania county to fish, that county would be Potter. Roadside signs at the county line announce, "You have entered God's country." For me, this is near the mark. There are more than ninety miles of *designated* Class A wild trout water—streams in which native trout reproduce and are no longer stocked by the Fish Commission. And there are many more unclassified small wild trout streams as well.

Most of Potter County's minimal population lives on farms in the valleys. Towns are small and the villages mere hamlets. There is only one stoplight in the entire county. Tourism is heavily focused on hunting—for bear, wild turkey, deer, and small game. There are acres and acres of state game and forest land, miles of snowmobile trails, and opportunities to view elk and to canoe through gorges and wide plains.

The headwaters of the Allegheny River are in Potter County, northeast of Coudersport on Route 49 near Gold. I was having a relaxed exploratory drive around when I stumbled onto the large billboard that announces the proximity of the headwaters. It was humbling to see this little spring spurting up from a cow pasture, then visualizing it by the time it becomes the huge navigable tributary of the Ohio River.

Potter County is a long haul from almost anywhere in the mid-Atlantic, but the five- to six-hour drive is well worth it if you can afford to spend three or four days. There are so many different angling opportunities that it requires careful advance planning and current local information to decide where to fish and when. In addition to the designated wild trout waters, the state stocks more than 150,000 trout in 800 other areas. There are Catch-and-Release, Heritage Trout, Delayed-Harvest, Selective-Harvest, and traditional Put-and-Take areas.

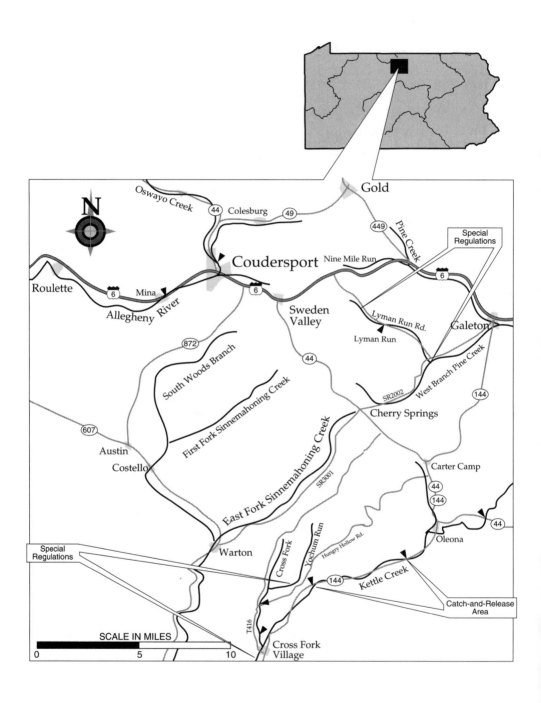

For the purposes of this book, I've listed the better-known streams that I have fished, as well as the ones to which I tend to return. On my initial trips, I'd often wonder by the end of the day whether I had enjoyed the fishing or the exploring more. Since then, I've settled on stretches of wild or Catch-and-Release trout water where I've done well and can quickly reorient myself after many months away from the area. Because of the abundant opportunities, I strongly recommend hiring a guide or going with friends on your first trip.

None of the rivers and streams described in this chapter are wider than forty to fifty feet (if that) where I fish them. Wading is usually not a problem, although there is always the possibility of high water early in the season.

Much of Potter County is situated on a high plateau, and streams have a relatively gentle grade. They are freestone with a rock, pebble, and sand bottom. Standard 3- to 6-weight trout rods from 6 to 9 feet long will cover all occasions. There's always a place for a small stream rod, such as a 7-foot, 4-weight, in Potter County.

The hatches and flies listed for Kettle Creek (below) will serve as a general guide for anglers visiting the area. However, many streams have special strengths, and these are noted when possible. Always consult local guides and fly shops for current conditions and advice on which streams are fishing well.

Regulations

As previously noted, there are many different regulations governing the streams of Potter County. I note some as part of the general description of the water; however, it is best to rely on the regulations manual provided with the fishing license.

THE UPPER ALLEGHENY RIVER

Where it fishes best, the upper Allegheny is about thirty to forty-five feet wide and runs through upland meadows and hardwoods north of Coudersport. Footing is stable. Chest waders should be used in the early season, as there are some deep pools.

Access

• Some of the best early-season fishing is downstream from Coudersport between the Reed Run Bridge and Mina. This water holds both stocked and wild browns. Take Route 6 west from Coudersport and enter the stream near the bridge, then fish upstream. (Note: Reed Run is posted.)

• After the early season, the Allegheny fishes best *above* Coudersport along Route 49 to Colesburg. Stocked and wild trout are both present. The

Delayed-Harvest area starts 4.1 miles from Coudersport and is 2.6 miles long. There is room to park on the wide shoulders of Route 49.

Hatches
Some of the best hatches on the upper Allegheny include Hendricksons, March Browns, sulphurs, and drakes. I once spent an outstanding June evening fishing a gray drake at dusk on the river behind Dr. Pete Ryan's house. Dr. Ryan is a dentist, fly tier, and longtime advocate for wild trout in Potter County. His leadership in the God's Country chapter of TU is legendary.

OSWAYO CREEK
This stream is also north of Coudersport (see DeLorme's *Pennsylvania Atlas and Gazetteer,* p. 33). It has a reputation for being extremely temperamental, giving up extraordinary numbers of trout one day and seeming sterile the next. The best fishing requires a short walk through meadows to the stream. The water runs between alders and other low bushes. There are lots of steep scoured banks, heavy brush, and deadfalls to protect trout.

Take Route 44 north from Coudersport to Coneville. Fish between Coneville and Millport for the largest trout. The main stem from the village of Oswayo to Clara Creek provides five and one-half miles of wild trout water.

Access
- At Calhoun Road in village of Oswayo.
- T354 bridge on Route 244 (fish upstream) (not on map).
- Bridge past the cemetery on Route 244 (not on map).
- T351 bridge on Route 44 near Clara Creek (not on map).

Hatches
Some noteworthy hatches on the Oswayo include Hendricksons, Blue Quills, sulphurs, green drakes, yellow drakes, and Tricos. The stream has excellent Trico hatches all summer long.

CROSS FORK
Cross Fork is one of my favorite Potter County streams. In fact, I enjoy fishing it more than my actual tally of trout taken there justifies. I've found Cross Fork somewhat wanting in fish more than ten inches long on my last two trips, but this could have been the result of drought.

I like the size of the stream (about twenty-five feet) and the combination of riffles, runs, and the occasional long flat pool, and there is just enough overhang to keep the water cool and the fish protected.

Regulations

Cross Fork is regulated by Heritage Trout Angling rules. For 5.4 miles from Bear Trap Lodge downstream to the Weed property (one mile above the village), fishing may be done with artificial flies and streamers only, tied on single barbless hooks. All trout must be released.

I usually begin at the area known as Hungry Hollow. Fishing upstream from the campsite will quickly take you into smaller water, with far less angling pressure. Downstream water is wider and deeper.

Access

Take Route 144 north to the village of Cross Fork. Just before the bridge, turn upstream along a track with a No Outlet sign. This stretch can be productive, but it is also very popular. Continue on Route 144 over the bridge and take the first right up the hill. This is T416, which I call Cross Fork Road. The water can be reached easily at the following points:

• At Elk Lick Bridge on Cross Fork Road. Park on the road and walk down to the water.
• At Windfall Run Road.
• At Hungry Hollow Road. Turn right and park.
• On Cross Fork Road behind Bear Trap Lodge.

YOCHUM RUN

This is an undesignated wild trout stream. It is a small tributary of Cross Fork, which enters the latter above the Heritage Angling stretch. A path along the water makes it more accessible than many other native trout streams. It's worth a good look.

LYMAN RUN

Lyman Run is one of the best-known wild trout streams in the county. Adjectives like "pristine," "gin-clear," and "springlike" abound when describing the water, while "very spooky" will suffice for the fish!

Lyman's reputation is well earned, as one will discover after landing one of the brilliantly colored ten-inch brown trout found in this twelve-foot-wide water. (A ten-inch fish really is a trophy here!) Anglers must move with stealth and will usually have to kneel in the water to hide their profiles.

The stretch just upstream from Lyman Lake is relatively open and permits easy casting—even if to wary fish. On at least one occasion I remember, this open water produced three times as many fish as the supposedly more popular section upstream.

I prefer to fish Lyman with high-riding dry flies, because I like to see eager brookies come up from the bottom of pools to snatch them, but Pheasant-tail nymphs are a good alternative if there are no rising fish. Lyman's Run gets a fair amount of pressure for such small water, and I do not recommend fishing it unless you are alone and believe you are the first through a particular stretch.

Regulations

From its mouth on Lyman Lake upstream four miles to Splash Dam Hollow, Fly-Fishing-Only, Selective-Harvest regulations apply. The daily limit is two trout; minimum size is nine inches for brook trout, twelve inches for brown trout. I cannot suppress my dismay at the fact that Lyman Run is not regulated as Catch-and-Release water. I suspect early-season anglers take more than permitted; it's no wonder the fish are so shy!

Access

From Coudersport, take Route 6 east and turn right onto Thompson Road (not on map) south (near Walton) to Lyman Run Road.

- Turn left and park near mouth of Splash Dam Hollow.
- Turn right and park on the shoulder where Jacob Hollow enters.
- Turn right and park near the road maintenance facility. Walk down to the stream and fish up or down.

From the south (Oleona—Kettle Creek), take Route 144 north to Galeton. Then take Route 6 east, make a left on Thompson Road, and proceed as directed above.

EAST FORK OF THE SINNEMAHONING CREEK

This wild trout stream was very kind to me and two other members of the Delaware Valley Women's Fly Fishing Association one day in late October. I was out with Erin Mooney and Susan Eggert, faced with the task of putting three of us on water I'd not previously fished. I had been directed to the stream by Al Zigarski, the manager of angling supplies at Wheary's Store in Waterville. Al reported the East Fork was fishing well and had done so all year. (The year was 1996, when there was no lack of rain in the east. The East Fork does not do well in drought years.)

We drove up and down the dirt road a couple of times, trying to see likely access places and where to space ourselves. "Fish Shinglebolt Hollow," Al Zigarski had said. We were left on our own to pick water we couldn't see from the road.

We dropped down in three separate places, leaving about a quarter mile of road between each of us. As it turned out, the stream switched back and forth, and we were nearly within hailing distance of one another. In the next two hours, Susan and Erin each took four fish, two on top and two beneath the surface, using tan or gray elk-hair caddis imitations and Green Weenies. They fished a relatively open, marshy area that alternated between shallow riffles and a few deep pools.

I fished in the woods, upstream of the open marsh, hoping for a good *Baetis* hatch that would make my little Blue-Winged Olive flies irresistible. No such hatch occured. However, I also took fish on caddis and Green

Weenies, although I saw only one or two insects on the water. I was fishing a very rich stretch of water, according to local anglers, one that could easily have produced more trout than the three recorded in my notebook.

Regulations
The 2.9 miles of the East Fork of the Sinnemahoning between Shinglebolt Hollow and Horton Run Road have been designated as Class A wild trout waters. All trout hooked must be released. Trout are no longer stocked in these waters. The stream is stocked from the town of Wharton upstream to Horton Run.

Access
From Oleona, take Route 44 north to Cherry Springs Park. Turn left on SR3001, which runs along the East Fork from Cherry Springs to Wharton.
* Look for a sign marking a Youth Trout Restoration Program. Park there, walk downstream half a mile or more, and fish upstream.
* Pull off anywhere along SR3001 below this sign. Drop over the bank, through the marsh grasses to the water. Fish up- or downstream.

KETTLE CREEK
The tale is told that Kettle Creek got its name from the curve of the stream; whether so dubbed by Native Americans or settlers I do not know. There is a plausible fullness of body that curves and narrows to a smaller stream that could be construed as the spout of a kettle.

Whatever the origins of its name, Kettle Creek has long been popular with trout fishermen. It is probably the best-known, most productive stream in Potter County. It bears the proud distinction of having the oldest Catch-and-Release area in the state. It's easy to wade much of its best water, and you will find plenty of company in the water during the green drake hatch in late May.

The stream has a higher-than-average pH level (7.0 to 7.3 throughout) compared with other Potter County streams (most of which are under 7.0). It has excellent hatches year-round. Stretches include water regulated as Class A wild trout, Catch-and-Release, and traditional Put-and-Take. There is ample parking near convenient access points that may be fished nearby or used as gateways to remote reaches.

Kettle Creek flows almost thirty-five miles from its headwaters (near Germania) down to the Susquehanna River at Renovo. Phil Baldaccino, owner of the Kettle Creek Tackle Shop, constantly emphasizes the fact that Kettle has good hatches of every important eastern mayfly from early to midseason (see below). Never widening to more than fifty feet above Cross Fork, the streambed offers secure footing for anglers and a productive configuration of riffles, pools, and run water. During rainy periods, the stream muddies, but then it clears up surprisingly soon, making it possible to fish before other waters.

Kettle's drawback is that it does not have a lot of cover and therefore tends to warm up in the summer. Nonetheless, fall fishing on Kettle can be excellent, as there are a number of large holdover trout on the move. Blue-Winged Olives, ants, and terrestrials continue to provide good sport until late in the season.

Regulations
The Catch-and-Release stretch is 1.7 miles upstream from about five hundred feet below the Route 144 bridge. Only artificial lures or flies are allowed, and barbless hooks are required.

Access
In my mind, I've come to divide Kettle into four different sections: the lower stocked water upstream from Kettle Creek Lake to above Cross Fork (ending below the Catch-and-Release area); the Catch-and-Release water from five hundred feet below the bridge over Route 144 upstream 1.7 miles; the lower end of the upper water, from the end of the Catch-and-Release upstream to the bridge on Route 44 (around Ole Bull State Park and Oleona); and the upper reaches above Route 44. Access points are obvious along Route 144 and Route 44, and the water may frequently be reached from the road:

- At Cross Fork Village.
- At the bridge on Route 144—lower end of the Catch-and-Release water.
- At the pull-off on Route 144 at the upper end of the Catch-and-Release stretch.
- At Ole Bull State Park.
- On Route 144 at Oleona.
- On Route 44, just east of Oleona. Park here and work upstream if you want to fish for the best of Kettle's wild trout population.

Hatches, Flies, and Best Times to Fish
Kettle Creek, like the great majority of Potter County streams, fishes best from early in the season (mid-April) through the third week of June and then again in the fall beginning in mid-September. This is not to say that the area cannot produce good fishing during the summer. It does, but the angler will have to range farther from the familiar paths and find spring-fed or well-shaded streams.

The following list of flies and when to fish them was compiled from several sources, but most of the information came from Phil Baldaccino (Kettle Creek Tackle) and Jack Mickiewitz (former owner of West Pike Outfitters in Galeton).

Spring
Mid-April to mid-May: Blue-Winged Olive (#18–#20), Blue Quill (#18), Quill Gordon (#14), Hendrickson (#14), tan caddis (#14–#16).

Mid-May to mid-June: Gray Fox (#14), March Brown (#14), blue dun (#18–#20), Blue-Winged Olive (#14), green drake and Coffin Fly (#10), brown drake (#12), slate drake (#14), yellow stonefly (#12), sulphur (#16–#18), Light Cahill (#14–#16).

Mid-June to mid-July: sulphur (#16–#18), Cream Cahill (#14–#16), yellow drake *(Potamanthus distinctus)* (#12), slate drake *(Isonychia bicolor)* (#14), chocolate dun or spinner (#16).

Summer (mid-July to September)
Trico (#20–#24), Blue Quill (#18), slate drake (#14–#16). Terrestrials: ants, beetles, grasshoppers.

Fall (September to November)
Flying brown ant (#14), Blue-Winged Olive (#18), tan caddis (#16), cream and olive midge (#20–#24).

IF YOU GO . . .
Coudersport is about six hours from Washington and New York and an hour less from Baltimore and Philadelphia. Pittsburgh is a four-hour trip. The trip to Kettle Creek (Cross Fork or Oleona) is about an hour less if approached from the south.

Find the best route to I-80 and Route 15, south of Williamsport. Take Route 44 toward the town of Jersey Shore (off Route 15). Take Route 44/220 west for about one mile, then take Route 44 exit north to Oleona (on Kettle Creek). To reach Coudersport, continue on Route 44 north to Route 6, then go left (west) on Route 6 to Coudersport.

From New York City, go to Binghamton and take Route 17 west to Route 220 south to Route 6. Continue west on Route 6 to Coudersport.

Tackle Shops and Guides
Cross Fork Tackle. Cross Fork Village. A small inventory. (717) 923-1960.

Davis Sporting Goods. Wellsboro. Barry Davis, proprietor. (717) 724-2626.

Kettle Creek Tackle Shop. Route 144 at Hammersley Fork. Phil Baldaccino, proprietor. Full tackle shop. Guides available. (717) 923-1416.

Northern Tier Outfitters. Galeton. Brad Bireley, proprietor. Flies and terminal tackle, guide service, custom rod builder. (814) 435-6324.

Slate Run Tackle Shop. Slate Run. Tom and Debbie Finkbiner, proprietors. A huge supply of Orvis products, clothing, general store items, and beautifully tied flies. Also a gift shop, bakery, and deli. (717) 753-8551.

Wheary's Country Store. Waterville. Al Zigarski, Fly Shop Manager. Clothing, tackle, flies, guide service. (717) 753-8241.

Where to Stay

First Fork Lodge. Costello, near Austin, on Route 872. Jack Krafft, proprietor. This old Victorian home houses a collectibles shop and a B&B, which can provide three meals. Excellent value. Inexpensive. (814) 647-8644.

Hotel Crittenden. On the square in Coudersport, the county seat. Private rooms and baths. Clean and convenient. Restaurant. Inexpensive to moderate. (814) 274-8320.

Kettle Creek Lodge and Susquehannock Forest Cabins. At the intersection of Routes 44 and Route 144 in Oleona on Kettle Creek. Stephen Benna, proprietor. Cabins as well as private rooms and baths in a lodge. Best value in the area. Inexpensive. (814) 435-1019.

Tom & Kathy's Bed and Breakfast. Oleona. Ten multiple-bed rooms. Two baths. Horseback riding offered. Inexpensive. (814) 435-8582.

Additional lodging can be recommended by Coudersport's Chamber of Commerce (see Resources, below).

Camping

Kettle Creek State Park. Off Kettle Creek Road, near Leidy. (717) 923-6004.

Ole Bull State Park. Oleona. (814) 435-5000.

Susquehannock State Forest. 264,000 acres in Potter County, with campsites available.

Contact Forest District, P.O. Box 673, Coudersport, PA 16915. (814) 274-8474.

Where to Eat

Hotel Crittenden. Coudersport. Good food and bar. Moderate. (814) 274-8320.

The Northern. Coudersport. Junction of Route 6 and Route 872. Burgers and other American fare. Bar, TV. No reservations. Moderate. (814) 274-8930.

Black Forest Inn. Route 44 about five miles east of Oleona. A barn of a restaurant and bar with a huge fireplace. Stick with basic food. Inexpensive. No reservations. (717) 769-7203.

Resources

Coudersport Chamber of Commerce. (814) 274-8165.

Potter County Tourist Promotion. (814) 435-2290. Order the vacation map of Potter County.

CHAPTER 10

Northwestern Pennsylvania: Oil Creek, Cherry Run, Porcupine Run, Upper Two Mile Run, Little Sandy Creek, Neshannock Creek, and Slippery Rock Creek

Venango County is northwestern Pennsylvania's answer to Potter County in the east: It boasts countless trout streams, many of which hold wild trout. The streams that do not hold wild trout owe their fate to pollution from the coal, oil, or timber industries. Northwestern Pennsylvania provided the raw materials for Pittsburgh, the great industrial center of those industries. Its streams could hardly have avoided pollution.

Working with business interests, local chapters of TU have done much to improve the water quality of the area—once one of the dirtiest areas in the country. Venango County is very beautiful: Plateaus and ridges overlook farmland, mountains, and continuous rolling hills, and there are few houses to mar the view.

The county seat, Franklin, seems to be thriving. Its streets are lined with huge old Victorian houses built by oil entrepreneurs and their wealthy managers more than a century ago. Solid brick buildings are owned by Elks, Moose, and other fraternal interests. The area is a favorite with Ohio anglers, who come from Youngstown and Cleveland to fish.

OIL CREEK

Oil Creek is one of the biggest, most beautiful rivers in Pennsylvania. The word "creek" is inappropriate here, for this is a big river. The water ranges from sixty to one hundred feet wide, running through gentle mountains from Lincolnville to Oil City, where it joins the Allegheny River. The Pennsylvania Fish Commission stocks thirty-three miles of water, and the Oil Creek chapter of TU supplements these stockings, particularly in the Delayed-Harvest stretch.

Oil Creek got its name because the large oil resource of northwestern Pennsylvania was found near its banks. Native Americans used to skim oil off the surface of the water. On August 27, 1859, Colonel Edwin Drake struck oil at a depth of nearly seventy feet. His well was the birthplace of

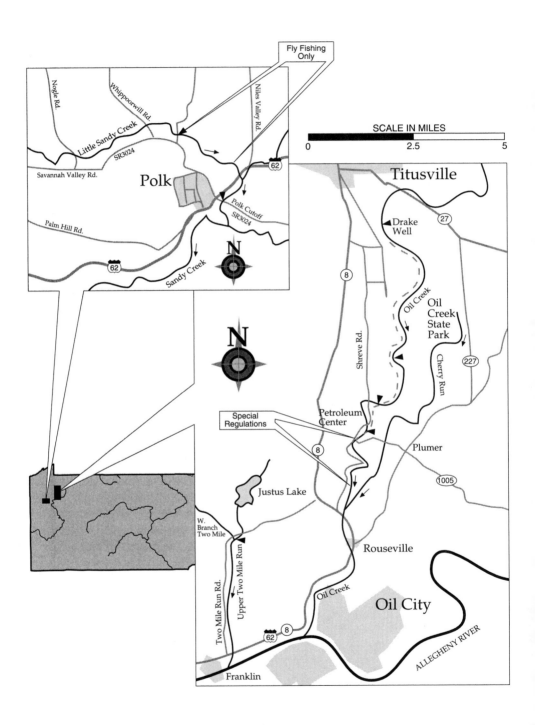

the oil industry, and a museum now stands on the site just south of Titusville.

Oil Creek is one of the best trout streams in northwestern Pennsylvania. At its best, it challenges anglers who prefer match-the-hatch angling. Oil Creek has the greatest variety of insects of all the streams in the area. Most of the major eastern mayfly, stonefly, and caddis hatches emerge here.

Mike Laskowski, owner of Oil Creek Outfitters, explains that Oil Creek has rebounded from its polluted days (when oil and acid frequently found their way into the stream) to an exceptionally rich aquatic environment. He describes an amazing sulphur hatch, which at its peak looks like a yellow-orange cloud hovering above the water. He also notes that the two insects the stream does not have, *Ephemera guttulata* (green drakes) and *Ephemera subvaria* (Light Hendricksons), are absent from many western Pennsylvania streams.

Summer temperatures render Oil Creek's water too warm for instream trout reproduction. Most Oil Creek trout are stocked or are stocking holdovers between nine and thirteen inches long. The tributaries, however, are worth exploring for their native populations of wild brook and brown trout.

I fished the Delayed-Harvest stretch downstream from Petroleum Center in September with my brother Dick McIntosh and Frank Malic, our guide from Oil Creek Outfitters. The fishing was challenging. We were nymphing and trout were selective. They seldom moved more than a foot from a lie to examine our offerings. Frank took four fish on nymphs. I lost two; Dick landed one.

The stream—except under high-water conditions—is easy to wade, despite its width. It's always advisable, however, to wear felt-soled waders and use a staff if you are a stranger to this water. There is a path along most of the Delayed-Harvest stretch.

Regulations

The 1.6-mile Delayed-Harvest, Artificial-Lures-Only Project is in the Oil Creek State Park just off Route 8 between Oil City and Titusville. It begins at the Petroleum Center bridge over Oil Creek (near Oil Creek Outfitters) and extends 1.6 miles downstream to the railroad bridge at Columbia Farm.

All fishing must be done with artificial lures or flies with a minimum size of nine inches, and there is a three-fish-per-day creel limit between June 15 and Labor Day. From the day after Labor Day until June 15 of the following year, all fish must be released. On the rest of the river, Put-and-Take trout-fishing regulations prevail.

Access
- In Petroleum Center at the bridge or behind Oil Creek Outfitters.
- Pioneer Road upstream two miles from the Fly-Fishing-Only section.
- The bridge on Miller Farm Road, five miles upstream from Petroleum Center.
- At Drake Well Museum, off Route 8 just south of Titusville.
- Below the Fly-Fishing-Only project at Blood Farm. This section receives little pressure and is a favorite with experienced local fly anglers.

Hatches, Flies, and Best Times to Fish
From February through September, Oil Creek produces insects that attract the brown trout population. During the late fall and early winter, a variety of midges may be used. Because Oil Creek warms in the summer (becoming good bass water), many prefer to fish it beginning in March with the little black stonefly and tapering off in June after the tremendous sulphur hatch.

I'm sure the sulphurs are worth a trip just to see the duns hovering like dust over the river, but try to go during the week, or whenever you can avoid the crowds. This emergence is very popular with anglers from Pittsburgh, Ohio, and the northwestern part of the state. The earlier spring hatches (stoneflies, Quill Gordons, Blue Quills, caddis) are also prolific.

According to Mike Laskowski, Oil Creek can be a world-class fishery between late September and February. The fall hatches are excellent, the crowds have diminished or disappeared, the water has cooled, and the surrounding countryside is in full fall foliage.

The list of hatches and flies below can be used on the other northwestern Pennsylvania streams mentioned in this chapter. Most of the streams will have fewer hatches than Oil Creek.

Winter (December to March)
Midges, little black stonefly (#18), early black stonefly (#14), early brown stonefly (#14).

Spring (April to May)
Blue Quill (#16), Quill Gordon (#14), grannom (#14), Black Quill (#14), small black caddis (#16), bright green caddis (#14), Gray Fox (#12), Blue-Winged Olive (#l6, #20), March Brown (#12), sulphur *(Ephemerella invaria)*, (#16), Light Cahill (#14), slate drake (#12).

Summer (June to August)
Brown drake (#12), sulphur *(Ephemerella dorothea)* (#18), Light Cahill (#18), Trico (#22), whitefly *(Ephoron leukon)* (#14), terrestrials (beetles, ants, and inchworm patterns such as the Green Weenie, #14).

Fall (September to November)
Cinnamon caddis (#14), terrestrials, midges.

CHERRY RUN
Cherry Run is a Class A wild trout stream. It flows into Oil Creek below Rouseville just after the stream crosses Route 8. It can be fished upstream along Route 227 to Pleasantville. Much of the land is on oil company property, and access is limited. Obey posted signs and ask the landowner's permission before crossing land.

PORCUPINE RUN
Porcupine Run (not on map) is the second best wild rainbow fishery in Pennsylvania. (First honors go the Falling Spring Run near Chambersburg in southcentral Pennsylvania.) It also holds brook trout and some browns. It is a small stream that empties into Hemlock Creek at McCrea Schoolhouse Road (SR2023). It can also be fished downstream from its headwaters along Route 157 near Hampton Station. Hemlock Creek is stocked from just above the mouth of Porcupine Run downstream to its mouth at the Allegheny River.

Access
To get to Porcupine Run, take Route 62 north from Oil City. Turn right onto McCrea Schoolhouse Road (SR2023) in the village of President.

UPPER TWO MILE RUN
This fifteen-foot-wide overgrown stream runs from just above Justus Lake downstream to the Allegheny River. The stream is stocked and also holds wild browns. In the fall, big browns often run up the short section above the lake to spawn.

I saw four fourteen-inch browns the third week of September lying upstream of the culvert at the junction of the West Branch of Two Mile Run and Upper Two Mile Run. They looked promising, but my brother and I had a commitment to move on to Little Sandy Creek.

Access
To access Upper Two Mile Run, take Route 8/62 north out of Franklin. Look for Two Mile Run Road on the left about one and one-half miles outside Franklin. Turn left on Two Mile Run Road, which runs along the stream. Just before this road crosses T448, the mouth of the West Branch

of Two Mile will be on the left. There is good fishing on Upper Two Mile Run to the dam on Justus Lake.

LITTLE SANDY CREEK
Little Sandy Creek is a small (fifteen to twenty feet wide) freestone stream near Polk, about one and one-half hours from Pittsburgh's South Hills. Little Sandy has long been a project of the Oil Creek chapter of TU. The chapter has made many in-stream structural improvements, creating pools, cover, and lies for fish in a lovely 1.3-mile Fly-Fishing-Only stretch. The stream is stocked by the state and TU. Delayed-Harvest regulations govern the fly-fishing section.

My brother Dick and I spent a very relaxing two hours late one afternoon in September. Guide Frank Malic advised us to walk from the parking lot downstream to the railroad trestle and fish back to the car. But the pools looked so lovely along the way that I never made it as far as the trestle.

I tried terrestrials, a Green Weenie, and a Woolly Bugger, and I believe I moved four trout. The fish were reluctant to do more than look at my flies from a distance. A fish would come out, take a look, and scoot back under the hemlock roots. It was obvious that other anglers had preceded us on the stream that day. I advise fishing Little Sandy early, hoping to be the first angler through the water.

Access
To reach Little Sandy, take Route 62 to Polk and the junction of SR3024 and Route 62. The stream crosses SR3024 just east of the intersection. Park there or on the shoulder of Route 62 and fish upstream.

To access the Fly-Fishing-Only upper area, take SR3024 north to the first road on the right up a hill. The road is lined by tall evergreens. It ends in a parking lot near the pump station for the Polk Center School and hospital across SR3024.

NESHANNOCK CREEK
Neshannock Creek is an hour and twenty minutes from Pittsburgh (see DeLorme's *Pennsylvania Atlas and Gazetteer*, p. 42). It is accessible, easy to wade, and popular with local urban (and suburban) anglers. The Neshannock is a freestone stream with moderate cover. It originates at Cool Spring and Otter Creek in Mercer County and flows southwest through Lawrence County, picking up tributaries and emptying into the Shenango River in New Castle.

The Neshannock is stocked with brown and rainbow trout. It is a good trout fishery until summer, when it becomes a very good stream for catching smallmouth bass and northern pike. Although it warms in summer and there is a lack of oxygen in the water, a number of browns and 'bows do hold over in the Neshannock. The stream averages thirty feet in width and is easy to wade. On rainy days, it clouds quickly, as it is subject to runoff from cultivated agricultural areas.

Access
A railroad grade follows the Neshannock south of Mercer, making access relatively easy. Slip into the water behind the Outdoor Shop and fish upstream. Or, drive downstream on Route 168, take a right on Gerber Road, and follow it to the parking area at the covered bridge that crosses the stream on Covered Bridge Road. Anglers can also find easy access by pulling off Covered Bridge Road near the railroad tracks and taking a very short hike to the stream.

Hatches, Flies, and Best Times to Fish
See Oil Creek for general hatch information.

Caddis imitations are very productive on the Neshannock. Try tan, olive, and dark brown flies (#16) in April and May, and green caddisflies from mid-May to mid-June.

Neshannock Creek has particularly good emergences of brown drakes (mid-May to mid-June), March Browns (mid-May), slate drakes (mid-May to mid-June), and Cahills (mid-May through June).

SLIPPERY ROCK CREEK
Slippery Rock Creek is less than an hour from downtown Pittsburgh (see DeLorme's *Pennsylvania Atlas and Gazetteer*, p. 43). I found myself in an isolated rural area long before I reached a fishable section of the water. The stream is at least as slippery as its name indicates. I have not fished it, because when I was looking forward to doing so, the water was too high and fast to wade. So I walked the banks of the gorge reaches and admired the boulders in the flatter water. And I spoke to Slippery Rock regulars who say that cleats or felt soles and a staff are a very good idea here.

Slippery Rock is nearly as wide as Oil Creek at many points and eighty to one hundred feet wide in most of its productive reaches. In the gorge stretch (downstream from Route 422 near Rose Point, past McConnell's Mill to the reach downstream of Eckert Bridge), the water becomes sixty to seventy feet of challenging froth—whitewater more to the liking of whitewater sportsmen than anglers. Wading is most difficult between Route 422 and Eckert Bridge. There are scenic trails and challenging reaches downstream from Eckert Bridge to Harris Bridge (over SR2030, near the upstream end of the Delayed-Harvest, Fly-Fishing-Only stretch).

Like the Neshannock, Slippery Rock has a siltation problem: It muddies very quickly after rain, and its rocks are covered with a slick paste of dirt and vegetation. One of the days I explored it, Slippery Rock was badly muddied by runoff from Hell Run, which enters about a mile above Armstrong Bridge. Slippery Rock was damaged by acid mine drainage in the 1960s, but since then the Department of Environmental Resources has installed a water treatment plant (liming device) at the headwaters near Harrisville, improving the water quality.

Access
　• To reach the gorge (upper) section, take I-79 north from Pittsburgh to Route 422 west. Cross under Route 19, and make the next left on T526, which will take you to the entrance and office of McConnell's Mill State Park. Follow the one-way park road to the mill. You will see the whitewater rushing under the covered bridge at McConnell's Mill. To continue downstream, stay on T526 until it ends at T399. Take a right on T399 until it ends at SR2013. Turn left at the T and follow to SR2030 (Mountville Road). Turn right on SR2030 and follow to Harris Bridge, four miles below Eckert Bridge.
　• To reach the Delayed-Harvest, Fly-Fishing-Only half-mile stretch from the north, take Route 19 to Portersville. Turn onto Route 488 west. Turn right onto SR2022 (Heinz Camp Road), and follow it to Armstrong Bridge (roughly in the middle of the special regulations section). Park and fish.
　• To reach the special regulations section from the south, take Route 488 out of Ellwood City and make a left on Armstrong Road (SR2007). Proceed to the bridge and park.
　The state stocks from Armstrong Bridge upstream fifteen miles to Route 173. Regular Put-and-Take regulations apply to all but the Delayed-Harvest, Fly-Fishing-Only stretch.

Hatches, Flies, and Best Times to Fish
This river fishes best in spring and fall—April and May, and again in September through October. It becomes a good smallmouth bass stream during the summer.
　Caddis provide Slippery Rock's best hatches. In spring, there is a good emergence of grannom and green caddis (#16), and tan and olive caddis, as well as midges and craneflies. Mayflies—such as bugs imitated by the Light Cahill, sulphur, Blue-Winged Olive, and in the upstream reaches, the brown drake—make respectable appearances.
　The whitefly (#14–#16) imitates the *Ephoron leukon,* which appears in mid-August, and fall brings *Baetis* (use Blue-Winged Olives, #20) in the morning and again in the afternoon.

OTHER STREAMS

Streams that I have not had a chance to fish but deserve attention include:

- Dennison Run (a wilderness trout stream), located in Clinton and Victory townships. Its mouth is one mile from the bridge at Kennerdell on the west side of the Allegheny River.
- Thompson Creek, a six-mile-long stream that holds stocked and streambred trout and supports a wonderful insect population. Access is upstream at Route 89 or downstream at Route 8.
- Caldwell Creek. This creek has a Delayed-Harvest, Fly-Fishing-Only section from the Selkirk Highway bridge downstream to Dotyville Bridge. The West Branch of Caldwell Creek is Catch-and-Release for 3.6 miles from West Branch Bridge upstream to Three Bridge Run. The creek has stocked and streambred trout.
- Cherrytree Run, a native trout stream that runs along Route 8 north of Oil Creek.
- Sugar Creek, a substantial stream (about thirty feet wide) that offers big stocked and holdover trout. Good mayfly hatches, but the grannom emergence is unusually heavy. Access is along Route 427, from Route 27 west of Chapmanville, south to Route 322 in Wyattville.

IF YOU GO . . .

From downtown Pittsburgh, take I-279 north. It will become I-79 north. Continue north to I-80. Then take I-80 east to Route 8 to Franklin. Continue through Franklin to Oil City. The trip to Oil Creek will take just less than two hours from Pittsburgh. Other trips described here will be slightly shorter and can be accessed by similar routes from Pittsburgh.

Tackle Shops and Guides

The Fishing Post. Pittsburgh. Orvis dealer. Full-service fly shop. (412) 364-2850.

The Fly Tyer's Vise. Pittsburgh. Tony Morasco, proprietor. Fly-tying and fishing supplies. (412) 276-2831.

Indiana Angler. Indiana. Woody Banks, proprietor. Woody is an experienced western Pennsylvania angler. His shop and guide service are respected throughout the state. (412) 463-2011.

International Angler. Pittsburgh. Tom Ference, proprietor. (412) 782-2222.

Oil Creek Outfitters. Petroleum Center (near Oil City). Mike Laskowski, proprietor. Mike lives on Oil Creek all year, and a phone call to him will tell you whether a trip to the river is warranted. He also follows Erie steelhead runs. The shop is located on the special regulations stretch of Oil Creek. (814) 677-4684.

The Outdoor Shop. Volant. Bob Shewey, proprietor. On the banks of Neshannock Creek. Fly shop and guide service. (412) 533-3212.

South Hills Rod and Reel. Pittsburgh. Very popular with Pittsburgh fly fishers. (412) 344-8888.

Where to Stay

Colonial Drake Hotel. Franklin St., Titusville. Restaurant on premises. Inexpensive. (814) 827-2267.

Cross Creek Resort. Titusville (near Oil Creek). Restaurant. Expensive. (814) 827-9611.

Franklin Motel. Franklin (near Oil Creek). Inexpensive. (814) 437-3061.
Holiday Inn. Oil City. Moderate to expensive. (814) 677-1221.
Inn at Franklin. Restaurant on premises. Inexpensive. (814) 437-3031.
McMullen House B&B. Titusville. Inexpensive. (814) 827-1592.
Quo Vadis House B&B. Franklin. Inexpensive. (814) 432-4208.

Camping

Oil Creek Campground. Titusville. (814) 827-1023.
Two Mile Run County Park. Dempseytown. (814) 676-6116.

Where to Eat

Benjamin Restaurant. In the Inn at Franklin. Moderate to expensive. (814) 437-3031.

Cross Creek Resort. Titusville. Moderate to expensive. (814) 827-9611.
Hoss's. Oil City. Inexpensive. (814) 677-3002.
Sportsman's Tavern. Petroleum Center. Route 8, north of Oil Creek State Park entrance. Wings and beer. Inexpensive. No reservations.

Resources

Franklin Area Chamber of Commerce. (814) 432-5823.

Oil Creek State Park office. Maps of park and Oil Creek. (814) 676-5915.

Pennsylvania Fish Commission. (814) 437-5774.

Venango County Area Tourism and Promotion Agency. 1-800-776-4526.

Western Pennsylvania Conservancy. (412) 288-2777.

CHAPTER 11

Southwestern Pennsylvania: Loyalhanna Creek, Bobs Creek, Stonycreek River, Clear Shade Creek, Yellow Creek, and Potter Creek

Route 30, the Lincoln Highway, runs southeast from Pittsburgh through the rural farmland of southwestern Pennsylvania to Philadelphia. It was the first transcontinental highway in the country, stretching from New York to San Francisco. In 1995, the governor of Pennsylvania announced the Lincoln Highway Heritage Park Corridor, the 145-mile stretch between Chambersburg and Greensburg. There are many postcolonial villages, country taverns, bed and breakfasts, and antique stores along this historic tourist route.

Trout anglers have plenty of options in Cambria, Westmoreland, Somerset, and Bedford Counties. There are several good freestone and limestone streams, all with plenty of public access. Acid mine drainage, the curse of the Appalachians, remains a threat to trout habitat; however, the problem has been addressed during the past decade. Water quality is improving as quickly as funding permits, but more than five thousand miles of unreclaimed native trout streams remain. It will be some years before these hold fish again.

LOYALHANNA CREEK
This river runs along Route 30 through Ligonier, an hour and a half east of Pittsburgh. It is a stocked freestone stream, thirty to forty feet wide on the regulated water in town. The water is easy to reach and to wade. I have caught nice trout here early in the season when other waters were closed for stocking. It warms up quickly with the onset of summer.

Angling author Charles Meck writes that he was introduced to the now-famous Green Weenie on the Loyalhanna. Loyalhanna hatches of note include little black stoneflies, March Browns, caddis, and green and brown drakes. Many fish are taken on streamers, Woolly Buggers, Muddler Minnows, and terrestrials.

Regulations
Delayed-Harvest, artificial-lures-only regulations apply from the bridge on Route 711 downstream to SR2045.

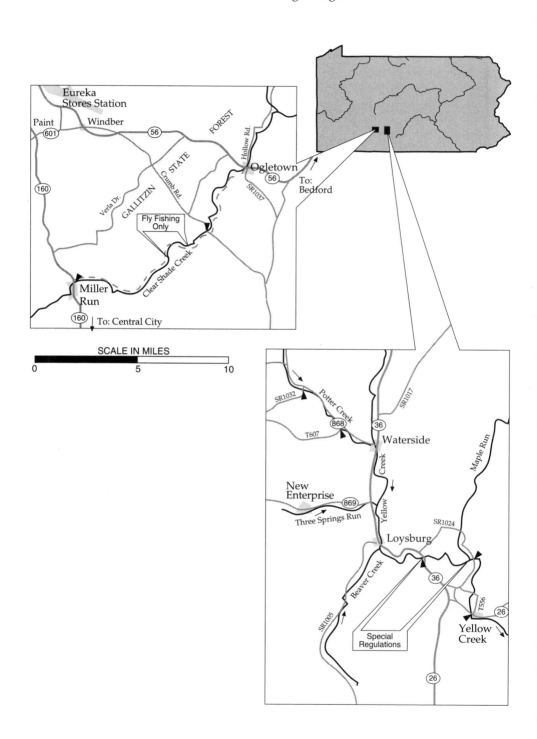

Access
- Route 30, one-half mile east of SR2045.
- Route 30, at a parking lot near Mill Creek.
- At the Route 711 bridge.

BOBS CREEK

Bobs Creek is the westernmost trout stream in the eastern Pennsylvania drainage (the Susquehanna River watershed; see DeLorme's *Pennsylvania Atlas and Gazetteer,* p. 74). It is a freestone mountain stream that runs through Blue Knob State Park near Pavia. Its narrow water is full of lovely runs, deep pools, and spurting rapids. It can be waded in hip boots.

Bobs suffered flood damage in the mid-nineties. It is stocked with browns and brookies, and wild trout hold in the upper section. Fish average between ten and twelve inches. There are no special regulations on Bobs Creek.

Access

The best fishing is above Pavia. Take Route 869 northwest from Pavia. Look for a dirt road on the right (T652) identified with a sign that reads, "The Lost Children of the Alleghenies."

The monument to the Lost Children of the Alleghenies commemorates a frontier incident. Three children who had been lost for weeks were found after a woman had a dream which revealed their whereabouts. Although they were no longer alive, her vision was considered miraculous and commemorated.

- T652 follows the stream up the mountain for eleven miles. There are pull-offs along the way. A steep bank drops to the water; once below, the grade is gentle.
- Berkheimer Road (SR3001) approaches the stream from the upper end.
- Access to the lower part of Bobs is available from the ballpark in Pavia downstream. Downstream from Osterburg, the stream heats up in the summer. It is best to fish this section before the end of June.

Hatches, Flies, and Best Times to Fish

Early in the season, Bobs can be difficult to fish, as spring runoff falls in torrents down the mountain. After the water level has dropped, it is very productive, nurturing a number of good hatches.

On April afternoons, fish Blue-Winged Olives (#20), Blue Quills (#18), and March Browns (#14). In May, look for a fantastic hatch of green drakes, as well as giant green and giant yellow stoneflies (#10) in the evenings, and #16 stoneflies during the day. In June and July, sulphurs, Cahills, slate drakes, and caddis work well.

STONYCREEK RIVER

The Stonycreek River is forty-three miles long, draining 466 square miles in Somerset and Cambria Counties (see DeLorme's *Pennsylvania Atlas and Gazetteer*, p. 73). It flows north from Pious Springs, near Berlin, to Johnstown, where it joins the Little Conemaugh to form the Conemaugh main stem.

Randy Buchanan, an expert tier of stonefly nymphs, and his friend, the outdoor writer Len Lichvar, fish this water often. They warned me that the stream would live up to its name. Randy loves this water. "A nymph fisherman's dream!" he exclaims. "Pocket water, pocket water, and more pocket water!"

Randy and Len took my brother Dick and me to the stream at Mostoller Station near Kimmelton. Moving into casting position required major assistance from my wading staff, and I had several near falls. In more than two hours, I stood secure enough to cast for about ten minutes. Pocket water, indeed, and rocks, rocks, boulders, and more rocks! The rocks have sharp, jagged edges designed to cut shins. Worse, they are covered with algae, making them exceptionally slippery.

Fortunately, the Stonycreek River has a good trout population. A thirteen-inch brookie took my *Isonychia* nymph on the fourth cast the day we fished. We all did well, with my brother reporting a foot-long rainbow. But I found the tedious negotiation of sharp and slippery rocks exhausting, and the fact that I had to wipe the algae off my fly every cast or two did little for my mood. Had the trout been actively feeding, I would not have given these deterrents much thought. As it went, the iced tea in the car was more welcome than usual. I'll save the Stonycreek River for periods of frenzied surface activity.

Reclamation of the Stonycreek River

The Stonycreek River watershed is the target for the reclamation of some of the most acidic water ever to result from coal mining in Pennsylvania. More than 150 years of acid mine drainage have devastated streams in the area, with negative impact on Paint Creek, Shade Creek, Bens Creek, and others, as well as Stonycreek.

The Mountain Laurel chapter of TU has joined many other groups in an umbrella project called Stonycreek-Conemaugh River Improvement Project (SCRIP). The organization is mitigating the effect of acid mine drainage by employing "passive" treatment methods—low maintenance techniques that use the natural environment to neutralize acid. SCRIP's Oven Run Project on the Stonycreek is a six-site, $5 million initiative that uses wetlands, holding ponds, and successive alkalinity-producing systems to remove toxic metals and improve the pH of the water. When complete, this project will restore more than twelve miles of river.

To date, trout have not reproduced in the Stonycreek River. However, the section known as the Upper Gorge, from Glessner's Bridge downstream, is managed under the Fish Commission's fingerling stocking program. It is a put-and-grow fishery. Anglers tell of hooking fifteen- and sixteen-inch rainbows that have grown up in the water.

Regulations

No special regulations apply on the Stonycreek River. In appreciation of reclamation efforts, many local anglers have adopted a no-kill policy. Access is primarily across private land, so be sure to observe No Trespassing signs, and leave property as you find it.

Access

- Gorge access at Shanksville, SR1001 and SR1007.
- Upper gorge access at Glessner's Covered Bridge, on Covered Bridge Road (T565) downstream from Shanksville.
- Lambertsville Road. Walk in three miles to the gorge.
- Mostoller Station at the highway bridge on SR1008, at the railroad crossing near Kimmelton. Walk down the tracks along the water.
- Stoystown Lions Community Park off Route 30, Stoystown.

Hatches, Flies, and Best Times to Fish

Anytime the water is running high and strong, the Stonycreek River will be difficult to negotiate. Remember to wear felt-soled boots with studs and carry a wading staff.

The best hatches occur on Stonycreek in June, when stoneflies (especially *Paragnetina media)* emerge profusely between the first and the middle of the month. Other outstanding hatches include gray and tan caddis in May and June, sulphurs, Light Cahills, slate drakes *(Isonychias),* and blue-winged olives (June), and a huge golden stonefly *(Pteronarcys,* #8) in August and September.

CLEAR SHADE CREEK

Clear Shade Creek in Somerset County is one of the most picturesque and secluded trout streams in southwestern Pennsylvania. It is also one of the most popular freestone streams in the Johnstown area and a frequent destination for local anglers. I've heard accounts of fine populations of wild trout in the past, but in recent years, the fish population has declined. No one culprit has been labeled the cause; in all likelihood, a combination of development, angling pressure, drought, and scouring from floods have taken their toll.

Clear Shade still holds a few wild trout but is best fished as an early-season stream. It warms up in the summer. Randy Buchanan, my brother, and I fished it late one afternoon. We left discouraged. We could count on the fingers of one hand the number of trout we saw. Had Len Lichvar not had a better experience two weeks before, I would have sworn the water was sterile!

Regulations
Fly-Fishing-Only from the inflow of Windber Reservoir upstream one mile.

Access
To reach Clear Shade, take Route 56 from Bedford to Ogletown. Then take a left on Verla Drive from Route 56 just west of Ogletown. Go to Crumb Road.

• Take a left on Crumb Road (T816) to an iron bridge at the stream. Fish up- or downstream.

• To reach the Fly-Fishing-Only water, take Route 56 to Windber. Then take Route 160 six miles toward Central City. A locked gate across an access road will be on the left side of the road. (Note: In recent seasons the gate has been unlocked from the first day of trout season to the end of May.) A two-mile walk upstream from Route 160 (or downstream from the iron bridge mentioned above) is required to reach the fly-fishing section.

YELLOW CREEK
Yellow Creek is one of the best trout streams in western Pennsylvania. It is by far the most productive fishery in the Bedford area and worth traveling some distance to fish.

Yellow is a limestone stream with a freestone influence. The banks are lined with hemlock, fir, and hardwoods. Large stones and slippery rocks cover the streambed, but in comparison to negotiating the Stonycreek River, Yellow Creek poses few problems. There is so much good holding water on Yellow that you don't have to move far to find good fish. Early in the year, the current is strong, and felt soles and a wading staff are recommended.

After a couple of years of promising to do so, Randy Buchanan, Len Lichvar, and I got together to fish Yellow Creek. We went in May, when the water was high and swift. I waded to deep holding water and tied on a mottled, beautifully ugly Buchanan stonefly nymph. After a little time, I felt a strike. And another. Or I thought I did. But nothing materialized when I lifted my rod. I began to watch Randy nymphing upstream.

Buchanan is the best nymph fisherman I've ever seen. His concentration is total; his sensitivity to the take appears psychic. Lichvar says he has watched Randy land fifty fish to other anglers' three! I'm sure this is no exaggeration. Len is no slouch himself, but he usually ends up a few fish shy of Randy's total.

We fished the river beginning about a mile downstream of Route 36 and working back to the bridge on the same road. The fish were not very active. Spring hatches were late, and the sulphurs we anticipated were not yet emerging. Later that summer, my brother and I spent a hot afternoon on the same stretch of stream. It was very productive. Trout readily took terrestrials.

Regulations
Delayed-Harvest, Fly-Fishing-Only regulations apply for 1.25 miles from the mouth of Maple (Jack's) Run upstream to the cable near Red Bank Hill. Yellow Creek gets a fair amount of pressure during major hatch periods such as green drakes, sulphurs, and *Baetis* (blue-winged olives).

This stream has sufficient in-stream trout reproduction, and the Fish Commission would do well to think about stopping all stocking. It has the potential to produce wild trout in similar numbers to Fishing Creek in Clinton County and Spruce Creek, and it should be protected and allowed to do so.

Access
To reach Yellow Creek, take Route 26 north from Route 30 (near Everett) to Route 36. Go left on Route 36 to Loysburg. The best fishing is between Loysburg and Yellow Creek. Ask permission of landowners to fish anywhere above Loysburg.

• To reach the lower end of the regulated water, turn off Route 36 onto SR1024 at the New Frontier Restaurant and follow this road across Maple (Jack's) Run to a bridge.

• The upper end of regulated water can be reached downstream from the Route 36 bridge.

• There is a productive section known locally as "the wall" on T556 (Yellow Creek Drive) in the village of Yellow Creek.

Hatches, Flies, and Best Times to Fish

Early season
End of April to early May: Blue Quills, Hendricksons, Blue-Winged Olives (#20), tan caddis (#16), black caddis, stoneflies, especially Buchanan's Large Apricot or Golden Stonefly nymph patterns (#10).

May 15 to June 15: Sulphurs, Cahills, green drakes (excellent hatch!), Coffin Fly, tan caddis (#14-#16).

Summer (June to September)
Terrestrials: beetles, ants, grasshoppers, caterpillars, inchworms (Green Weenies). Sulphurs (#16–#18), slate drake (#12–#14), Cahills (#14–#16),

and whitefly (#14) imitations. Upper Yellow Creek has an excellent Trico hatch beginning in July and continuing through September.

Fall (September to October)
Blue-Winged Olives (#20–#22), slate drake (#14), stoneflies (#8–#10), tan caddis.

POTTER CREEK
Potter Creek is a small limestone tributary of Yellow Creek that joins the latter at Waterside. Not stocked since 1990, it is the site of habitat improvement by the Mountain Laurel chapter of TU in cooperation with local landowners. Much of the stream runs through private farms where cattle have polluted the water and collapsed the banks. Cattle are now fenced out, limestone and granite stabilize the banks, and in-stream structure, as well as bushes and saplings, provide cover for trout.

It's a good idea to walk well back (fifty feet) from the water on Potter. Some of the banks are deeply undercut, and footsteps will easily spook the trout.

I took one of my best-of-the-year fish on Potter about 9:00 on an August morning. It was a seventeen-inch brown that sipped a Trico I could hardly see. I was kneeling at the base of the bank, half in the water, half out, to avoid detection. To get a drag-free drift, I had to drop the little fly at the far bank just under the branches of an apple tree and let it float down to the fish.

I could hardly see what I was doing, because the sun reflected like steel on the water. After my umpteenth cast, as if by instinct, I lifted my rod as a huge brown trout began to thrash about in a very small patch of water. I scrambled to my feet and reeled in quickly, hardly able to believe my success!

Potter is known for its exceptional sulphur spinner falls and Trico hatches. Take Route 868 upstream off Route 36 at Waterside. Ask permission of landowners to fish, or park along the road and enter the stream at one of the small bridges.

IF YOU GO . . .
From Baltimore or Washington, take I-70 or I-270 to Breezewood to Route 30. To reach the Stonycreek River, take Route 30 west to Lambertsville Road one mile east of Stoystown. For Yellow Creek, take Route 30 west to Route 26 north. Then bear left on Route 36 toward Loysburg.

From Pittsburgh, take Route 30 east to Everett. Take Route 26 north from Everett to Loysburg.

Tackle Shops and Guides
The Fishing Post. Greensburg. John McAdams, proprietor. (412) 832-8383.

Harts Sporting Center. Johnstown. Clarence Hart, proprietor. Reports Stonycreek River water conditions. (814) 288-5099.

Indiana Angler. Indiana. Woody Banks, proprietor. An excellent fly shop in westcentral Pennsylvania. (412) 463-2011.

South Hills Rod & Reel. Pittsburgh. (412) 344-8888.

Where to Stay

Bedford House B&B. Bedford. Lyn and Linda Lyon, proprietors. Moderate. (814) 623-7171.

Covered Bridge Inn. Bedford. Greg and Martha Lowe, proprietors. Moderate. (814) 733-4093.

Days Inn. Richland (near Johnstown). Moderate. (814) 269-3366.

Ligonier Country Inn. Laughlintown, near the Loyalhanna River. Restaurant. Moderate. (412) 238-3651.

The Murphy Inn. Richland (near Johnstown). Moderate. (814) 266-4800.

The Holiday Inn. Johnstown. Moderate to expensive. (814) 266-8789.

Waterside Inn B&B. Woodbury (near Loysburg on Yellow Creek). Barbara Leighty, proprietor. Wonderful hostess, big breakfast! Three of the double bedrooms are in a separate house, which has a living room and kitchen and can be rented in its entirety. Inexpensive to moderate. (814) 766-3776.

Camping

Blue Knob Campground. Bedford area. (814) 276-3576.

Shawnee Sleepy Hollow Campground. Schellsburg. (814) 733-4218.

Where to Eat

The Creekside Inn. On Route 30 just before Roaring Spring and Hollidaysburg. A steak and seafood restaurant. Moderate to expensive. (814) 696-0377.

Jean Bonnet Tavern. Everett. Moderate. (814) 623-2250.

Frontier Restaurant. Loysburg. A family restaurant serving breakfast, lunch, and dinner. Particularly handy for a lunch break on Yellow Creek.

Ligonier Country Inn. Laughlintown. Moderate. (412) 238-3651.

There are other places to eat in Bedford, Johnstown, Ligonier, and Greensburg.

Resources

Bedford County Conference and Visitors Bureau. 1-800-765-3331.

Fallingwater. P.O. Box R, Mill Run, Pennsylvania 15464. (412) 329-8501.

Johnstown Chamber of Commerce. (814) 536-5107.

Laurel Highlands Visitors Bureau. Ligonier. (412) 238-5661.

SCRIP. P.O. Box 153, Johnstown, Pennsylvania 15907. (412) 445-4652.

Western Pennsylvania Conservancy. 1-800-732-0999.

New Jersey

OVERVIEW

Yes, there is good trout fishing in New Jersey. The state stocks more than two hundred rivers, lakes, and streams with 600,000 trout annually. While stocked streams constitute the majority of New Jersey trout waters, there are also thirty-one wild trout management areas regulated to protect the fish that reproduce in these streams. (See the regulations listed below.) The streams with the best water quality are located in the westcentral and northwestern parts of the state and flow into the Delaware River. The New Jersey Bureau of Freshwater Fisheries has done much to improve trout habitat for recreational anglers. Warm water, silt, and runoff from developments and cultivated land are the primary enemies of water quality in this, the nation's most populated state. The fisheries staff is doing a good job against tough odds and an exceptionally strong lobby of Put-and-Take anglers.

Patricia L. Hamilton, a state senior fish biologist, is familiar with several habitat improvements. Rocks held in place by logs have been put in streams to deflect water and create holding areas, trees have been planted to shade and cool the water in the summer, and banks have been stabilized using several bioengineering techniques. In many cases, TU volunteers enhance and improve what the state is doing.

If it comes as a surprise that there are trout streams in New Jersey, you may be more amazed to learn of the *wild* trout streams. In 1990, the New Jersey Fish and Game Department initiated a wild trout management program. A number of streams that had been identified as containing a naturally reproducing trout population began to be regulated as wild trout streams.

Artificial flies and lures only may be used, and except from Opening Day until September 15 (when two fish more than seven inches may be kept), all trout must be returned to the water. The trout in these fragile waters are largely left in place to reproduce and increase their numbers.

Thirty-one streams are classified as wild trout streams. Occasionally, when the data warrants, a stream is added. The program attests to the integrity of the staff in attempting to protect and preserve wild trout.

As more New Jersey anglers come to practice catch-and-release fishing, it is hoped that additional streams in which trout can hold over or reproduce will come under restrictive regulations. In the meantime, state officials are doing a good job of providing a balance of resources for all interests: traditional bait anglers, spin fishermen, fly anglers, and those that prefer catching streambred fish.

Lisa Barno, a senior fisheries biologist who manages the Raritan Drainage, explained the various classifications of trout water in the state. Water classification is one of several factors taken into consideration when determining regulations. Where trout cannot survive warm summer temperatures, variations of Put-and-Take regulations are in place. Where stocked trout can survive from year to year, or on streams where fish reproduce, the number of trout taken is restricted.

The rules are complex, but they illustrate the enlightened policies of the department and the consideration they have given the issue.

General trout regulations. The creel limit is six fish per day for the first seven weeks of the season, four fish per day thereafter. Minimum fish size is seven inches.

Trout-stocked waters with no in-season closures. Daily creel limit of six trout at least seven inches long for the first seven weeks of the season, four per day thereafter.

Trout-stocked waters with closed in-season stocking dates. Closed to fishing 5:00 A.M. to 5:00 P.M. on dates listed for stocking. Again, the creel limit is six fish per day for the first seven weeks of the season, four fish per day thereafter. These regulations govern some of the largest trout rivers, many of which get a lot of pressure.

Wild trout streams. The water quality of these streams supports natural trout reproduction. They are classified as wild trout streams and are no longer stocked. Fishing is permitted all year. All fish must be released except from Opening Day (in April) to September 15, when two seven-inch or longer fish may be kept per day. There is a twelve-inch minimum on brown trout in Van Campens Brook and the Pequannock River. Only artificial lures or flies may be used.

Year-round trout conservation areas. Anglers may keep one fish fifteen inches or longer per day except during in-season stocking closures, when all fish must be released. Only artificial lures and flies may be used.

Seasonal trout conservation areas. Anglers may keep one fish fifteen inches or longer per day from approximately the third week of June until the third week of March of the following year. Only artificials may be used during this period. From Opening Day until the third week of June, six fish per day, seven-inch minimum size, may be kept.

Fly-Fishing-Only areas. Only flies and fly tackle may be used, and fish less than seven inches must be released. Creel limits and stream closure periods vary. (See regulations book.)

SOME TIPS FOR TROUT FISHING IN NEW JERSEY

Most New Jersey trout waters are stocked. The warm summer temperatures and insufficient flow prevent trout from living through stressful drought periods in much of the state. Therefore, the best fishing in New Jersey is early in the season, from early April until mid-June, while the fish are still vigorous.

Steve Varga, owner of Steve's Bait & Tackle in Hopewell, explained his spring angling calendar. It is based on fishing ahead of warming water and provides an easy way to remember the order in which New Jersey trout are at their best.

Steve starts with the South Branch of the Raritan and fishes it until early June. By mid-May, he shifts west to the Musconetcong and the Paulinskill, where the water is cool through June. Next he drives to Big Flat Brook and the other northern trout streams for the best fishing in mid to late June. Finally, he fishes the upper Delaware River or goes east to salt water.

HATCHES, FLIES, AND BEST TIMES TO FISH

All the New Jersey trout streams described in this section have similar hatches. Therefore, I am providing a list of generally effective flies based on information from the guides and fly shop owners who helped me with my research.

Timing of hatches on individual streams will differ according to the year, the weather, and location of the water. Bugs will appear first on streams to the east. Different environmental characteristics will make some insects more prevalent on one stream than another, but there is sufficient uniformity to make this a useful guideline. Always check with local fly shops for up-to-date hatch information.

Les Shannon, owner of Les Shannon's Fly & Tackle in Califon, has created a complete Mayfly Hatching and Pattern Chart for the South Branch of the Raritan and its tributaries. The chart also works for most streams in the central and western part of the state.

Bill Feddock's hatch chart, printed in *Fishing New Jersey Trout* by John Panola, is also excellent. I have incorporated both of these documents. But for the hatch-matching angler, they are worth seeking out because they include detailed information on specific species and subspecies and the proper Latin terminology.

Late Winter (February to March)
Little black stonefly and dark midge imitations.

Early season (late March to April)
Quill Gordon (#12–#14), Iron Blue Quill (#14–#16), Hendrickson (a strong hatch in much of the state, #12–#14), Blue-Winged Olive (#16–#20).

Spring (late April to early June)
Little black caddis and olive caddis imitations (#16), Blue-Winged Olives (#16–#20), black midge (#18–#20), March Brown (#12–#14), Gray Fox (#12–#14), tan caddis (#16), grannom (#14–#16), green caddis (#16), sulphur (#16–#18), stonefly nymph patterns, green drake (#8) (drakes appear for the most part only on streams that hold wild trout).

Summer (June to September)
Light Cahill (#12), golden drake (#12–#14), mahogany drake (#8–#12), brown caddis (#14–#16), terrestrials (ants, beetles, hoppers, and cricket imitations), Tricos (#18–#22) (not everywhere), whitefly (mid-August) (#12–#14), slate drake (#12).

Fall (October to November)
Little Blue-Winged Olive (#18–#22), little Brown Quill (#12–#14), midges.

STATEWIDE RESOURCES

New Jersey Division of Fish, Game, and Wildlife. (908) 236-2118.

New Jersey State Park Service. Information about public campgrounds. 1-800-843-6420 or (609) 292-2797.

Camping New Jersey. A complete directory of private campgrounds. New Jersey Campground Owners Association. (609) 465-8444.

New Jersey Department of Natural Resources. (908) 236-2118.

New Jersey Travel and Tourism. 1-800-JERSEY-7.

Panola, John A. *Fishing New Jersey Trout*. Madison, New Jersey: Outdoors USA., Inc., 1994. A good fishing guide book.

Perrone, Steve, ed. *Discovering and Exploring New Jersey's Fishing Streams*. Somerdale, New Jersey: New Jersey Sportmen's Guides, 1994. A good fishing guidebook.

Complete New Jersey Trout Waters. Gogal Publishing and Alfred B. Patton, Inc. This is a map that marks all trout streams and special regulations. In a state without a DeLorme atlas, it is invaluable. (215) 722-1410.

Meck, Charles. *Mid-Atlantic Trout Streams and Their Hatches*. Woodstock, Vermont: Backcountry Publications, 1997.

County road maps of Sussex, Warren, Morris, Somerset, and Hunterdon Counties will be essential to an angler who has recently moved to the area or who wants to fish New Jersey extensively. Maps by Hagstrom and Patton are sold at local bookstores, convenience stores, and gas stations, or contact the Boards of Chosen Freeholders in each county.

CHAPTER 12

Northcentral New Jersey: The South Branch of the Raritan River and Its Tributaries—Beaver Brook; Drake's Brook; Hickory Run; Stony, Tetertown, and Willoughby Brooks; and the North Branch of Rockaway Creek

SOUTH BRANCH OF THE RARITAN RIVER

The South Branch originates at the outflow of Budd Lake in Morris County and flows nearly forty miles to the town of South Branch, where it joins the North Branch to form the main stem of the Raritan. This is New Jersey's best-known trout river. It is thirty to forty feet wide for most of its length. The Ken Lockwood Gorge, named for a famous conservationist, is a very pretty stretch of swift runs and pocket water coursing between banks lined with evergreen and rhododendron. This section is the most celebrated and heavily fished trout water in the state.

In the gorge, the river is difficult to wade. Its slippery bottom and scuzzy boulders can be dangerous in high water. During storms, the gorge stretch rises quicker than the rest of the river (and also drops sooner). Wear felt soles (with cleats if you have them), and take a wading staff. The South Branch is stocked (by the state and the Ken Lockwood chapter of TU) with rainbow trout in the upper section (above Califon), where brook and brown trout reproduce.

The Claremont stretch of the Raritan near the village of Long Valley is also under special regulations (Year-Round Trout Conservation). This section is not stocked and supports brook and brown trout. I prefer this section to the gorge. The wading is much easier, and I have caught several fish here. The river is narrower (about thirty feet wide), the grade gentle, and the footing secure.

One April afternoon, I watched my fishing buddy, Mary Kuss, catch eight-inch, twelve-inch, and fifteen-inch brownies—all on a #12 Gold-Ribbed Hare's Ear nymph. The last was a big, fat fighting football of a trout.

The South Branch of the Raritan below Clinton is a good smallmouth bass fishery in summer. The North Branch of the Raritan holds a few

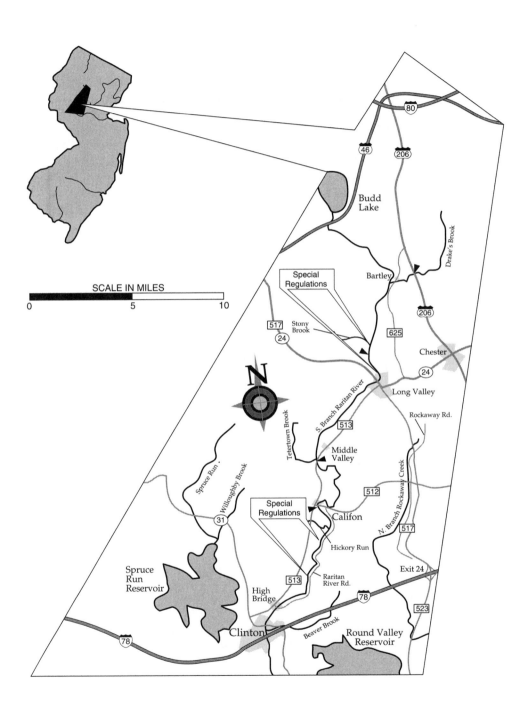

brown trout in the upper reaches and has sections well stocked with rainbows and browns, but it is no match for the South Branch.

Access

• Califon Island Park. Take Bank Street in the village of Califon to the park. The river runs slow and deep here, and it is a worm angler's paradise.

• The Fly-Fishing-Only stretch in the gorge, which begins on Raritan River Road downstream from the bridge in Califon. There are one- and two-car pull-offs between trees. The gorge area begins just below the Hoffmans Crossing Road bridge and continues 2.5 miles downstream to private land.

The lower end—from Cokesbury Road upstream into the gorge—is private and posted as such. At the end of Cokesbury Road, if you take a left on Fairview Avenue, you will circle into Clinton once more.

• The Claremont stretch. To reach this, take Route 512 out of Califon to Route 513 (Struder Road) north to Long Valley. Take a left on Route 24/517 and an immediate right onto Fairview Avenue. (There is a firehouse on the right.) Go .375 mile from the firehouse, and turn right onto a dirt road that looks like a driveway. Each time I was there, two large garbage containers and a short post-and-rail fence marked the entrance. This road leads to another dirt crossroads—a former railroad bed. Turn left onto it, and the stream will be on your right.

Hatches, Flies, and Best Times to Fish
In the introduction to this section, I listed the major hatches in northern New Jersey and the best flies to use. Most of these are applicable to the South Branch of the Raritan. The best South Branch hatches include several subspecies represented by drakes—green, gray, yellow, golden, and olive drakes. The South Branch also has plentiful caddis hatches.

In the winter, there are thousands of midges, fewer people, and a good hatch of early black stoneflies in February.

In the spring, Quill Gordon, Hendrickson, Blue Quill, March Brown, Gray Fox, green drake, and sulphur flies will all work, in roughly that order. Try fishing the South Branch during the Hendrickson hatch in April and during May, when the best sulphur hatch in the state occurs.

In June, Light Cahills and big brown drakes (*Hexagenia limbata*, #6–#10) emerge. This is the renowned "Hex" hatch that also appears on the Au Sable in Michigan and other midwestern waters. Cream drakes (*Potamanthus neglectus*, #12–#16) and golden drakes (*Potamanthus distinctus*, #8–#10) also appear. (Latin names as whimsical and amusing as these deserve to be used.) Tricos begin to appear mid-July and last through November.

In summer, some drake patterns still work, as well as terrestrials and Tricos. The whitefly *(Ephoron leukon)* hatches on mid-August evenings, and later in the month, the slate drake fly is effective. In September, continue with the late summer patterns (except for the whitefly), and try dark Blue-Winged Olives and Brown Quills (#14–#16).

Regulations

The two-and-one-half-mile Fly-Fishing-Only stretch of the Raritan is in the Ken Lockwood Gorge area, along River Road. Only artificial flies are allowed, except on Opening Day and the following eight days when bait may be used.

The Year-Round Trout Conservation area is the Claremont section, 1.1 miles from the Anglers Anonymous property downstream to the mouth of Electric Brook. One fish, fifteen inches or longer, may be kept per day. Only artificial flies and lures may be used.

The South Branch has a number of small tributaries that support streambred trout. Those listed below are the most accessible and can withstand some angling pressure.

BEAVER BROOK

This stream joins the South Branch on Main Street in Clinton. It is very inviting water, and there are reproducing brook trout above the Annandale Reformatory sewage treatment plant. The stream is stocked three times a year below the plant.

DRAKE'S BROOK

This stream can be found by taking Route 513/24 east from Long Valley toward Chester.

Take a left on Bartley Road (Route 625), and continue to a school on the right. Drake's Brook flows under the bridge on the road just past the school. The only parking is on the shoulder or on school property as permitted.

Drake's is one of Les Shannon's favorite small brook trout streams. It's possible to cast without hanging up your fly or going to your knees, there is little pressure, and the fish are there.

HICKORY RUN

Hickory Run is managed as a wild trout stream and contains streambred rainbows! A farmer stocked his pond a century ago and the rainbows slipped into the stream. They have been reproducing ever since. It is a tributary of the South Branch of the Raritan and enters the stream in Califon.

STONY BROOK, TETERTOWN BROOK, AND WILLOUGHBY BROOK

Wild trout regulations apply on all three of these brooks. Stony Brook enters the South Branch at the beginning of the Claremont stretch. Tetertown Brook is a very small, wild trout stream on the upper South Branch. It holds many seven-inch brown trout. Willoughby Brook (aka Buffalo Hollow Brook) runs along the edge of Voorhees State Park, near Buffalo Hollow Road, into Spruce Run Reservoir. All these streams are small and tough to fish, but those that enjoy finding trout in the wild will be rewarded.

NORTH BRANCH OF ROCKAWAY CREEK

New Jersey shad chaser Ted Ziegert took Mary Kuss and me to this stream one sunny Sunday in mid-April. We caught several brilliantly colored brookies on beadhead nymphs and dark (brown or black) caddis dry flies (#16–#18). Trout reproduce here, and the water is regulated as a wild trout stream.

The North Branch of Rockaway Creek is a fifteen- to twenty-foot-wide stream that flows through woods and pastures. Much of the stream runs through posted land in Hunterdon County, an upscale area with many resident anglers. It's pleasant fishing, provided you can find open water without too many other anglers. Even with restricted regulations, the fish are under lots of pressure. Many die from manhandling and hook wounds, as well as from warm summer water temperatures and other natural causes.

Access

Take Rockaway Road off Route 517 (Old Turnpike Road); north off I-78 at exit 24 to King's Road Park at King's Road bridge. Fish anywhere along Rockaway Road that is not posted.

Regulations

Wild Trout Stream regulations. Catch-and-Release, except from Opening Day until September 15, when two trout larger than seven inches may be kept. Artificial lures and flies only.

Hatches, Flies, and Best Times to Fish

The flies recommended in the introduction to this section work for this stream. The best time to fish it is in the spring, early in the morning, before anyone else has waded through the water.

IF YOU GO . . .

From New York City and northern New Jersey, take either I-80 west or the New Jersey Turnpike and I-78 west. Look on the map for Route 31 (north-south) and Route 46 and follow local directions (above). Philadelphia is two and one-half hours from Clinton, and Baltimore is about three and one-half hours. Take I-95 north to I-295 west. Bypass Trenton and take Route 31 north to Clinton.

Tackle Shops and Guides

Sportsmen's Center. Bordentown. Robert Attick, proprietor. Attick is a guide and source of good information on New Jersey trout streams. (609) 298-5380.

Delaware River Outfitters. Route 31, Pennington. Mark Dettmar and Bruce Turner, proprietors. Full-service fly shop, fly-tying materials, and Orvis equipment. Guide service includes Delaware River trips for shad and trout. Mark and Bruce also run angling schools. (609) 466-7970.

Shannon's Fly & Tackle Shop. Califon. Les Shannon, proprietor. Les is the old-timer among New Jersey's many new destination fly shops. He knows (and will tell you) more about the South Branch of the Raritan than almost anyone. Les has a large supply of fly-tying materials, as well as an inventory of nine thousand flies. He created the complete Mayfly Hatching and Pattern Chart for the South Branch of the Raritan. (908) 832-5736.

Steve's Bait & Tackle. Hopewell. Proprietor Steve Varga carries a few flies but mostly spinning tackle. He has fished northcentral New Jersey for thirty years. He knows the water, the fish, and the lies and is an excellent day-to-day source of stream information. (609) 466-4611.

There are many more tackle shops in eastern New Jersey. I have included only those near the streams described in this section.

Where to Stay

Fountain Motel. Lebanon. On Route 22, near Whitehouse. Basic and clean. Inexpensive. (908) 236-6322.

Holiday Inn Select. Clinton. Route 173. Breakfast, restaurant, and lounge. Expensive. (908) 735-5111.

Neighborhood House B&B. Long Valley. Moderate. (908) 876-3519.

Round Valley Motel. Route 22, Whitehouse. Inexpensive. (908) 534-2640.

Camping

Round Valley State Park. Lebanon, near Clinton. (908) 236-6355.

New Jersey State Park Service. 1-800-843-6420 or (609) 292-2797 for public campgrounds.

Voorhees State Park. Glen Gardner, north of Clinton. (908) 638-6969.

Where to Eat

Chesapeake Bay Seafood Company. Long Valley. Moderate. (908) 876-3922.

Clinton House. Clinton. Good atmosphere and service, carefully prepared food. Expensive. (908) 730-9300.

Hunan Wok. Long Valley. Moderate. (908) 876-9680.

Inn on Schooley's Mountain Road. Califon. Routes 24/517. Inexpensive. (908) 876-9111.

Spinning Wheel Diner. Route 22, Whitehouse. Spiffy art deco design. A good place for breakfast or lunch. Inexpensive. No reservations.

The Muddler Minnow. Main Street, Clinton. Unusual combinations of health food. Good takeout fare. Bakery on premises. Inexpensive. No reservations.

Tomato Grill. Route 31, near Clinton, opposite entrance to Spruce Run Reservoir. Moderate. (908) 249-1199.

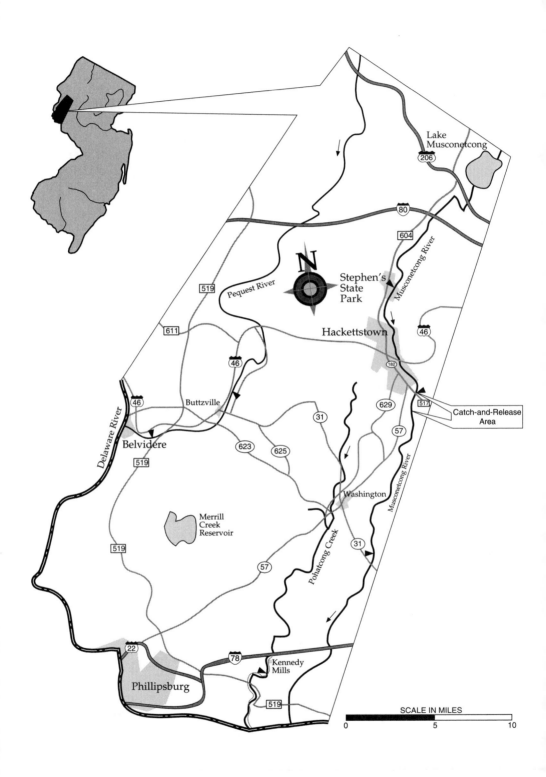

Lake
Musconetcong

[206]

[80]

[604]

Musconetcong River

[519]

Pequest River

N

Stephen's
State
Park

[46]

Hackettstown

[611]

[46]

[182]

[46]

[517]

Buttzville

[31]

[629]

Catch-and-Release
Area

[57]

Delaware River

[46]

Belvidere

[519]

[623]

[625]

Merrill
Creek
Reservoir

Washington

Musconetcong River

[519]

Pohatcong Creek

[31]

[519]

[57]

[22]

[78]

Kennedy
Mills

Phillipsburg

[519]

SCALE IN MILES

0   5   10

CHAPTER 13

Westcentral New Jersey:
The Musconetcong River,
Pohatcong Creek, and the Pequest River

THE MUSCONETCONG RIVER

In the no-kill (Fly-Fishing-Only) area near Hackettstown, the Musconetcong (called the "Musky" locally) is about fifty feet wide and a relatively flat piece of water with lots of undifferentiated riffles and runs. The special regulations section is the only water in the state managed as a no-kill (Catch-and-Release) *and* Fly-Fishing-Only area. Year-round fishing is possible here from the Route 24 (Schooley's Mountain Road) bridge in Hackettstown downstream for one mile. Farther downstream from the no-kill section, the Division of Fish, Game, and Wildlife is acquiring property to increase the number of public angling opportunities.

The Musky was the first stream in New Jersey to receive Wallop-Breaux funds for habitat improvements awarded to the New Jersey Bureau of Freshwater Fisheries. In 1995, two stream deflectors were placed in the Musky near Hackettstown to improve trout habitat during periods of low flow.

The Musky has better mayfly hatches early in the season than the South Branch of the Raritan, whereas the latter has better caddis. It is a freestone stream. However, lots of grass grows along its bottom, so scuds, shrimp, and cress bugs work here all year.

The stream is stocked frequently in spring and fall with brook, brown, and rainbow trout in the ten- to eleven-inch range. It warms up quickly, so the best time to fish is from March to the middle of June.

Regulations

The Fly-Fishing-Only, no-kill stretch starts at the Route 24 bridge (not on map) in Hackettstown and continues downstream for one mile. Only single barbless hooks are permitted. This stretch may be fished all year, except during in-season stocking closures.

The rest of the river is regulated as stocked trout water with closed in-season stocking dates. For the first seven weeks of the season, six trout per day may be kept; thereafter, there is a four-fish-per-day limit and a seven-inch minimum size.

Access

• To reach the Musconetcong Fly-Fishing-Only, no-kill stretch near Hackettstown, take Route 31 north of Clinton, to Route 57. Take a right on Route 57 east to its end at Route 182. This junction is in the middle of the special regulations section. Go right (south) on Route 182/24, and the river will be on the right. The special regulations stretch is well marked. Route 182/24 will also take you to Route 517/24 (Schooley's Mountain Road) and Califon.

• Below the special regulations section, there is good fishing downstream (toward Washington) from the Fly-Fishing-Only section. There is access to the water along Route 57. Deep holes and sizable riffles make good trout habitat.

• There is a productive stretch upstream from the bridge on Route 31.

• There is a good reach at the graphite mill off Route 31 near Asbury.

• The upper Musky can be fished in many locations, most notably in Stephen's State Park off Route 604 between Hackettstown and Netcong. Route 604 can be accessed from Route 206 at its northern end and Route 46 to the south. Take Willow Grove Road off Route 46 in Hackettstown and go about two miles to the park.

Either park at the main park office and fish upstream or park at the farthest lot upstream from the office and fish downstream. The water is thirty to forty feet wide, shaded by evergreens and hardwoods, and alternates between long riffles, runs, and pocket water. It is a much prettier part of the stream than the no-kill section. Wading is not difficult, but a local angler told me the quality of the fishery has declined in recent years.

Hatches, Flies, and Best Times to Fish.
Because it warms up in summer, it is best to fish the Musky in spring and late fall. In the no-kill section, midges appear all winter. Scuds, shrimp, and cress bugs work on the Musky in addition to the mayflies listed in chapter 12.

THE POHATCONG CREEK
The Pohatcong Creek is a twenty- to thirty-foot-wide freestone stream that flows through agricultural land in Warren County. It is an inviting-looking stream, with long quiet pools, fast runs, and lots of riffles meandering between treelines dividing rural farms and restored old properties. The grade is gentle, and the stream is very easy to wade.

The problem with the Pohatcong is that much of its best water is posted, and there are no special regulations on the open water. The Pohatcong Sportsman's Club controls more than a mile of the lower water upstream from the Delaware River. This is the section about which I heard stories of big browns migrating in the fall.

Hoping for public access, I walked downstream along the club water. I saw wonderful holding areas and prayed the posted signs would come to an end. It was not to be. I was soon at the Delaware, blinded by its dazzling expanse under a bright September sun. I felt as if I had walked out of a cave into an impressionist painting. As two canoes and an outboard swept by, I longed for a boat, a big fish, and a good fight. I needed to tangle with something major to reverse the bad mood incurred by having to pass up the private water. I cast into the side eddies of the river for more than an hour, gradually calming down and becoming mesmerized by the currents and the trees in full fall color.

After I returned to my car, the posted signs were no sooner behind me than I saw the cast-off worm cups and chewing tobacco pouches of bait fishermen. I realized I was within spitting distance of the water. I continued upstream and walked to the stream where it ran five hundred yards from the road. The banks were mashed down and the water looked empty. Upstream a few miles, I did locate productive water.

Regulations

The Pohatcong is a General Trout Stream with closed in-season stocking dates. The entire length is stocked, from the headwaters near the Rockport State Game Farm many miles downstream to the Delaware. For the first seven weeks of the season, six trout per day may be kept; thereafter there is a four-fish-per-day limit and a seven-inch minimum size.

Access

The Pohatcong can be accessed at several spots along its route downstream. Route 57 south from Washington and Pleasant Valley parallels the stream for several miles. Although these roads do not appear on the map, there are access points at the bridge at Winter's Road and Creek Road, the junction of Mountain Road and Creek Road, and the junction of River Road and Creek Road. This water is leased by the Sportsman's Club. There is some access above the posted stretch. On Route 31, just above Kinnaman—Jackson Valley Avenue (Route 628) in Washington.

Hatches, Flies, and Best Times to Fish

The Pohatcong has good hatches of standard mayflies and caddis. Consult the list of flies in chapter 12 or local fly shops for specific recommendations.

THE PEQUEST RIVER

Few people realize that this midsize trout water originates in Sussex County as a spring creek. Near Newton (Routes 611 and 603), water gushes through the ground to form the headwaters of the Pequest. Sow bugs and cress bugs will take fish here, as will freshwater shrimp. The spring is located on private property but can be fished with permission from the owner.

As the Pequest flows downstream, it becomes more and more influenced by freestone tributaries. There is lots of pocket water and easy access along Route 46. The most productive stretches are between Belvidere and Buttzville and near the Pequest Hatchery. I fished with Mark Dettmar, Chuck Salvani, and Chris Scrivens from a particularly productive spot. Take the first left north of Hot Dog Johnny's. Park and fish upstream or down.

The first time I waded the river, I fell flat on my face. It was April and the water was up. I guess I gave my guides their laugh for the day. They were all catching fish, but I couldn't get anything going. And it didn't get any better after my fall! I've since discovered the river fishes better when it's about a foot lower. In fact, I prefer the Pequest to the Musconetcong despite the restrictive regulations on the latter.

The Pequest is fifty to sixty feet wide in many places, and it gets low and clear in the summer. The trout are still there, but they get spooky until the fall rains raise the water level. Some anglers fish upstream from the Delaware at Belvidere in the fall, when spawning browns come up and mix with the fall stockies.

The Pequest Trout Hatchery is about seven miles west of Hackettstown. It is a rich resource for those who wish to enjoy New Jersey outdoor life. There are educational programs for children, models of local animals, and "how to" workshops, including beginning fly fishing, hiking, and turkey hunting. Large trout swim around in tiled pools outside the entrance to the resource center. At the parking area, there is a fishing site for the disabled built by the North New Jersey chapter of TU and Ramsey Outdoors.

The Division of Fish, Game, and Wildlife has purchased property downstream from the hatchery. There is a sluice of cold (54 degrees Fahrenheit) water that comes from the hatchery into the Pequest about one-quarter mile upstream of the entrance.

The Pequest is unprotected and flat in the Great Meadows area, but as it nears the hatchery, the cover and holding water improve.

Regulations

From its source downstream to the Delaware (except for the Seasonal Trout Conservation Area at the Hatchery), four fish per day may be kept from June 1 through mid-March of the following year, and six fish may be kept from Opening Day through May—seven-inch minimum size—except on days listed for stocking, when the stream is closed.

The Seasonal Trout Conservation Area starts at the railroad bridge upstream of Pequest Hatchery Road and extends downstream one mile to Route 625 (Pequest Furnace Road). In this stretch, one fifteen-inch fish per day may be taken from mid-May through mid-March of the following year. Only artificials may be used. From mid-March until mid-May, regulations for the rest of the stream apply.

Access
- At the entrance to the Pequest Trout Hatchery, Route 46, seven miles west of Hackettstown.
- The first road on the left north of Hot Dog Johnny's.
- Numerous pull-offs along Route 46 between Belvidere and Buttzville.

Hatches, Flies and Best Times to Fish
The hatches on the Pequest are much the same as those listed in chapter 12. Also try cress bugs, amber shrimp, and scuds on the upper Pequest.

IF YOU GO . . .
The Musconetcong, Pohatcong, and Pequest are northwest of I-78 in Warren County. Take Route 31 north from I-78, pass Clinton, and follow directions to the specific streams.

Tackle Shops
Delaware River Outfitters. Route 31, Pennington. Mark Dettmar and Bruce Turner, proprietors. Large tackle shop, clothing, fly-tying materials, and guide service. (609) 466-7970.

Shannon's Fly & Tackle Shop. Califon. Les Shannon, proprietor. (908) 832-5736.

Where to Stay
Days Inn. Route 46, near Hackettstown and the Pequest and Musconetcong. Inexpensive. (908) 496-8221.

Econocourt. Near Hackettstown. Inexpensive. (908) 637-4176.

Camping
Stephen's State Park. North of Hackettstown. (908) 852-3790.

Where to Eat
Inn on Schooley's Mountain Road. Route 24/517. Inexpensive. (908) 876-9111.

Hot Dog Johnny's. Route 46, Buttsville, on the Pequest. A local legend famous for its hot dogs and buttermilk! Inexpensive. No reservations.

Pane et Vino. Route 46, just west of Hackettstown. Has a good local reputation. Moderate. (908) 813-8535.

Spinning Wheel Diner. Route 22 east, between Whitehouse and Lebanon. Inexpensive. No reservations.

Tomato Grill. Route 31, opposite entrance to Spruce Run Reservoir. Moderate. (908) 249-1199.

Washington House. Route 31, Washington. Steaks, chops, seafood. Moderate. (908) 689-9846.

CHAPTER 14

Northwestern New Jersey: Big Flat Brook, Van Campens Brook, Dunnfield Creek, and the Paulinskill River

The streams described in this chapter flow through New Jersey's most rural areas and are the state's best trout streams. All have special regulations sections that improve the angling for those who prefer fly fishing under catch-and-release and creel limit restrictions.

BIG FLAT BROOK

Big Flat is the favorite of many New Jersey fly anglers. It runs through miles of rural countryside and state holdings in the Walpack Valley between the Kittatinny Mountains and the Delaware River. The Flat Brook–Roy and Walpack Wildlife Management Areas are maintained for sporting purposes. Big Flat Brook traverses wooded land, abandoned fields, working farms, and orchards. From the lower reaches, the Big Flat Brook takes its name. It creates a shallow, fifty-foot-wide ribbon down the Walpack Valley.

The Blewett Tract of Big Flat Brook is one of the most popular fly-fishing areas in the state. The property was originally owned by William Blewett, a conservationist and fly fisherman who, while he was alive, allowed the New Jersey Fish, Game, and Wildlife Department to stock his water and opened it to public fishing as long as only fly tackle was used. Upon Blewett's death, the government purchased most of the property for the Delaware Water Gap Recreational Area. Under the stipulations of his will, Blewett's former property remains a public Fly-Fishing-Only stretch.

Although the Blewett Tract is only half a mile long, it withstands considerable angling pressure. I watched a nymphing angler catch and release twenty trout in less than an hour one afternoon in early May. I was astounded, and I never did discover his secret weapon! I took four eleven-inch browns on a Pheasant-tail nymph and felt like a bumbling idiot by comparison.

Big Flat Brook also fishes well from Flatbrookville to Walpack Center. Perhaps because there are no special regulations, this area is underused and is a good place to stalk browns migrating upstream from the Delaware to their fall spawning grounds.

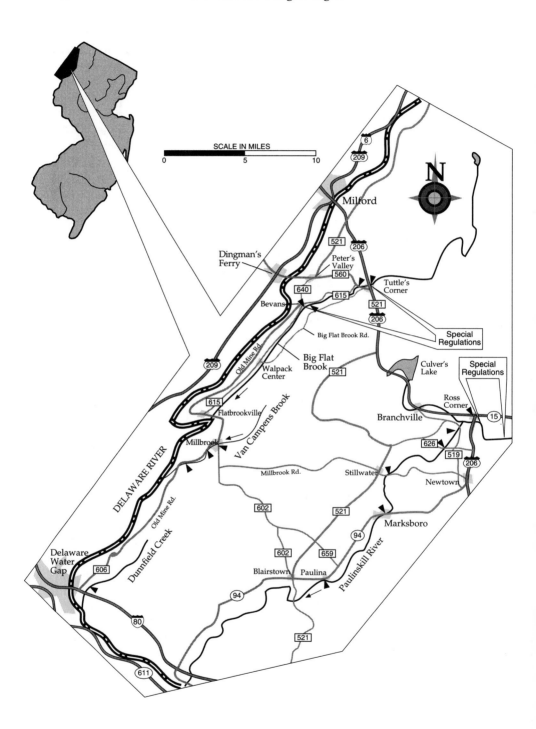

Big Flat Brook is amply stocked throughout the spring and fall. Though the water does warm up in the summer, there are numerous holdover trout. Wading is not difficult, but the rocks can be slippery. Felt-soled shoes and a staff are a good precaution. The Flat Brook muddies easily in a storm but recedes quickly. Upper Flat Brook stays clear even after heavy rains.

Regulations
The Fly-Fishing-Only section runs from the Route 206 bridge downstream about four miles to the Roy Bridge on Mountain Road. It includes the Blewett Tract. Regulations stipulate that only flies may be used year-round, and fishing is not permitted during in-season stocking closures. From January 1 to March 23 (when stocking begins), anglers may keep four trout seven inches or longer per day. No fishing is permitted between March 24 and Opening Day.

From Opening Day for about two weeks—until the next stocking— any tackle may be used, and six trout, seven inches or longer, may be kept per day. From the third week of April through Memorial Day, six trout, seven-inch minimum length, may be taken per day, and from June 1 through New Year's Eve four trout, seven-inch minimum, may be kept per day.

The remainder of Big Flat Brook is regulated as Stocked Trout Water with in-season closure dates for stocking. Big Flat Brook is stocked from one hundred feet above Steam Mill Bridge on Crigger Road in Stokes State Forest downstream to the Delaware River.

Access
To reach Big Flat Brook from the north, south, or east, take I-80 to exit 33 (Route 15 north). Take Route 15 north to Route 206 north to Tuttle's Corner.

To access Big Flat Brook from the west, take I-80 to exit 4, Route 94, north to Blairstown. Then take Route 602 from Blairstown to Millbrook Village and Route 615 to Flatbrookville, then Walpack Center. Look for Mountain Road and Big Flat Brook Road off Route 615 north of Walpack Center.

• If you continue on Route 206 from Tuttle's Corner, you can access the upper end of the Fly-Fishing-Only area at the Route 206 bridge (Shaefer's Bridge). The regulated reach extends four miles downstream.

• If you turn *left* at Tuttle's Corner onto Route 560, the road will cross the stream and Big Flat Brook Road in the Fly-Fishing-Only area. There is parking on the north side of Big Flat Brook Road.

• The Blewett Tract, which is regulated as Catch-and-Release (as well as Fly-Fishing-Only), is contained within this four-mile stretch. It begins at Three Bridges Road and continues upstream one-half mile, just above the confluence of Little Flat Brook. To reach it, take Route 521 through Peters Valley. About one mile south of Peters Valley, there is a sharp right bend in the road. *Continue straight*, taking the dirt road, which leads to the Three Bridges parking lot and the downstream boundary of the Blewett Tract.

• The "bait" stretches abut the Fly-Fishing-Only areas, from Roy Bridge downstream to the Delaware River and upstream of Route 206.

• Additional access points can be found along Big Flat Brook Road between Route 206 and Walpack Center.

Hatches, Flies, and Best Times to Fish

Big Flat Brook has good hatches of mayflies and caddis. The best fishing is from April through June and September through October. The hatch list at the beginning of this section can be used for Big Flat Brook.

VAN CAMPENS BROOK

A thirteen-inch brown trout startled me from an early-morning daze on Van Campens late one May morning. The trout took my Patriot dry from the surface of a small pool under the hemlocks in the upper reaches.

ANN MCINTOSH

Van Campens Brook

That was the first time I fished Van Campens, but not the last. Since then, it has become my favorite New Jersey trout stream. It is one of the best wild trout fisheries in the state, supporting in-stream reproduction of rainbows, browns, and brook trout. It is also the prettiest and one of the most remote places to fish in New Jersey. A tributary of the Delaware River, it's a good spot to stop and fish en route to the Delaware or even the Catskills.

Van Campens is only ten to fifteen feet wide. It runs off the western slopes of the Kittatinny Mountains seven miles to the Delaware River. It is shaded throughout and has not been stocked since the late 1960s. Because it is not stocked, it doesn't receive much pressure from put-and-take anglers. However, because it is small and somewhat fragile, it's the kind of stream on which I like to be the first angler through the water in the morning.

Hip boots will keep one dry on Van Campens. Even wading shoes will suffice, but it's best to stay out of the water. Be sure to take a small stream rod if you have one. The canopy along the stream is high enough to permit a good cast. These are feisty fish that will make a delicate rod a joy to fish. Van Campens trout do not come to hand easily.

Regulations

Throughout its length, Van Campens is regulated as a wild trout stream. All trout must be released, except from Opening Day through mid-September, when one rainbow or brook trout, seven inches or longer, may be kept per day. The minimum length for brown trout is twelve inches.

Access

To reach Van Campens Brook from the south, take Route 606 (Old Mine Road), the last New Jersey exit east of the Delaware River, about twelve miles north toward Millbrook.

- After twelve miles, there will be a road to the right with a park sign for picnics, hiking, etc. Pull in, park, and fish upstream. This is the most picturesque part of the water and very popular.
- Continue up Old Mine Road and park near the gate to the park hiking trail (marked).
- There is access to the stream in Millbrook at the end of Old Mine Road, from the Blairstown-Millbrook Road bridge.

Hatches, Flies, and Best Times to Fish

Because there is in-stream reproduction and the water does not warm to critical temperatures in the summer, there are trout feeding in Van Campens all year. Hatches follow the eastern hatch timetable. (See the introduction to this section and Al Caucci's hatch chart for the Delaware River, in chapter 1.) The stream has good hatches of mayflies, caddis, and stoneflies.

DUNNFIELD CREEK

The first time I fished Dunnfield Creek, I was alone except for two intrepid campers huddled under a tent next to the parking lot off I-80 at the Delaware Water Gap. It was 38 degrees Fahrenheit that mid-April morning!

A mountain trail parallels the stream, and there are many spots from which to drop down to fish. The water consists of steep falls dropping into deep pools—a very pretty setting. But given the air temperature, I was not surprised that I didn't get a nibble.

I returned three weeks later in May. Families with kids swarmed up the mountain. Some were swimming in the brook with their dogs, others necked on top of boulders—picture-perfect boulders and pools, teeming with teenagers and dogs.

I found a large, very deep lagoon of a pool and wasted my time trying to sink a nymph deep into it while a bunch of kids giggled and gaggled and asked why I wasn't catching anything. If you fish Dunnfield Creek, go early in the season (but not too early), when only serious hikers will be there.

Surveys show that the numbers of trout in Dunnfield rival those in Van Campens, but you can't prove it by me. Perhaps they had been put down for the day. I'm sure I should have hiked up the mountain at least a mile to fish for the wild brook trout I know are there. But, given this stream's popularity with nonanglers, I'll stick to Van Campens.

Regulations

Dunnfield is now regulated as a wild trout stream (like Van Campens, except the minimum length for all trout is seven inches).

Access

To reach Dunnfield Creek, take the first exit off I-80 on the New Jersey (east) side of the Delaware at the Delaware Water Gap and locate the parking lot where hikers park, opposite the Visitors Center.

Hatches, Flies, and Best Times to Fish

Fish Dunnfield as you would Van Campens, realizing, however, that its fish may have been spooked by nonanglers playing in the water. If it is difficult to locate trout in the lower reaches, there are plenty of brookies in the headwaters above the crowds.

THE PAULINSKILL RIVER

The first time I saw the Paulinskill, it was high and muddy and three feet over its banks. I was told that this is not unusual for the Paulinskill. Much of the river is difficult to wade whenever there has been heavy rainfall. Its banks are swampy in many reaches, and much of the streambed is steep in silt.

The Paulinskill looks like ideal bass water, but some of the biggest trout (breeders) the state stocks are said to be put here and in Big Flat Brook. Although it warms in the summer, the Paulinskill temperatures are not as marginal for trout as those of the lower Musconetcong.

The Paulinskill has its champions; however, I've not yet had the opportunity to fish with one. There is a lot of deep stillwater on the Paulinskill, and I will need some extended stream time, or a good local guide, to learn its secrets. While there are runs and riffles, the angler should be prepared to fish this stillwater to catch the biggest fish.

The river is fifty to sixty feet wide, with lots of deep slow runs. There are beautiful, absolutely flat hundred-foot-long pools that—on calm days —reflect every detail of the landscape. On a clear fall day, one can see every color of each turning leaf in its surface. Unless you are casting to rising fish, make sure to get your nymph near the bottom in a drag-free drift. I'm told the fish are most likely to respond at that level.

Jack Decker of Stillwater has fished the Paulinskill regularly for years. He explains that it comes from limestone base at its headwaters and then is influenced by many freestone tributaries on its way to the Delaware. He fishes scuds and olive or green shrimp patterns all year and mayflies in the spring.

There is private property along much of the Paulinskill, but if you ask permission and leave the land as you find it, landowners will let you fish.

Regulations

The East Branch of the Paulinskill in Sussex County near Ross Corner is regulated as a Year-Round Trout Conservation Area from the Limecrest Railroad spur bridge downstream 2.25 miles to the West Branch of the Paulinskill at Wabasse Junction. One trout, fifteen inches or longer, may be taken per day using artificials only between January 1 and the beginning of the stocking period. All trout must be released during stocking periods. After mid-April, regulations revert to one fifteen-inch trout per day, using only artificials.

The rest of the river is regulated as stocked trout water with closed in-season stocking dates. For the first seven weeks of the season, six trout may be kept per day; thereafter, there is a four-fish-per-day limit. There is a seven-inch minimum size.

Access

Maps of Warren and Sussex Counties will serve you well on the Paulins-kill. Use them to find access points where the river crosses county roads.

Take Route 94 north off I-80 at Columbia. Use Warren and Sussex County Routes 614, 610, and 521 to find the water and its public access points. Look for the Division of Fish, Game, and Wildlife signs for Trout Stocked Waters to identify water open to the public.

• Some of the most popular reaches are between Paulina and Marks-boro. Access these from Route 94 and from Paulina at the lower end of Paulinskill Road. Also experiment in Paulina below the dam. The middle reaches of the Paulinskill consist of wide flat water running through open meadows. Casting is easy, but wading the soft silted bottom is less than desirable. Also, the lack of cover warms the water and keeps the trout at the bottom of big holes.

• There is a productive section near Ross Corner.

• There is access from Route 15 in Lafayette Village.

• There is access at the bridge on Route 519 near Branchville and downstream at Balesville on Route 626. There is a lot of posted land in this area, so be sure to ask permission to fish.

• One of the best access points is from Route 648. (Use a Sussex County map.) Park at the automobile repair shop and walk along the rail-road tracks to the water. This is a Year-Round Trout Conservation Area.

In its upper reaches, the Paulinskill is a surprisingly small, intimate, overgrown stream—given its broad belly downstream. Even small-stream devotees will find it a challenge to wade with stealth, without spooking fish.

Hatches, Flies, and Best Times to Fish

Matching the hatch is important on the Paulinskill, and that fact (as well as the potential size of the catch) is part of its allure. It fishes best early in the season (April and May) and again in the fall (late September and October), when water temperatures have cooled and browns swim up the river to spawn.

IF YOU GO . . .

Big Flatbrook is about one and one-half hours (seventy-five miles) from New York City (in moderate traffic). Take I-80 west to exit 33 for Route 15 north to Route 206 north for Big Flatbrook. I-80 is within easy reach of all four streams described above.

Tackle Shops and Guides

There are no nearby fly shops. The closest is listed below. (Also refer to lists in chapters 12 and 13.)

Shannon's Fly & Tackle Shop. Califon. (908) 832-5736.

Where to Stay

Budget Motel. East Stroudsburg, Pennsylvania. AAA. Exit 51 off I-80. Nice, but no complimentary breakfast. J. R.'s Green Scene restaurant on site. Moderate. (717) 424-5451.

Days Inn. East Stroudsburg, Pennsylvania. Interstate 80, exit 52. Moderate. (717) 424-1771.

The Inn at Millrace Pond. Hope, at the junction of Route 611 and Route 519. Restaurant and lodge. Moderate to expensive. (908) 459-4884.

Shannon Inn and Pub. East Stroudsburg, Pennsylvania. Interstate 80, exit 52. Expensive. 1-800-424-8052.

Camping

Worthington State Forest Campgrounds. Sites on the Delaware River near the Water Gap. (908) 841-9575.

Where to Eat

There are few restaurants in the area. Either cross the Delaware River into Pennsylvania at the Delaware Water Gap and Stroudsburg to find restaurants, or use the eateries listed in chapters 12 and 13.

Delaware

OVERVIEW

The state of Delaware is not known as a travel destination for trout anglers. The bulk of it lies on the Delmarva Peninsula, a flat, sandy chunk of land south of Wilmington and Philadelphia and east of the Chesapeake Bay. The best fishing opportunities are for striped bass, bluefish, and other sport fish, both onshore and off.

However, if you find yourself in Wilmington in need of some fresh air and casting practice, there are six stocked streams, and they all provide viable springtime fishing. White Clay Creek is by far the most satisfactory, and it receives most of the fish stockings. Brandywine Creek is an excellent summer smallmouth bass fishery.

Information about fishing the Delaware River can be found in the Pennsylvania section of this book. Flowing through New York, Pennsylvania, and New Jersey to its mouth in Delaware, the river cannot be claimed by any single jurisdiction. The best fly fishing I've found on the Delaware, however, is in the northeastern corner of Pennsylvania, rather than in the river's namesake state.

STATEWIDE RESOURCES

Delaware Department of Natural Resources and Environmental Control (Fish and Wildlife). 89 Kings Highway, P.O. Box 1401, Dover, Delaware 19903-1401. (302) 739-5295.

Delaware Department of Tourism. 99 Kings Highway, P.O. Box 1401, Dover, Delaware 19903-1401. 1-800-441-8846.

Maryland Delaware Atlas and Gazetteer. DeLorme, P.O. Box 298, Freeport, Maine 04032. (207) 865-4171.

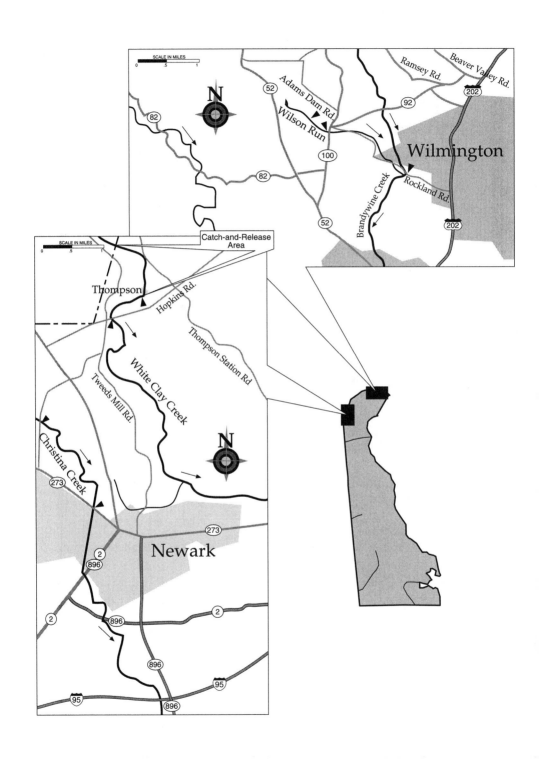

CHAPTER 15

Delaware Trout Streams:
White Clay Creek, Christina Creek,
and Wilson Run

Considering the limited cold-water resources with which it has to work, the Delaware Department of Natural Resources (DNR) has used what it has to good advantage. Most of Delaware's fresh water flows through the northwestern part of the state from Pennsylvania into New Castle County and the lower reaches of the Delaware River. All six designated trout streams are stocked. The water warms so much in the summer that trout cannot survive, let alone reproduce. Anglers are encouraged to keep their fish, which will likely expire in the water otherwise.

The staff of the Fish and Wildlife Division of the DNR has undertaken several education initiatives. Laura Madara, the assistant superintendent in Brandywine Creek State Park, has worked with other staff members to develop an angling instruction program for young people and special populations. The department also hosts a program that trains adults to teach kids to fish. The result of these efforts, Madara and her colleagues hope, will be knowledgeable, conservation-minded anglers who will value the natural resources wherever they find trout.

The state stocks about thirty-one thousand brown and rainbow trout in April and May. The fish average eleven inches, but five hundred trophy rainbows fourteen inches or longer are released in April. About 90 percent of the total stock population is released on White Clay Creek, the best trout water in the state.

Opening Day in Delaware is usually the first Saturday in April. Anyone wanting to experience an enthusiastic Opening Day crowd need only come to Delaware's White Clay Creek near Newark. More than four thousand anglers have been known to appear along Tweeds Mill Road, casting elbow-to-elbow to fish that have barely had time to learn to find food in the wild. I'm told the smell of Power Bait hovers, and Styrofoam worm containers abound!

WHITE CLAY CREEK

White Clay, a modest trout stream by other states' standards, is Delaware's best trout stream. It traverses woodlands, marshes, and open meadows. There is a lot of silt on its bottom, but numerous deadfalls and trees provide cover throughout the spring months.

I spent a nice afternoon on White Clay in April. It was my first day fishing that season, and I landed three eleven-inch browns on the Fly-Fishing-Only regulated water near Tweeds Mill Road. Because this marked the beginning of my angling year, I was content. Also, I was there during the week, so I was alone on the stream. The trout put up a good fight, indicating they had been given time to acclimate to the natural surroundings.

Access
To access White Clay from Wilmington, take Route 2 south to Newark and make a right on Tweeds Mill Road. Tweeds Mill Road runs near the water upstream to the Pennsylvania line. There are several places to access the water from the road across private land, but be sure to obey posted signs and ask permission to fish. You may wish to try the following:

- Catch-and-Release area from Thompson Bridge on Chambers Rock Road (not on map) near Thompson.
- The access point at Hopkins Road.

Anglers may also want to consider fishing the East Branch of White Clay on the Pennsylvania side in the White Clay Creek Preserve. Access there is from the Landenberg Store on Penn Green Road, as well as at Good Hope Road and at Broad Run Road. (Remember, you will need a Pennsylvania fishing license.)

Regulations
The Fly-Fishing-Only section is one mile from Thompson Bridge on Chambers Rock Road upstream to the Pennsylvania state line. Four trout a day may be taken. Many fly anglers practice catch-and-release in this area—at least until mid-June. All Delaware trout streams—except the Fly-Fishing-Only stretch of White Clay Creek—have a daily limit of six trout. No fishing is permitted on any stream within two weeks of Opening Day (the first Saturday in April).

Hatches, Flies, and Best Times to Fish
As soon after Opening Day as the crowds recede is the best time to fish for Delaware trout. If possible, go after work, during the week, early in the season. The trout will be feisty, and you will avoid the popular weekends.

Good flies to try on White Clay include San Juan Worms, Woolly Buggers (#12), Green Weenies, Gold-Ribbed Hare's Ears, and Pheasant-tail nymphs (#14–#16); attractor patterns such as the Royal Coachman and the Patriot (#12–#16); and elk-hair tan or olive caddis (#14–#16) in the spring. Streamer patterns work well early in the season when the water is high.

CHRISTINA CREEK

This small stream runs through northwestern Delaware until it becomes the substantial Christina River at Wilmington. It is stocked from Rittenhouse Park in Newark upstream to the Maryland line.

Access

• Near the intersection of Routes 72 and 2, east of Newark; south of Salem Church Road and north of Route 40.

WILSON RUN

Each year, on the fourth Saturday in April, the Delaware Trout Association, Brandywine Creek State Park, and the Division of Fish and Wildlife hold a fishing derby on Wilson Run. Physically and mentally challenged individuals are given a chance to fish, assisted by staff and volunteers from the local chapter of TU. Although the stream is only fifteen feet wide, it is deep and holds big trout through the spring. It flows through a meadow on the Du Pont farm that supported Winterthur. All the structures, including the barns and stone walls, were built by Italian masons in the late 1800s and have been preserved.

Wilson Run is stocked at the junction of Route 92 and Route 100 (Thompson's Bridge Road), at the main entrance to the park off Adams Dam Road, and at a bridge in the park maintenance area (also off Adams Dam Road).

Access

To reach Wilson Run, take the Route 202 exit off I-95. Go left (north) on Route 202 (Concord Pike). After approximately two miles, take a left on Route 141. At the second light, go right on Rockland Road and, bearing left, cross Brandywine Creek. Stay straight over the bridge on Adams Dam Road. Brandywine Creek State Park is one mile farther along on the right.

Delaware stocks three other streams with trout: Beaver Run, Mill Creek, and Pike Creek. They are less productive than the ones described above.

IF YOU GO . . .

There is much for nonanglers to do in this area. In fact, the attractions are much better than the trout fishing! So, if you find yourself in Wilmington with a few hours to spare, visit the Winterthur Museum, Longwood Gardens, the Brandywine Museum (featuring paintings by Andrew Wyeth), or the excellent antique shops in the area. The area can be reached by

I-95, Route 1, or Route 2. Locate one of these major arteries from Philadelphia, Wilmington, or Newark, then refer to local directions and maps.

Tackle Shops and Guides

The Sporting Gentleman II. 5714 Kennett Pike (Route 52), Centerville. Judy Laurie and Barry Staats, proprietors. In Frederick's Country Center. An Orvis dealer with a complete line of tackle, clothing, accessories, and gifts. (302) 427-8110.

Austin Reed Outfitters. 3832 Kennett Pike (Route 52), Greenville. Austin Reed, proprietor. Excellent supply of salt- and freshwater rods, tackle, and top-of-the-line angling gear and clothing. (302) 654-6515.

Where to Stay

Dugal's Inn B&B. Mortonville, Pennsylvania. Moderate to expensive. (610) 486-0953.

Hotel Du Pont. Wilmington. Very attractive. Good restaurant. Expensive. (302) 594-3156.

The Inn at Montchannin Village. Montchannin, Delaware, near Winterthur and Brandywine Creek State Park. Crazy Cats restaurant inside. Luxurious and expensive. (302) 888-2133.

Where to Eat

This area is replete with gourmet country-style restaurants. A few favorites are mentioned below. More modest places are easily found.

The Back Burner. Hockessin. Expensive. (302) 239-2314.

Buckley's Tavern. 5812 Kennett Pike, Centerville, Delaware (near Kennett Square, Pennsylvania). Good atmosphere and wine list. Moderate. (302) 656-9776.

Farm House Restaurant. Avondale, Pennsylvania (5 miles south of Longwood Gardens, near the White Clay and Christina Creeks). Expensive. (610) 268-2235.

Dilworthtown Inn. West Chester, Pennsylvania. Expensive. (610) 399-1390.

La Cocotte. West Chester, Pennsylvania. Expensive. (610) 436-6722.

Longwood Inn. Kennett Square, Pennsylvania. On Route 1, just north of Route 82. Moderate to expensive. (610) 444-3515.

Kennett Square Inn. Kennett Square, Pennsylvania. Moderate to expensive. (610) 444-5688.

.and

...d has enjoyed a rebirth since 1986, when the
... Natural Resources (DNR) made the protection
...reams a priority. This policy was the result of an
...nes W. Gracie, then president of Maryland TU,
... of TU, and the DNR. It states that any stream in
...can reproduce will no longer be stocked with
hatchery fish. The policy is based on the theory, supported by numerous
studies, that when hatchery-raised fish are stocked in wild trout streams,
the wild fish population suffers. Stocked trout disrupt wild trout, interfere
with their means of survival, and eventually dominate the stream.

The policy has resulted in 825 miles of trout water in Maryland. Thirty
miles (nine streams) are managed under special regulations (Catch-and-
Return, Trophy Trout, and Delayed Harvest), and an additional 29 miles
(seven streams) are Put-and-Take fisheries. Trout reproduce in the remaining 766 miles, which are no longer stocked or regulated.

The emergence of Big Gunpowder Falls in northern Baltimore County
as an important wild trout river has brought national attention to the
state. There are more than nine miles of Catch-and-Return wild trout
water on the Gunpowder, and it is generally considered one of the ten
best trout streams in the East.

Western Maryland's Savage River has been managed as a trophy
trout stream for many years, nurturing exceptional numbers of wild fish.
The North Branch of the Potomac is in reclamation from decades of pollution from acid mine drainage, and its comeback is nothing short of miraculous. The other wild trout streams exist in eleven of Maryland's
twenty-three counties. They are too small and too numerous to include in
this book, but enterprising local anglers fish them regularly.

The Youghiogheny, usually associated with Pennsylvania, originates
in West Virginia and flows north through western Maryland, dropping
one thousand feet in the first thirty miles. The Maryland stretch has

recently become a recreational cold-water fishery. Although it does not support trout reproduction, it is an astonishingly beautiful river.

The Gunpowder, Savage, North Branch of the Potomac, and Youghiogheny constitute Maryland's big four trout rivers, but there are several others worth exploring along the way. Big Hunting Creek north of Frederick is couched in angling history and filled with challenging trout. It is the only stream in the state that has demonstrated its ability to sustain trout reproduction where fish are stocked. (The stream is so popular that state officials made an exception and stock trout for the pleasure of the many anglers who come here.) The DNR, several chapters of TU, and the Federation of Fly Fishers have devoted countless hours and multiple resources to improving the habitat on Hunting Creek.

I credit DNR official Robert Bachman and his colleagues, Robert Lunsford, Charles Gougeon, Kenneth Pavol, and Howard Stinefelt, staff of Maryland's Fresh Water Fisheries, with the consistent, long-term vision that supports the state's freshwater fisheries program. They have based their activities on the 1986 policy, often in the face of formidable opposition.

When the state of Maryland retained Bachman, renowned for his studies of brown trout on Pennsylvania's Spruce Creek, it moved to the forefront of wild trout and cold-water resource management in the East. In order to reclaim polluted streams, Bachman has been resourceful in his promotion of innovative techniques. For example, he promoted the use of limestone dosers in western Maryland. This method, which puts limestone into streams to raise pH levels, has sweetened a number of waters, including tributaries of the North Branch of the Potomac.

Bachman and his colleagues have juggled the conflicting interests of bait anglers, fly fishermen, and catch-and-release advocates to provide good recreational angling for all. Despite proximity to the nation's capital, Baltimore, and Philadelphia, Maryland's trout streams are not yet as crowded as the limestone creeks of southcentral Pennsylvania or the free-stone streams of the Catskills. And stream mile for stream mile, I'd challenge anglers from any other state in the region to find as many healthy, fat, wily wild trout per mile as Maryland has to offer.

STATEWIDE RESOURCES

Maryland Delaware Atlas and Gazetteer. DeLorme, P.O. Box 298, Freeport, Maine 04032. (207) 865-4171.

Maryland Department of Natural Resources. (410) 974-3061.

Maryland Office of Tourism Development. (410) 333-6611.

runs dominate the first mile and a half. Then the stream relaxes into the classic pool-riffle-run configuration.

I grew up on a farm along the Gunpowder near Monkton. As a girl, I had little appreciation of the river's potential as a trout stream. It was a warm-water fishery that we used for inner-tubing. Parents and children of all ages floated five miles of river, gossiping on the quiet stretches and screeching down the rapids. It never crossed my mind that I was swimming in what would become one of the best wild trout fisheries in the East—the source of pleasure for anglers from Baltimore, York, Washington, and northern Virginia. If I fished at all then, I fished on bass ponds. There were no trout in the Gunpowder.

In 1986, Maryland TU signed an agreement with the city of Baltimore to provide a minimum release of cold water from the bottom of Prettyboy Reservoir. The flow rate was based on existing studies that illustrate what trout require to live and reproduce in the habitat. The agreement guaranteed a minimum volume (flow rate) of 11.5 cubic feet per second throughout the year. Although this is not big volume, it seems adequate. Currently, in-stream studies are planned to ensure that the most advantageous flow rate for the fish is maintained. The average year-round water temperature in the Gunpowder is 52 degrees Fahrenheit.

In 1983, the first brown trout fingerlings were stocked in Big Gunpowder Falls. These trout grew and thrived. In 1985, the first brown trout eggs were planted. In 1986, the first fry hatched from eggs planted in the riverbed. In 1987, there was a good young-of- the-year (YOY) population, and—that same year—the first Catch-and-Return regulations went into

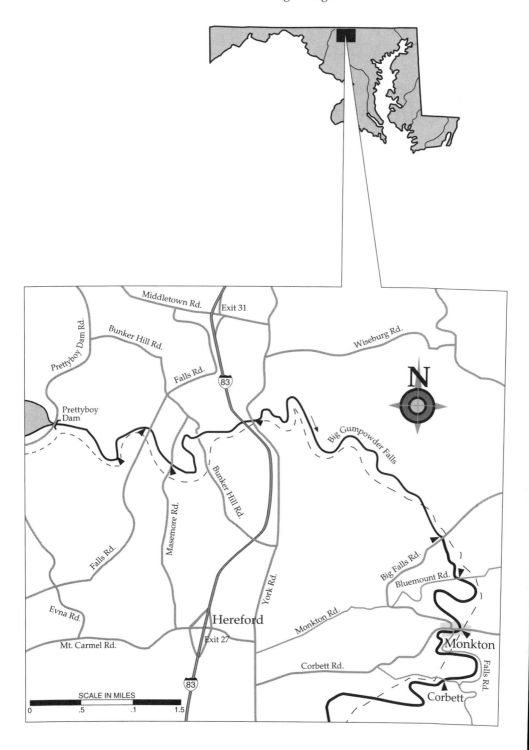

effect. The final stock of brown trout and I
were released in 1990. The first eight miles
have not been stocked since.

The fish population is monitored ever
shows an increase in the streambred trout
revealed an average population of more tha
150 pounds per acre) in the Catch-and-Retur
those of great western rivers such as the Big
4,000 trout per mile.

Over time, brown trout have dominated
constitute 96 percent of the fishery, with bro
bows (2 percent) accounting for the remainde
all found in the upper section of the Catch-a
mile below the dam. This upper section is also
midge hatches. It can be reached by descendi
parking lots on Falls Road (see map).

The Gunpowder is an exceptionally scenic
wood and hemlock shade banks covered with
and limestone rock. On humid summer evenir
over the water, caused by the collision of hot ai   ... Ducks,
geese, deer, and other wildlife abound. Late one Sunday afternoon, I
encountered a small black bear.

The Gunpowder is not difficult to wade, except in the deepest pools,
or when the dam is partially open and a volume of water is being
released. There are footpaths on either side of the river from Falls Road
downstream to Big Falls Road. Hikers and mountain bikers also use
these, and in the summer inner-tubing and canoeing remain popular.

The Gunpowder can be fished all year, although I find the action
somewhat sluggish from mid-November to February on all but the
warmest days. Nonetheless, I have caught trout with ice in the guides of
my rod. Stacey Smith, who guides for On the Fly, likes to fish Clouser
Deep Minnows whenever the fish are not active—including midsummer.

The Gunpowder illustrates that managing streams for recreational
fishing and wild trout results in a population of educated fish. Because
they forage for themselves from birth, the fish learn to be careful about
when and what they eat. They are used to humans—hikers, anglers,
canoeists, and so on—but they seem to have developed keen sensors that
detect real predators (for example, herons and artificial flies).

Gunpowder anglers complain of canoes putting the fish down. But
I've found that if I wait a few minutes after a *quiet* canoe passes, rising
fish resume their routine (not so with splashy tubers and inexperienced
canoers). On the other hand, I may wait twenty minutes or half an hour
for a trout that *I* have put down to resume feeding.

There is no question that the trout in the Gunpowder are very selective and very difficult to fool. I've met many local anglers who have gone fishless and given up on the river. New generations of trout are growing up acclimatized to the presence of humans, wary of our entire arsenal of threats. My subjective feeling is that it is very hard to surprise Gunpowder trout. They seem to sense trouble and lock their jaws. Stacey Smith describes them as cautious, not spooky. I find them intolerant of all but the best presentations of artificials.

As with many great rivers, the fish are taken from the most difficult spots. Anglers should fish the back eddies along the banks, where the fish lie near cover and just outside the main current. Smith has had repeated good results with Clouser Deep Minnows, although the Gunpowder does not have a lot of minnows. He also uses little shrimp patterns (for example, a #18 tan scud) in the first half mile below Prettyboy Dam. The algae in the water there nurture freshwater shrimp.

Regulations
From the base of Prettyboy Dam downstream to Bluemount Road, flies or artificial lures only may be used, and Catch-and-Return policies apply. From Bluemount Road to Corbett Road, an angler may keep two fish over sixteen inches per day.

Access
There is access to ten miles of Catch-and-Return water at eight roads that cross the river. Parking is available at all of them (see map).

Hatches, Flies, and the Best Times to Fish
The best time to fish the Gunpowder—if you prefer dry-fly fishing and hope to catch these educated fish off guard—is during the sulphur hatch, which begins in the third week of May and continues in profusion through June. While sulphurs come off the Gunpowder all summer, the May-June period is the most productive. There are three sulphur emergences on the Gunpowder: *Ephemerella invaria*, *E. rotunda*, and *E. dorothea*. Begin with larger patterns (#14) and work down to #16–#18 (and even #20) by early June.

The Gunpowder is also an excellent stream on which to fish terrestrials. In the summer, it's best to be the first angler through a given reach of water. Mahogany spinners and beetles, ants, and hoppers work well. Whenever I get on the river at first light, I count many more fish at the end of my angling day than had I not ventured onto the water until mid-morning. This success has little to do with hatch activity. It is strictly the result of the fish being a little less wary in low light—after a good night's rest and a hungry awakening!

DOUGLAS LEES

Big Gunpowder Falls

I've caught some of my best Gunpowder trout in September and October. There are fewer anglers, and small tan caddis, terrestrials, and Blue-Winged Olives are effective. I remember a certain broad-backed brown that gulped my grasshopper pattern from the top side of a leaf one mid-September morning. And I remember numerous other trout that I worked on for more than forty minutes before one or the other of us succumbed!

More trout are taken from the Gunpowder with nymphs and large streamers than with dry flies. The Woolly Bugger outperforms other patterns year-round. Pheasant-tail nymphs, Green Weenies, and beadhead and Serendipity patterns all take their share of fish.

Major hatch activity and rising fish on the Gunpowder can be found during emergences of Hendricksons, Gray Fox, sulphurs (third week of May through June), caddis, and—on the upper section below the dam—midges (year-round). When you find a Gunpowder trout feeding on the surface—in all but the most prolific of hatches—keep your profile low and leaders and tippets long. Sometimes I think these trout have eyes in the back of their heads and lockjaw at the mere suspicion of a nearby fly angler. I have never had as many false takes as I have experienced on the Gunpowder during sulphur season! It is as if every fly flashes a last-minute warning just as the fish commits itself to the food.

Winter (December through March)
Little black flies (#20) (they look like miniature houseflies). *February:* little black stonefly and stonefly nymph (#14–#18), Adams (#14–#18), midges and midge larva.

Spring (April through mid-June)
April: little black stonefly, Little Blue Quill (#18–#20), Tellico nymph, Dark Hendrickson, Red Quill.

Late April to early May: Hendricksons, Quill Gordons, March Browns.

Mid-May to mid-June: Gray Fox (#14–#16), sulphurs (#14–#20), Light Cahills (#12–#14), elk-hair caddis (#14–#18).

Summer (June to mid-September)
Sulphurs and Cahills continue, getting smaller over time. White-gloved Howdy *(Isonychia bicolor)*, slate drake, rusty or mahogany spinners (#14–#16), terrestrials (beetles, ants, hoppers—Stimulators #14–#16), caddis and caddis emergers (#14–#18).

Fall (September to November)
Blue-Winged Olives (#20–#22), midges, ants, caddis (sporadic).

Year-round favorites:
Black Flashabou Woolly Bugger (#8–#12), San Juan Worm, the Patriot, Green Weenie, Pheasant-tail nymph, Gold-Ribbed Hare's Ear, midges in upper section (black, peacock herl, Griffith's Gnat #20–#24). Little white or tan scuds (#18–#20) often work well in the plunge pool below Prettyboy Dam.

IF YOU GO . . .
Take I-83 north from Baltimore or south from York, Pennsylvania, to exit 27—Mt. Carmel Road (Hereford). Go left at the exit to fish from Masemore or Falls Road. Go right one-quarter mile and left on York Road to fish from the Bunker Hill and York Road access points. Go right on York Road and take an immediate left on Route 138 (Monkton Road) to On the Fly shop or for access to the river from Big Falls, Bluemount, Monkton, and Corbett Roads.

Nonfishers may wish to visit Ladew Topiary Gardens on Route 146 nine miles east of Monkton. Nationally acclaimed topiaries, including fox-chasing scenes, appear in clipped boxwood bushes. Open April to October. Lunch. The National Aquarium and Baltimore's Inner Harbor are also popular tourist destinations. The city is about thirty-five minutes from the Gunpowder.

Tackle Shops and Guides

On the Fly. Monkton Road, Hereford. Wally Vait, proprietor. Fly shop and guide service. This is *the* destination fly shop for the Gunpowder River. Vait hung up his shingle in 1992 in response to the needs of Gunpowder fly anglers and is still going strong. (410) 329-6821.

Fisherman's Edge. Catonsville. Joe Bruce, proprietor. Extensive inventory of tackle and flies, both freshwater and saltwater. Bruce keeps up with central Maryland's fresh- and saltwater conditions. 1-800-338-0053.

Old Village Fly Shop. 25 South Main Street, Shrewsbury, Pennsylvania (just over the Maryland line). Charles King, proprietor. Flies, rods. (717) 235-9020.

Tochterman's. 1919 Eastern Avenue, Baltimore. Mostly saltwater and spinning tackle. (410) 327-6942.

Tollgate Tackle. Bel Air (near I-95). Norm Bayer, proprietor. Fly and tackle shop. (410) 836-9262.

Trout & About. Arlington, Virginia. Phil Gay, head instructor and guide. (703) 536-7494.

Wolf's. Ellicott City. Scott Wolf, proprietor. Full fly shop. 1-800-378-1152.

Bill Wolf. Baltimore. A Gunpowder guide. (410) 377-6759.

Where to Stay

Gunpowder B&B. Monkton. Angling hostess. Twenty minutes to the Gunpowder. Moderate. (410) 557-7594.

Hill House Manor B&B. 19301 York Road, Parkton. Use exit 31 from I-83. Moderate. (410) 357-8179.

Hampton Inn. Hunt Valley, off I-83, five miles south of the river. Part of the no-frills chain. Moderate. (410) 527-1500.

Marriott's Hunt Valley Inn. Hunt Valley, also off I-83, five miles south of the river. Restaurant. Expensive. (410) 785-7000.

Wiley Mill Inn B&B. White Hall, near Hereford. Moderate. (410) 329-6310.

Where to Eat

Manor Tavern. Near Monkton, Maryland, about five miles east of the river. Moderate. (410) 771-8155

Milton Inn. 14833 York Road (Route 45), Sparks. About five miles south of Hereford. Very good four-star restaurant in a limestone farmhouse. Reservations required. Expensive. (410) 771-4366.

Pioneer House. York Road, Hereford (opposite Bunker Hill Road). Good place for refreshments or lunch. Inexpensive. No reservations.

Monkton Bagel Shoppe and Deli. York and Mt. Carmel Roads, Hereford. Breakfast, lunch, or takeout. Inexpensive. No reservations.

Wagon Wheel. Route 45, Hereford. Breakfast and lunch. Inexpensive. No reservations.

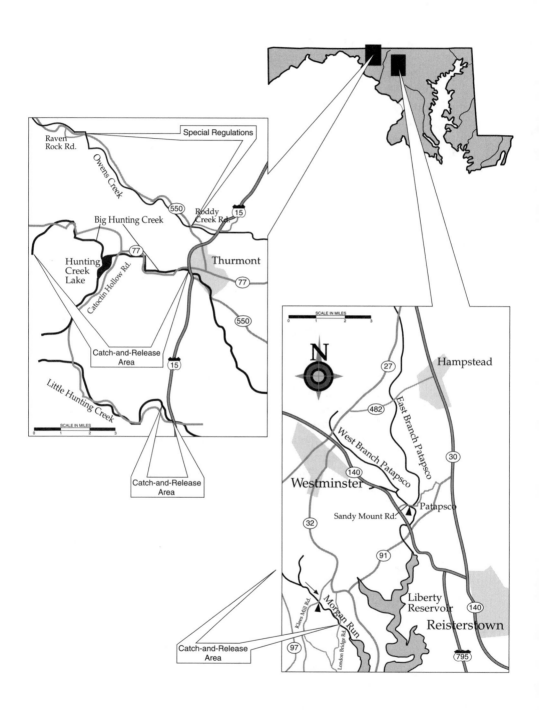

Special Regulations

Raven
Rock Rd.

Owens Creek

550

Roddy
Creek Rd.

15

Big Hunting Creek

77

Hunting
Creek
Lake

Catoctin Hollow Rd.

Thurmont

77

550

Catch-and-Release
Area

15

Little Hunting Creek

SCALE IN MILES
0   1   2   3

Catch-and-Release
Area

SCALE IN MILES
0   1   2   3

N

27

Hampstead

482

East Branch Patapsco

30

West Branch Patapsco

140

Westminster

Patapsco

Sandy Mount Rd.

32

91

Liberty
Reservoir

140

Reisterstown

K005 Mill Rd.

Morgan Run

London Bridge Rd.

97

795

Catch-and-Release
Area

CHAPTER 17

Central Maryland:
Big Hunting Creek, Little Hunting Creek, Owens Creek, Morgan Run, and the East Branch of the Patapsco River

The streams of central Maryland do not have the good water quality of the Gunpowder and the Savage, the North Branch of the Potomac, or the Youghiogheny, but they are worth fishing if you are near Frederick, Hagerstown, or Westminster.

BIG HUNTING CREEK

Big Hunting Creek is north of Thurmont and Frederick in the Catoctin Mountain range. Distilling moonshine, milling pulp, and berry picking were the major industries a century ago. During the 1930s, the federal government purchased ten thousand acres in the area, including the land where Camp David is now located. Big Hunting Creek begins on the east slope of the Catoctin Mountains, crosses Route 77, and enters Hunting Creek Lake (a recreational impoundment).

Below the lake, the stream courses under hardwoods and hemlocks, past the Visitors Center and the Joe Brooks Memorial, eventually empty-ing into Frank Bentz Memorial Lake. Rainbows are the dominant species on Big Hunting Creek, followed by browns and occasional brook trout.

Big Hunting Creek's fame stems from the fact that in 1940 Joe Brooks founded the Brotherhood of the Junglecock here. His creed is chipped into the Joe Brooks Memorial on Route 77 opposite the Visitors Center. Its tenets are worth restating:

> . . . enjoying, as we do, only a life estate in the out of doors, and morally charged in our time with the responsibility of handing it down unspoiled to tomorrow's inheritors, we individually undertake annually to take a least one boy a-fishing, instructing him, as best we know, in the responsibilities that are soon to be wholly his.

Brooks continues:

[We have] as a common goal—the conservation and restoration of American game fishes. . . . Creel limits shall always be less than the legal restrictions and always well within the boundaries of nature herself.

To my way of thinking, Brooks's creed is irrefutable. The fact that it is chiseled in granite next to this mountain stream in northern Maryland brings legend to the area. It is fitting that Big Hunting Creek became Maryland's first Fly-Fishing-Only stream and later its first Catch-and-Return regulated area. I take exception to the exclusion of girls from the club, but I like to think that—had Brooks issued his decree in the latter part of this century—he would have included us.

Big Hunting Creek is very popular with Baltimore, Washington, and northern Virginia fly anglers. Enthusiastic fans such as Douglas Lees, the photographer from Warrenton, Virginia, like to sight fish. Lees maintains that if you pick your spots and focus closely on the fish, use long lines, light tippets, and small nymphs, you'll hardly be aware of other anglers.

Lees is particularly fond of the stream in late fall and winter, and he has taken sixteen-inch fish on Presidents' Day. When I fished with him one Friday late in June, we found several other anglers on the stream. The fishing was challenging. Hatches were few and rises infrequent. But I saw one leviathan more than two feet long lunge through the surface of a pool after a microscopic midge. I worked on him for more than an hour and never saw him again.

Lees and I fished one huge, deep pool near the Brooks Memorial for several hours. Other anglers came and went behind us. Douglas was more successful with small nymphs than I was using drys and emergers. He landed three nice fish more than a foot long. I was in one of my dry-fly moods, determined to fish drys on the beautiful water where I knew the trout could also see them. The easy access and wading, challenging casting, and difficult catching defined Big Hunting Creek for me that day, and I have remained seduced ever since.

Jim Gilford, who has made a lifetime commitment to conserving Big Hunting Creek (often using controversial stream restoration methods), feels there is much too much pressure on the stream and would like to find a way to reduce its popularity. He fishes only on weekdays, when there are no dogs or hikers and few other anglers.

Gilford points out that Big Hunting Creek is not the pristine mountain stream many imagine. There was no sediment control during the four years it took to build the Hunting Creek Lake dam in the 1930s, and there are still lingering problems because of this. He emphasizes that the stream has not been "pristine" for twenty-five or thirty years.

To maintain the stream for trout, Gilford and his allies insist, manmade structures are required. Log jack dams and wing deflectors have been placed in the stream to protect the banks and create holding areas for trout. Sixty tons of limestone have been installed on the bank near the Joe Brooks Memorial to mitigate erosion.

Although wild trout reproduce in the stream above and below the dam (browns in the ten- to fourteen-inch range spawn, and fry are observed here), Gilford believes these must be supplemented with hatchery stocks to maintain a sufficient number of trout to satisfy recreational anglers. Moreover, he sees no concrete evidence that stocked trout overtake and harm wild trout in this fishery.

Whether stocked, catchable-size hatchery fish disrupt the wild trout environment and displace them remains controversial despite the state's policy of not releasing stockies over wild trout. Big Hunting Creek is the exception—it is the only Maryland stream where stocked trout are released and wild trout are known to reproduce. TU and other conservation groups argue that stocking catchable-size trout in a stream that can maintain a population of naturally reproducing trout negatively affects the wild population. Gilford and others maintain this an attitude, not a proven fact.

About fifteen hundred catchable-size trout are stocked on the stream annually by private, nonprofit angling organizations. The umbrella group, known as the Friends of Big Hunting Creek (with members from Maryland Fly Anglers, Potomac Valley Fly Fishermen, and the Northern Virginia chapter of TU), stocks the water and maintains stream improvement structures.

Access and Regulations
Big Hunting Creek is the only stream in Maryland with Fly-Fishing-Only *and* Catch-and-Return regulations. (All others permit artificial lures as well as flies.) There are pull-offs along Route 77 between Thurmont and Hunting Creek Lake.

LITTLE HUNTING CREEK
This small tributary of Big Hunting Creek is no longer stocked and provides excellent brook trout angling. Much of the stream is private, but there is a short section that may be reached from Cat Rock Trail at the park entrance opposite the Catoctin Mountain Zoo Park on Route 15 near Thurmont. Catch-and-Return regulations apply from Route 15 upstream one-half mile to the Cunningham Falls State Park Manor Area.

OWENS CREEK
Owens Creek is located in wild, boulder-filled territory in the Catoctin Mountains. It has good hatches. Stream width varies considerably, from tight runs with low overhanging bushes to deep pools and flats up to forty feet wide.

Access and Regulations
From the main stem on Raven Rock Road downstream to Roddy Creek
Road, Owens Creek is regulated as follows: From March 1 through May
31, the daily creel limit is five trout, no minimum size. From June 1
through the last day of February, Catch-and-Return regulations apply,
and flies and artificial lures only are permitted. Access from Route 550
west of Thurmont, which follows the stream.

MORGAN RUN
Morgan Run, a small twenty-five-foot-wide stream south of Westminster
in Carroll County, has fished surprisingly well through several recent
warm summers. It is stocked annually with catchable-size hatchery-raised
trout, so it is not surprising that many fourteen- to sixteen-inch trout are
reported.

Morgan Run is a freestone stream running through woods and farmland. It falls gently and is easy to wade. Water temperatures climb into the
seventies in summer, but tributaries cool the water, making it fishable
except in extraordinarily hot years. It muddies quickly and clears up
equally fast.

Patapsco Valley TU chapter member Timothy Feeser explained that
Morgan Run is one of the few places in Maryland where one can catch
stocked browns, rainbows, *and* cutthroat trout! Trout do not reproduce
well in Morgan Run, whether because of negligent farming practices in
the headwaters or other factors. The Maryland DNR is currently investi-
gating the factors limiting reproduction.

Feeser likes to fish midges during the fall when the leaves are turning
and the stream is very colorful. Summer is another of his favorite times,
when ants, beetles, and inchworms work well.

Morgan Run has gained notoriety in Maryland as the first Project
Access site in the state. Project Access is a national effort to build sites
designed for disabled anglers, especially those fishing from wheelchairs.
Maryland TU board member Tom Gamper worked with disabled veteran
Art Nierenberg and the Patapsco Valley chapter of TU to build a fishing
platform, ramp, and parking area on Klees Mill Road off Route 32, about
five miles southeast of Westminster. The 1996 flood wiped out the structure, but it was fully rebuilt by midsummer.

Access and Regulations
Catch-and-Return regulations apply on Morgan Run from the bridge on
London Bridge Road upstream to the bridge on Route 97. One and a half
miles above and two miles below the Catch-and-Return stretch are
restricted to two fish per day, no minimum size.

EAST BRANCH OF THE PATAPSCO RIVER

Tim Feeser was brought up on a farm on the upper East Branch of the Patapsco. As a boy, he caught numerous bass and chub but no trout. Trout only appeared in the 1970s when a farmer stocked a small tributary and the state stocked Cascade Lake. In keeping with state policy, once the DNR realized that trout were reproducing on their own, all stocking ceased. The East Branch has been managed for wild trout since 1993.

The East Branch is tough to fish. There are very few hatches (a few caddis and midges) because of agricultural runoff upstream. East Branch trout are meat eaters: They like crayfish, hellgrammites, frogs, and minnows. The smart ones get very fat. Browns between fifteen and twenty inches are not uncommon. A twenty-seven-inch brown was taken in Aspen Run, a tributary of the East Branch.

Access

This stream runs almost entirely through private property, and one must have permission to fish. However, anglers can drive to the little town of Patapsco by taking Sandy Mount Road off Route 140 in Westminster. The east and west branches of the Patapsco converge there to form the main stem.

Hatches, Flies, and Best Times to Fish

The following information was provided by the Rod Rack in Frederick and the Friends of Big Hunting Creek.

Winter (November to April)
Little black stonefly and stonefly nymph (#14–#18); early brown stonefly; streamers (#6–#10) such as Hornbergs, Woolly Buggers, and white marabous.

Spring (April to June)
Early April: Blue Quill (#16–#18), little blue dun (#18–#20), Hendricksons, Red Quill, green caddis.
Mid-April to May: Quill Gordon, March Brown, Gray Fox, big brown stonefly (#10–#12), sulphur (#16–#20), Light Cahill (#12–#14).
June: green drake, yellow drake, White-Gloved Howdy, cream drake (*Potamanthus distinctus*), elk-hair caddis.

Summer and fall (July to November)
Small cream drake (*Potamanthus neglectus*), big brown drake, whitefly (*Ephoron leukon*, #14–#16 in late July and early August), Tricos, terrestrials (ants and beetles).

Fall (September to November)
Blue-Winged Olive (#20–#22), midges, little black stoneflies, Tricos, ants.

IF YOU GO . . .
To reach Frederick and Big Hunting Creek from Washington and northern Virginia, take I-270 from the Washington Beltway (I-495) to Frederick, then Route 15 north to Thurmont. Route 77 runs along the creek northwest from Thurmont. From Baltimore, take I-70 to Frederick. Proceed as above. Frederick is about 45 miles from both Baltimore and Washington.

To reach Morgan Run from Baltimore, take I-795 to Route 140 to Westminster. Turn on south Route 97, then take Route 32 south to Klees Mill Road, which crosses Morgan Run. Park at the bridge and fish up- or downstream. The bridge is about in the middle of the special regulations area.

To reach the East Branch of the Patapsco, take I-795 north to Route 140 to Westminster. Then take Sandy Mount Road east to the town of Patapsco.

Nonanglers may wish to hike in the Catoctin Mountain National Park or the Cunningham Falls State Park, or visit the Historic District in Frederick, the Antietam Battlefield, Harpers Ferry and the C & O Canal, and Gettysburg, Pennsylvania (thirty miles). There are also good antique shops in the area.

Tackle Shops and Guides
    Angler's Hollow. Westminster. Near Morgan Run and the Patapsco. (410) 751-9349.
    Keystone Sporting Goods. Hagerstown. (301) 733-0373.
    Laurel Fishing & Hunting. Laurel. Larry Coburn, proprietor. (301) 725-5527.
    The Rod Rack. Frederick. Rob Gilford, proprietor. Guide service and large selection of tackle, flies, and clothing. (301) 694-6143.
    Thurmont Sporting Goods. Thurmont. A small destination shop for Big Hunting Creek. (301) 271-7404.
    Trout and About. Arlington, Virginia. Phil Gay, head instructor and guide. Also guides on the Gunpowder, in Shenandoah National Park, and on Spruce Creek, Pennsylvania. (703) 525-7127.

Where to Stay
    There is an association of bed and breakfast inns in the Hagerstown-Frederick area with prices ranging from moderate to expensive. Call Inns of the Blue Ridge, Ltd., at (301) 694-5926, for general information, or try one of those listed below.
    Beaver Creek House. Hagerstown. Don and Shirley Day, proprietors. Expensive. (301) 797-4764.

Bluebird on the Mountain. Blue Ridge Summit (near Thurmont). Expensive. (301) 241-4161.

Spring Bank Inn. Frederick. Rates vary according to number of people and whether a private or shared bath is requested. Moderate. (301) 694-0440.

Tyler-Spite Inn. Frederick. 1814 Federal house in historic Courthouse Square. Very expensive. (301) 831-4455.

Comfort Inn. Frederick and Westminster. Moderate. 1-800-228-5150.

Days Inn. Frederick and Westminster. Moderate. 1-800-DAYS-INN.

Rambler Motel. Thurmont. AAA. Inexpensive. (301) 271-2424.

Super 8 Motel. Thurmont. Inexpensive. (301) 271-7888.

Camping

Cunningham Falls State Park. (301) 271-7574.

Catoctin Mountain Park (USFS). (301) 663-9388.

Where to Eat

Cockey's Tavern. Main Street, Westminster. Country cooking and cocktails. Moderate. (410) 848-4202.

Mountain Gate Family Restaurant. Thurmont. Inexpensive. (301) 271-4373.

There are many good restaurants in Frederick. Some of the most popular include the following:

The Brown Pelican. Expensive. (301) 695-5833.

Jennifer's. Inexpensive to moderate. (301) 662-0373.

J. T. Ashley's. Inexpensive to moderate. (301) 662-5141.

Resources

Tourism Council of Frederick County. 1-800-999-3613.

Maryland Delaware Atlas and Gazetteer. DeLorme, P.O. Box 298, Freeport, Maine 04032. (207) 865-4171.

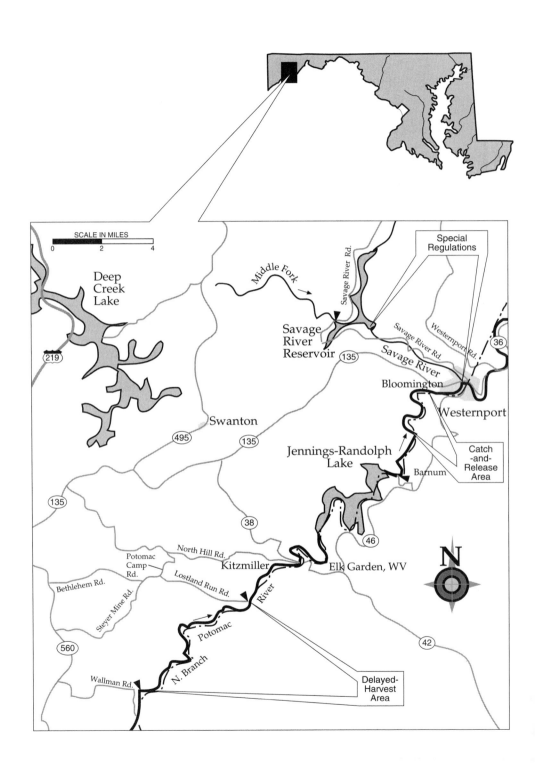

CHAPTER 18

Western Maryland I:
The Savage River, Middle Fork, and
the North Branch of the Potomac River

Western Maryland, one of the state's primary recreational areas, is within a three-hour drive of Washington and Baltimore. In addition to angling opportunities, there are boating on Deep Creek Lake, canoeing and rafting on the Savage and Youghiogheny Rivers, and skiing at WISP resort near Oakland.

There are more than 320 miles of water in Garrett and Allegany Counties, the state's two westernmost counties. The area is experiencing a resurgence of interest in fly fishing, spurred by stream restoration projects on the North Branch of the Potomac and the Youghiogheny Rivers. The combined efforts of anglers living in small western Maryland towns and the DNR have resulted in the reclamation of abandoned mines and investment in sewer treatment plants.

Maryland DNR official Robert Bachman maintains that had he searched the entire country for potential fisheries, he would have selected Garrett County. The area offers miles of stream and rivers and an incredible variety of water, from small mountain brooks to big rivers like those in the West, and everything in between.

THE SAVAGE RIVER

The Savage is the premier wild trout fishery in western Maryland. It is a rough-and-tumble tailwater with lots of rocky runs and rapids. The river lives up to its name. Its bottom is lined with big boulders that shrug off boiling water into swirling pockets and large, deep pools. There is a slick, pasty vegetation on the rocks that makes wading tricky. I fish here carefully, always with a staff and cleated felt-soled boots.

The Savage has been managed as a Trophy Trout stream since 1987. It was the Maryland DNR's first experiment in wild trout management. The river's predominant fish is the brown trout, although brook trout held sway at one time. It is not stocked and contains a tremendous population of native brookies averaging nine inches and fourteen-inch browns. DNR surveys show an average fish stock of sixty pounds per acre over the last five years.

The river receives water running between 50 and 150 cubic feet per second from the bottom of Savage River Reservoir. Stream temperatures seldom exceed 65 degrees Fahrenheit, and the river never freezes, making it an excellent year-round fishery. The Savage gets murky only after a tremendous amount of rain, enough to muddy the reservoir, which, in turn, releases off-color water into the Savage. When this happens, it takes some time for the river to clear.

MIDDLE FORK

The Savage River State Forest contains numerous small tributaries that run into the Savage River above the reservoir, and they all contain wild brook trout. The Middle Fork is the best. Maryland TU members Jim Gracie and Richard Schaad have taken their sons camping on the Middle Fork every spring for a number of years. There are twenty-four hundred trout per mile in the water, making it a great place for kids to fish. Gracie cautions that there is a forty-five-minute hike down a long steep incline, but the quality and quantity of wild fish cannot be exaggerated or surpassed in Maryland. (The stream can also be approached from its lower end, but to reach the best fishing, walk in at least two miles.)

Access

To reach the special regulations sections of the Savage River from the north or east, take Lower New Germany Road (I-68 exit 24) south to Westernport Road. Turn left on Westernport Road to Savage River Road. Make a right on Savage River Road along the upper Savage (Put-and-Take section), past the Savage River Reservoir to the special regulations section. There are several pull-offs along the road.

To reach the Savage from the southeast, take Route 135 through Westernport and look for Savage River Road on the right.

Regulations

There are two trophy trout sections contiguous to one another on the Savage below the reservoir. From the river's mouth near Luke, Maryland, 2.7 miles upstream to the lower suspension bridge (Allegany Bridge), artificial lures and flies may be used. Two fish may be taken daily; brookies must be at least twelve inches and browns must be at least eighteen inches.

The artificial Fly-Fishing-Only Trophy Trout section begins at the base of the dam and continues downstream 1.5 miles to the Allegany Bridge. Numbers and size of fish that may be taken are the same as for the lower section.

Hatches, Flies, and Best Times to Fish

The Savage River can be fished all year but is most productive from February through September. Because the bottom is treacherous, felt soles and chest waders are a must, and a wading staff and cleats provide additional security. The telephone number for dam releases on the Savage River is (410) 962-7687. Always call before making the trip.

Joe Metz, a member of the Nemacolin chapter of TU, recommends visiting western Maryland in the fall on warm days in October and November. Some of the best hatches on the Savage and Casselman are *Baetis* species. Metz gets on the stream by 1:00 P.M. for the hatch, which lasts until about 4:00 P.M. Sometimes he will use two flies, a #16–#18 Royal Coachman (or another attractor pattern) as the top fly and a Hare's Ear or Pheasant-tail nymph on a two-foot dropper.

Wally Vait, proprietor of On the Fly in Monkton, likes to go to the Savage in the late spring when the slate drakes appear. He claims that fishing this fly will boost the ego of any fisherman, because there is no wrong way to fish it. The more shallow the water and the greater the drag, the more fish you will catch!

Winter (February to March)
Little black stoneflies (#16–#18).

Spring
Early season–April: Blue Quill (#16–#18), Hendrickson (#12), Quill Gordon (#14–#16), Blue-Winged Olive (#18), midges (#20–#24), streamers (#10).

May to June: caddis (#14–#18), Blue-Winged Olive (#18–#20), sulphur (#16–#18), slate drake (nymph and dry fly, #14–#16).

Summer (July to September)
Green and brown caddis (#14–#18), midges (#24–#26), terrestrials (ants and beetles); Pheasant-tail, Bird's Nest, and Hare's Ear nymphs (#14–#18).

Fall (October to November)
Little Blue-Winged Olives (#18–#22), midges, Hare's Ear or Pheasant-tail nymphs (#18–#20), attractor patterns.

THE NORTH BRANCH OF THE POTOMAC RIVER
The North Branch of the Potomac River originates from a spring near the Fairfax Stone in West Virginia in the upper reaches of the Allegheny plateau. From there it flows eighteen miles to the man-made Jennings-Randolph Lake, an impoundment designed for flood control. Below the dam, the North Branch cuts a serpentine path through the eastern Allegheny mountains. First, it flows northeast through Bloomington, Luke, and Westernport, Maryland, then on to Keyser, West Virginia, and Cumberland, Maryland. At Cumberland, the water turns southeast and is

joined by the South Branch at South Branch, West Virginia, from whence it flows past Hancock, Maryland, and turns southeast once more on its way to Washington and the Chesapeake Bay.

The stretch of eight miles of trout water downstream of Jennings-Randolph Lake is becoming one of the outstanding tailwater fisheries in the East. It is an impressive reclamation project, given that the North Branch was completely lifeless from the 1930s until the mid-1980s, when the Jennings-Randolph Lake came into being. The lake mitigated the acidic water that entered it from the North Branch, resulting in an outflow of quality water with a pH of 6.0.

The river was first stocked below the dam by the Maryland DNR at Barnum, West Virginia, in 1987 on an experimental basis to see whether trout could live in the water. When Robert Bachman, the director of resources management of the fisheries division of the Maryland DNR, realized that the experiment worked and trout could live in the North Branch below the dam, he began to focus interest on a major reclamation project. The Conservation Fund bought six thousand acres of land in West Virginia that would otherwise have fallen to development, as well as a narrow strip in Maryland (between the railroad tracks and the river) to ensure that the new resource could remain intact.

The state has continued to raise trout in net pens below the dam. "This is the only place in the country where trout are being raised in the effluent of an Army Corps of Engineers dam, and an acidic one at that!" Bachman boasts. When the purchase was made, Catch-and-Return regulations were put in place from the dam one mile downstream. This section remains closed by the Army Corps, but when opened (expectations are that this will soon happen), the reach will be one of the most exciting tailwater trout fisheries in the state.

Meanwhile, the DNR has continued to improve the water quality of the North Branch. Once the potential began to be realized, Bachman and his colleagues persuaded others to let them treat the major sources of acid above the Jennings-Randolph Lake with limestone "in order to put a tourniquet on the sources of acid." Once dosers were placed on Lost Land Run, Laurel Run, the main stem at Kitzmiller, and at Gorman, the pH level improved from 6.0 to 7.0. The limestone not only purified the water, it also fostered parasites in the water that in turn nurtured the mayflies, stoneflies, and caddis that trout like to eat.

Once these four dosers went on line, the entire North Branch from its headwaters downstream has never dropped below a pH of 6.0 and is much closer to 6.5. Bachman adds, "We are now looking into the possibility of not just maintaining the pH, but of increasing the alkalinity, because the productivity of a trout stream is a direct result of the excess alkalinity in the river. This is where DNR involvement is now."

ROBERT BACHMAN

The North Branch of the Potomac

Bachman admits that although the recovery of the river and its ability to sustain trout is miraculous, it will take more time to develop into a mature trout fishery. He explains it this way:

> Below the lake, the insect population hasn't responded quite as well as we hoped. We think the reason is that we are getting nitrogen saturation from the highly concentrated, powerful out-flow of water from the dam. The dam was not designed with any life in mind, either in the reservoir or downstream. Now we have to fix that. It will be expensive, but not difficult. We need to reduce the force of the water that falls down forty feet and carries air (nitrogen) to the bottom, resulting in something like a fizzing can of soda pop.

The North Branch is stocked annually with brown, rainbow, and cut-throat trout in catchable sizes in the Put-and-Take reaches and with fin-gerlings in the Catch-and-Return sections. Brook trout are *not* stocked and are reproducing naturally in the river. The presence of brook trout con-firms that the water quality is acceptable.

In the eight miles below the Jennings-Randolph Lake and the five miles on the North Branch below the mouth of the Savage, anglers have the rare opportunity to land a grand slam—brook, brown, rainbow, and cutthroat trout—all in the same day! Bachman points out that there are few, if any, other places where such a catch could take place in the East, and in the West, perhaps only on the Gallatin.

There is evidence that browns and rainbows are reproducing in the main stem, and it is not the intent of the DNR that the cutthroat trout do so. The cutts are there for recreational purposes, to bite when nothing else will. It will take a number of years for sufficient bugs and grasses to develop to nourish the huge numbers of trout that could live and reproduce in this water. At this writing, neither Bachman nor anyone else will guess how long. Nonetheless, the North Branch is so breathtaking, the water so dramatic, that it is worth the wait.

Floating the North Branch

I floated the North Branch with my brother, Dick McIntosh, late in June. Harold Harsh of Spring Creek Outfitters in Oakland was our guide. We got to Barnum at 9:30 A.M. The air and water temperatures were ideal. The thermometer read 75 degrees Fahrenheit and the water was 62 degrees Fahrenheit. The flow from the bottom of the Jennings-Randolph Dam was 250 cubic feet per second—a good flow resulting in a depth of three to four feet of water.

As soon as we rounded the first bend, I understood why floating the river is so superior to wading. The bugs are just beginning to come back in this big water. There are not a lot of flies (or grown fish) for the size of the expanse, and anglers need to cover a lot of water to find targets.

Harold soon had us casting large dry flies like Stimulators and Sofa Pillows. Perfect drift and precise timing were critical. As I cast a Stimulator to cutthroat under the rock ledges, it reminded me of a day on the South Fork of the Snake River in Idaho, the scene of the best float trip I've ever had. Now I hold high hopes for an equally magnificent fishery closer to home.

The river flows through a near-wilderness area, and the vegetation is lovely. Wild azaleas and mountain laurel cover the banks. Shrubs sporting yellow, red, and white flowers jut out from ledge rock. Throughout the day, we alternated casting to the riverbanks, looking for shady spots.

I have never seen a guide work harder than Harold Harsh. He spent more time out of the raft than in it. He got through tough, boulder-strewn runs by dangling his legs off the back of the raft, kicking, pushing, and pulling us off and over boulders and shoals. It was often a roller coaster of a ride through steep drops and turbid whitewater, and I have no idea how Harold stayed with the raft.

The river was not generous the day Dick and I floated it. But we caught enough fish to be satisfied, and I missed enough others to realize that the fish are there and are challenging to catch.

Proximity to the nation's capital has resulted in much well-deserved publicity and angling pressure on the North Branch. However, the river is more than a hundred feet wide below the dam, filled with boulders and rough riffles as well as very deep pools. There is plenty of room for a number of anglers to fish in relative proximity to one another. Wading it is not for the faint-hearted, and in many places, it is impossible. Personally, I'll go by raft whenever I can afford to do so.

Access

Twenty-one miles of water above and eight miles below the Jennings-Randolph Lake are managed trout water.

• Access at Barnum to the North Branch below the dam is through Elk Garden, West Virginia, from the west, or via Westernport, Maryland, from the east. From Elk Garden, take Route 46 to Barnum Road. Turn left at the two churches. From Westernport, take Route 135 west to Luke. Turn left on Route 46 and continue for about five miles, bearing right at all intersections. At the second of two white churches at the top of a hill, turn right onto Barnum Road. Follow Barnum Road through the hamlet of Barnum to a large parking area. Park and walk downstream along an old railroad bed. The best fishing begins in the big riffle below the concrete bank. It is not possible to wade across the river along most of this section.

Above the Jennings-Randolph Lake, there are two access points in Maryland: Lostland Run Area and the Wallman Area. (A Garrett County topographical map should be used here.)

• To get to Lostland Run, take Route 495 south from I-68 exit 19 approximately twenty miles to Swanton. Make a right at the stop sign and proceed ten miles to Loch Lynn Heights (Route 495 will become Route 135). Turn left at the traffic light and follow Route 560 south two miles to Bethlehem Road. Turn left on Bethlehem Road (watch for signs to Potomac State Forest). Go two miles, then turn right onto Steyer Mine Road. Go about one mile to Combination Road and turn left. After about one-half mile, turn left on Potomac Camp Road. Continue past the state forest headquarters about one-half mile; turn right on dirt road marked Lostland Run access. The road dead-ends at a parking lot next to the river.

• To reach Lostland from the west (Deep Creek Lake, Oakland, Mountain Lake Park), take Route 135 east from Mountain Lake Park to Route 560 and proceed as directed above.

• To get to the Wallman area, continue on Route 560 south three miles past Bethlehem Road, and turn left on White Church–Steyer Road.

Go one mile until the road turns abruptly right. Continue straight on Audley Riley Road. Bear right at fork and follow signs to Wallman.

• On the West Virginia side, railroad tracks run parallel to the entire river. The river is too strong to cross. Felt-bottom soles with cleats, chest waders, and a staff are advised.

Regulations

Maryland and West Virginia have reciprocal agreements on the North Branch, so a valid license from either state will suffice. Whitewater releases for recreational rafting are made four weekends in April and May, so fishing below the Jennings-Randolph Lake is almost impossible at these times. The schedule of releases can be found by calling (301) 962-7687.

The Catch-and-Return area is managed as a Put-and-Grow fishery: Only fingerling brown, cutthroat, and rainbow trout are stocked, released to mature in the wild. The regulated stretch begins at a red post located 1.2 miles downstream of the parking lot at Barnum (just below the "Blue Hole" pool) and ends downstream about four miles at the confluence with Piney Swamp Run.

The state stocks catchable-size trout on the Put-and-Take sections above and below the Catch-and-Return reaches; rainbows, browns, and cutthroat trout may be taken there.

Above the Jennings-Randolph Lake, the trout water is managed as a Put-and-Take, Delayed-Harvest fishery. This section runs from the lower boundary of Potomac State Forest near Lostland Run upstream to the upper park boundary at Wallman. From January 1 to June 15, only artificial lures and flies can be used, and all fish must be returned to the water. From June 16 to December 31, two trout may be taken each day (no minimum size). This area is stocked several times during the spring and early summer.

Flies, Hatches, and Best Times to Fish

There is a two hundred-cubic-feet-per-second minimum release of cold water from the reservoir year-round. The best times to fish the North Branch above the Jennings-Randolph Lake are spring and fall. In the summer, look for the best sport in the Catch-and-Return area below the dam. Notable hatches remain sparse; however, the water quality is improving.

Spring (April to mid-June)

March Brown, sulphur, stonefly nymph (#8 imitation of a *Perlida*)—especially in Delayed-Harvest area. A big (#8) black-and-yellow stonefly nymph tied with an orange thorax (*Stenocron*). Harsh and Nolan call this the No Value fly because Art Flick writes that it is of little value in the East. It has found value around dark on the North Branch of the Potomac.

Summer (July to September)
Beetle, cricket, sulphur, slate drake, Dun Variant, caddis, and caddis emergers.

Fall (October to November)
Blue-Winged Olive (#22–#24), caddis, caddis emerger.

IF YOU GO . . .
Frostburg is about 150 miles from Baltimore, Washington, or Pittsburgh. Take I-70 (from Baltimore) or I-270 (from Washington) to I-68 west to Cumberland, Frostburg, and points west. From Pittsburgh, use I-79 south to I-68 east.

There is plenty for the nonangler to do in western Maryland. Cumberland abounds with Revolutionary War history (for example, George Washington's Headquarters), and antiquing is good throughout the area. Parks and other recreational areas abound. Hike, bike, ski, canoe, kayak, or ride horses.

Tackle Shops and Guides

Spring Creek Angler. Oakland. Harold Harsh and Allen Nolan, proprietors. Full-service fly shop. Provides guide service on the Savage, Casselman, and Youghiogheny, as well as pack and float trips on the North Branch and float trips on the Youghiogheny. (301) 334-6409.

Pop's Bait and Tackle Shop. Barnum, West Virginia. This is *the* ultimate destination shop for spin-tackle anglers on the North Branch of the Potomac. Pop provides up-to-date water reports and carries a small selection of flies for the North Branch. No phone.

Where to Stay

Brookside Inn. Near Aurora, West Virginia, only twenty minutes to Oakland via the recently improved Route 50 (George Washington Highway). Charming B&B in Victorian summer resort house. Fabulous breakfast. Dinners cooked to order. Moderate. (304) 735-6344 or 1-800-588-6344.

Starlite Motel. Oakland. Next to Denny's restaurant. Inexpensive. (301) 334-8686.

Town Motel. Oakland. An old standby. Inexpensive. (301) 334-3955.

Point View Motel. Deep Creek Lake. 1-800-244-1598. In the Frostburg-Grantsville area (near the Savage and Casselman Rivers).

Casselman Valley Farm. Grantsville. Off I-68 1.5 miles south on Route 495. Convenient and great views! Shared baths. Inexpensive. (301) 895-3419.

Casselman Inn. Grantsville. Amish-run and very convenient. Restaurant. Inexpensive. (301) 895-5266.

Comfort Inn. Frostburg. Moderate. (301) 689-2050.

Holiday Inn. Grantsville. Exit 22 off I-68. Moderate to expensive. (301) 895-5993.

Walnut Ridge B&B. Grantsville. Restored 1860s farmhouse. Moderate. (301) 895-4248.

Camping

Statewide camping information: (301) 461-0052.

Big Run, Casselman, New Germany, and Savage River State Parks. Near the Savage River. New Germany (301) 895-5453 and Herrington Manor (301) 334-9180. State parks have cabins.

Little Meadows Campground. Grantsville. (301) 895-5675.

Deep Creek Lake State Park. Swanton. Near the Youghiogheny and the North Branch. (301) 387-5563.

Potomac State Forest. Oakland. On the North Branch. (301) 334-2038.

Where to Eat

Au Petit Paris. Frostburg. Dinner only. Chef Louis Philip St. Marie is a rare find. Expensive. (301) 689-8946.

Casselman Inn. Grantsville. Good food. No cocktails. Inexpensive. (301) 895-5266.

Cornish Manor. Oakland. Very attractive restaurant in Victorian house with wraparound porch. Moderately expensive, but worth getting off the stream for! (301) 334-3551.

The Old Depot. Frostburg. An oak-and-fern bar. Inexpensive to moderate. (301) 689-1221.

L'Osteria. I-68, Exit 46. In an antebellum manor one mile east of Cumberland. Good food. Moderate. (301) 777-3553.

Penn Alps. Grantsville. Craft shop and home cooking. Moderate. (301) 895-5985.

Josie's Family Restaurant. Route 135, Mountain Lake Park. Inexpensive. No reservation.

McClive's Restaurant and Lounge. Oakland. On Deep Creek Lake. No reservations. Moderate. (301) 387-6172.

Silver Tree Restaurant. Deep Creek Lake. On the waterfront. Bills itself as the "biggest, busiest, best place to eat in the area." Moderate. (301) 387-4040.

Resources

Allegany County Visitor's Bureau. 1-800-872-4650 or (301) 777-5905.

Garrett County Promotion Council. (301) 334-1948.

Western Maryland Freshwater Fisheries. (301) 334-8218.

CHAPTER 19

Western Maryland II: The Casselman and the Youghiogheny Rivers

THE CASSELMAN RIVER

The Casselman and the Youghiogheny are the only rivers in Maryland that flow into the Ohio River basin. Located near Grantsville, the Casselman River is the easternmost stream in the Mississippi-Ohio River drainage. The river originates between Frostburg and Grantsville west of the Eastern Continental Divide and joins the Youghiogheny at Confluence, Pennsylvania.

The Casselman is a wide sixty-foot swath of water that is easy to access and to wade for most of its length in Maryland. It is very popular with Maryland, Pennsylvania, and West Virginia anglers. I like to go to the Casselman as soon as the water become fishable in the spring. The river is regulated as a Delayed-Harvest stream. Before June 15, all fish must be released.

The Casselman is stocked with three thousand brown and rainbow trout annually, many in the four- to five-pound class. Gary Yoder, liaison for the DNR in western Maryland, claims it is not unusual to catch more than forty fish per day during the Catch-and-Return period, and the size of the browns can be surprising. I've never caught fish in these numbers; however, I did see a father and son team nearly do so within the confines of a single eight-by-twelve-foot pool only two hundred yards from the main road.

At least once a year, I fish the Casselman from the ledge rock in front of the Meshack Browning Club, the dusty beer bar named after Meshack Browning, the renowned hunter whose rifle is on view at the Smithsonian Institution. Every spring, I'm surprised to see the wooden shack that houses the bar still standing.

Lack of shade makes the Casselman subject to warm water temperatures in the summer, mitigating against the possibility of in-stream reproduction. The river is best fished downstream of the I-68 overpass north about five miles to the Pennsylvania line. From I-68 take exit 19, Grantville, and proceed one-half mile north to Route 40. Turn right on Route 40 and continue one mile to the Casselman River. Take River Road north from Route 40. The road runs along the river, and there are frequent parking pull-offs.

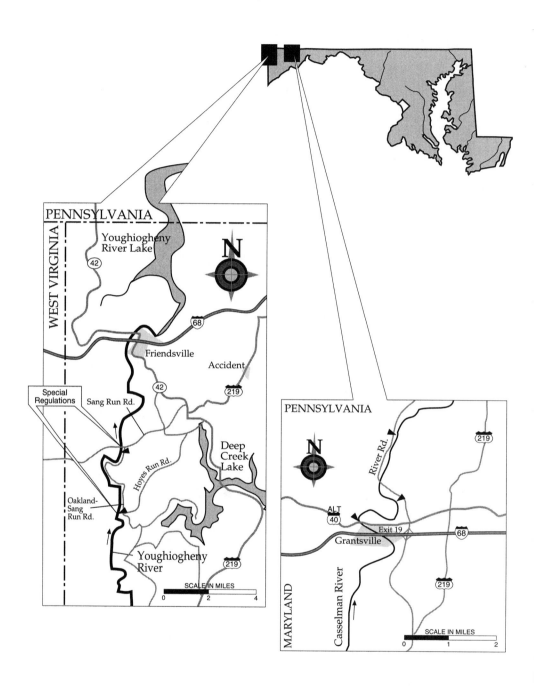

Hatches on the Casselman are similar to those on the Savage and other western Maryland streams. (Refer to the list in chapter 18 and the one below.)

THE YOUGHIOGHENY RIVER

This river, fondly referred to as the "Yough" (pronounced "Yock"), is a favorite with whitewater sportsmen and anglers. Native Americans named the water "a river that flows in a contrary direction," because the Yough runs north in an area where most rivers flow south.

In 1996, after twenty-eight years of classification as the state's only "wild and scenic river," Garrett County adopted a formal plan to protect the watershed. More than forty-seven hundred acres and twenty-eight miles of water cannot be developed, and habitat supporting wildlife is guaranteed intact in perpetuity.

Ken Pavol, western region manager for the Maryland DNR, has taken the lead in converting the Yough to a trout fishery. He played a key role in establishing the Catch-and-Return fishery between the Deep Creek Lake Power Plant and the Sang Run Bridge. He and the Youghiogheny chapter of TU negotiated an agreement with PennElec (the company that owns the power plant) to provide a minimum flow (forty cubic feet per second) of cold water so that trout can live in the river through periods of low flow and high temperatures.

Pavol and I drove to the river one hot July morning. As we left Oakland, he explained the state's plan: to stock fingerling browns and an experimental strain of warm-water rainbows in the Yough between the power plant and the Sang Run Bridge, where Catch-and-Return regulations would be enforced. The DNR wanted to create a challenging Catch-and-Return fishery on one of the state's most productive waters.

Despite the low flow that summer, we saw rising trout and the water was clear. We did not fish, however, not wanting to stress the trout during the hottest part of the day. I have since caught twelve-inch trout on the Yough during the summer, but I recommend fishing early in the morning or in the evening, when trees on either side shade the water.

Allan Nolan, co-owner of Spring Creek Outfitters, has caught rainbows up to twenty inches in the Hoyes to Sang Run stretch. Pavol and Gary Yoder, a DNR colleague, have had fall evenings when they caught and released more than twenty twelve-inch-long trout each. Green drakes, which have always shown up in respectable numbers on the river, are now profuse—or else would seem so from the trout's point of view. Look for them in late May and June. The Yough is becoming one of the best places in the state to fish the drake hatch.

The strain of warm-water-tolerant rainbows is flourishing in the Yough. Fourteen-inch-long fish have weighed in at two pounds. Spring Creek Outfitters reported an eighteen-inch brown weighing four pounds!

Apparently, these rainbows expand their girth even as they grow longer, for these are unusually heavy fish for their length.

Pavol explained that sediment (dirt, topsoil) prevents the Yough from being able to sustain streambred trout. The DNR has documented spawning fish but currently has no plan to mitigate the sediment load. This huge load of runoff enters the Yough from agricultural and developed property. It smothers roe that would otherwise hatch in the river and help establish wild trout. Though the growth rate of fingerlings illustrates that there is enough food and sufficient cold water to support streambred trout, fish will not be able to reproduce until runoff from agricultural and developed land is greatly reduced.

The first year that PennElec released cold water from the power plant on a regular basis was 1995. In the fall of that year, when the DNR executed its annual trout census, the standing crop of trout had doubled from the previous year. In other words, Pavol and his colleagues counted twice as many trout as had been at the same stations in 1994, before cold-water releases were instituted. This was the highest number of trout per mile ever documented on the Yough in Maryland.

The following year (1996), high water prevented electroshocking and a statistical count, but Pavol and others have gathered sufficient anecdotal information to support their estimate of more and bigger fish in the Yough than in the preceding year. The fishery is becoming Maryland's newest quality Put-and-Grow trout fishery, in no small part because of the quality of the surroundings and the water itself.

Access

To reach the Catch-and-Return stretch of the Yough, take Route 219 south from I-68. Just before Deep Creek Lake, turn right on Sang Run Road. It leads to the river. The four-mile Catch-and-Return area can be accessed here, and there is ample parking.

• The section from Hoyes Run to Sang Run provides the most consistent fishing. Park at Sang Run parking lot and walk north through the field, cross Sang Run, and continue another twenty minutes on an unimproved trail next to the river to the overhead power line. This short hike will put you on one of the most productive, little fished reaches of the river.

• There is another access point at Hoyes Run, but parking is more limited. To reach the Hoyes Run area, take Oakland Sang Run Road about four miles from the Sang Run area. Park in the small pull-off marked by a wooden sign describing Youghiogheny River trout regulations. The stretch between the power plant and Hoyes Run tends to be swift. It is filled with pocket water, and the best fishing is right at the edges of the water.

• The Yough is stocked with catchable-size fish in about fifteen miles of its Put-and-Take fishery. Pavol says that after the first blush of the season, these fish are often ignored by anglers. He recommends searching them out anytime after Memorial Day.

Unlike the North Branch of the Potomac and the Savage, the Yough is easy to wade *when there is no water being released from the Deep Creek Lake power generating plant.* The river is about eighty feet wide with a moderate gradient and bed of cobble and occasional boulders. Generating times vary widely during the year, and there are no warning alerts. Pavol says that the releases usually come early in the morning and late in the evening, but the schedule is spontaneous. *Before fishing, call (814) 533-8911 for water release schedule.* The water is swift and can be dangerous during release periods.

It takes two and one-half hours for the releases to reach the downstream limit of the special regulations section. Wading is treacherous during release periods. Suddenly this wide, otherwise friendly water becomes a rush of unseen pitfalls: invisible holes and trenches, slimy boulders, and greasy rocks. For stability, take a wading staff, and wear studs if you own them.

Note: The Yough can also be fished downstream in southwestern Pennsylvania. Good access is available at Ohiopyle State Park. There is a Rails-to-Trails bike path that runs from Ohiopyle to the takeout above Connellsville.

Regulations
The Catch-and-Return regulated water begins at a red post approximately one hundred yards upstream of the Deep Creek Lake tailrace and extends downstream four miles to the Sang Run Bridge.

Flies, Hatches, and Best Times to Fish
The best time to fish the Yough is any time between mid-April and the end of October. Ken Pavol stresses the importance of caddis hatches on the Yough. He takes eight out of ten fish there with caddis patterns. Use nymphs, emergers, soft-hackle wet flies, and drys. Gary LaFontaine's Tan Emerger—fished dry on top of the water—is a particularly effective pattern.

Fish pursue midges on the Yough all year. Gnat clusters, such as the Griffith Gnat in sizes #20–#22, work well.

Spring (mid-April to June)
Blue Quill (#16–#18), Quill Gordon (#14–#16), Hendrickson, March Brown, Blue-Winged Olive (#18), caddis, streamers (#10), Woolly Buggers, alewife patterns, minnow imitations.

The green drake usually appears between Memorial Day and the end of the first week in June and continues for two weeks. It may become the best green drake opportunity in the state.

May to June: Caddis (#14–#18), Blue-Winged Olives (#18–#20), sulphurs (#16–#18), slate drake (nymph and dry fly) (#14–#16), Cream and/or Dun Variants (#14–#16).

Summer (July to September)
Caddis, midges, terrestrials.

IF YOU GO . . .
To reach Oakland and Deep Creek Lake from Baltimore or Washington, take I-70 or I-270 to I-68 west to Route 219 south. From Pittsburgh, use I-79 south to I-68 and east to Route 219 south. The trip is about four hours from the Baltimore-Washington metropolitan area and about three and one-half hours from Pittsburgh.

Tackle Shops and Guides
Spring Creek Outfitters. Oakland. Harold Harsh and Allen Nolan, proprietors. Tackle shop specializing in wading trips on the Savage and Casselman and float trips on the Yough and the North Branch of the Potomac. (301) 334-6409.

Where to Stay
Brookside Inn. Near Aurora, West Virginia, only twenty minutes to Oakland via the recently improved Route 50 (George Washington Highway). Charming B&B in Victorian summer resort house. Fabulous breakfast. Dinners cooked to order. Moderate. (304) 735-6344 or (800) 588-6344.

Starlite Motel. Oakland. Next to Denny's restaurant. Inexpensive. (301) 8686.

Town Motel. Oakland. An old standby. Inexpensive. (301) 334-3955.

Point View Motel. Deep Creek Lake. 1-800-244-1598.

Camping
Deep Creek Lake State Park. Swanton. Near the Yough and the North Branch. (301) 387-5563.

Potomac State Forest. Oakland. On the North Branch. (301) 334-2038.

Where to Eat

The Deep Creek Lake–Oakland resort area (convenient to the North Branch and the Yough) has many restaurants.

Cornish Manor. Oakland. Very attractive restaurant in Victorian house with wraparound porch. Moderately expensive. Unless a major hatch is on, leave the water for this food. (301) 334-3551.

McClive's Restaurant and Lounge. Oakland. On Deep Creek Lake. No reservations. Moderate. (301) 387-6172.

Silver Tree Restaurant. Deep Creek Lake. On the waterfront. Bills itself as "the biggest, busiest, best" place to eat in the area. Moderate. (301) 387-4040.

Twila's Old Mill. Friendsville. Home-style cooking. Good place for a lunch break while fishing the Yough. Inexpensive. No reservations.

Resources

Garrett County Promotion Council. (301) 334-1948.

Garrett State Forest. Oakland. (301) 334-2038.

Western Maryland Freshwater Fisheries. (301) 334-8218.

Virginia

OVERVIEW

According to Larry Mohn, a regional manager with the Virginia Department of Game and Inland Fisheries (VDGIF), Virginia has more than twenty-eight hundred miles of trout streams, including more than twenty-three hundred miles of wild trout water. Most of the state's trout are found in its western region, in the Blue Ridge and Allegheny Mountains, where the elevation is high enough that the streams stay cool through the summer. Also between these two ranges are limestone subsurface formations that produce the water that feeds productive spring creeks.

The state's trout management program is three-fold:

1. Catchable-size fish are stocked from October through May in most of the state's trout streams.

2. Fingerling trout are stocked in waters that have sufficient food and adequate habitat to hold fish year-round but don't have good enough water quality to support in-stream reproduction. This portion of the state program is important, because it serves to educate anglers in the advantages of fishing for prey that is largely raised in the wild.

3. The wild trout program identifies and, when necessary, tries to enhance habitat on trout streams where trout can breed and increase their numbers. As in many other areas of the region, the biggest threat to wild trout in Virginia is siltation and warm water temperatures in summer. (Mohn points out that as little as a quarter inch of silt over trout roe can result in 100 percent mortality.) In the last twenty years, habitat degradation (a result of poor logging techniques, lack of riparian buffers on agricultural land, and stream channelization) has slowed, and the VDGIF has become more effective at protecting the trout environment.

Virginia's native brook trout population is the state's most valuable cold-water asset. There are hundreds of mountain streams where the adventurous angler can find these fish, which are so fragile and so beautiful that it makes one sad to see the slightest sign of damage from an angler's hook. These bright brookies account for 80 percent of the trout on twenty-three hundred miles of wild trout streams. Mohn and his colleagues maintain that Virginia has more miles of native brook trout streams than all other southeastern states combined. In any event, they are a gem and certainly worth a visit to the state.

One of the nicest things about trout fishing in Virginia is that it is year-round: In fall, winter, and spring, there is usually somewhere to go. Whether you go to the Jackson River (a tailwater fishery) or to Mossy Creek (a spring creek), there are trout streams in Virginia that maintain constant water temperatures for most of the year.

The state is attempting to implement more effective wild trout management policies, as the efforts of the Shenandoah National Park indicate. In the last few years, many more park streams have been opened to year-round fishing under Catch-and-Release regulations. Virginia trout fishing has also been boosted by a year-round season, which eschews Opening Day in favor of letting Put-and-Take as well as Catch-and-Release anglers catch fish all year. Fisheries biologists say the continuous season also improves trout management by clearing fish tanks before diseases develop.

STATEWIDE RESOURCES

Camuto, Christopher. *A Fly Fisherman's Blue Ridge.* New York: Henry Holt and Company, 1990.

Murray, Harry. *Trout Fishing in the Shenandoah National Park.* Edinburg, Virginia: Shenandoah Publishing Company, 1989. (To order a copy, call (540) 984-4212.)

Slone, Harry. *Virginia Trout Streams: A Guide to Fishing the Blue Ridge Watershed.* Woodstock, Vermont: Backcountry Publications. 1991.

Virginia Department of Game and Inland Fisheries. 4010 Broad Street, P.O. Box 11104, Richmond, Virginia 23230. Licenses, permits, information.

Virginia Department of Game and Inland Fisheries. P.O. Box 996, Verona, Virginia 24482. Larry Mohn, Regional Fisheries Biologist. (540) 248-9360.

USGS Survey Maps. Box 25286, Federal Center, Denver, Colorado 80225. (303) 236-7477.

Virginia Atlas and Gazetteer. DeLorme, P.O. Box 298, Freeport, Maine 04032. (207) 865-4171.

State and county road maps. Virginia Department of Transportation. 1401 East Broad Street, Richmond, Virginia 23219.

CHAPTER 20

Streams of the Shenandoah National Park

In the spring, the mountain streams of Virginia's Shenandoah National Park cascade down the steep slopes of the Blue Ridge Mountains, running through Catoctin gray-green stone, hemlocks, and hardwoods. In March, the water tumbles through the pools and overflows the boulders. By April, wildflowers appear in the moss, their blooms reflected in the morning dew. Beginning in late April and early May, if the water conditions are conducive, the fishing is very good. By May and June, the water recedes; boulders are bone dry and riffles very shallow.

Like the streams, which range from seven to twenty feet wide, the trout are small and very beautiful. All brook trout in the park are a wild native strain, their colors as bright as the water they inhabit. As adults, they average six to ten inches and seldom exceed eleven inches. (The browns grow to fourteen inches.)

Angling for brook trout in these mountains is an experience to be treasured. The brookies are a native American strain that has been in these streams for centuries. An angler accustomed to western rivers will have to hone his skills to a finer point here. The streams require exact delicate casts, often while kneeling behind a boulder. Food is scarce in the park, so trout are hungry. They anxiously take drys, shooting up from deep pools to snatch their prey.

Most park streams fish best in their upper reaches. The nicest way to fish them is to hike in and, if possible, camp overnight. If you park at the lower end of a stream, the farther upstream you walk, the more productive the fishing will be. There will be fewer anglers, and the trout are less susceptible to drought and low water. Nearly all the streams listed here can also be approached by hiking down from Skyline Drive. Ask the local tackle shop owners for the best approach and stream conditions when you go.

Tactics for fishing these mountain streams are described simply and clearly by Harry Murray in "Reading the Water," a chapter of his book *Trout Fishing in the Shenandoah National Park.* Murray describes where fish lie in the pools and riffles and how to approach them to get the most out

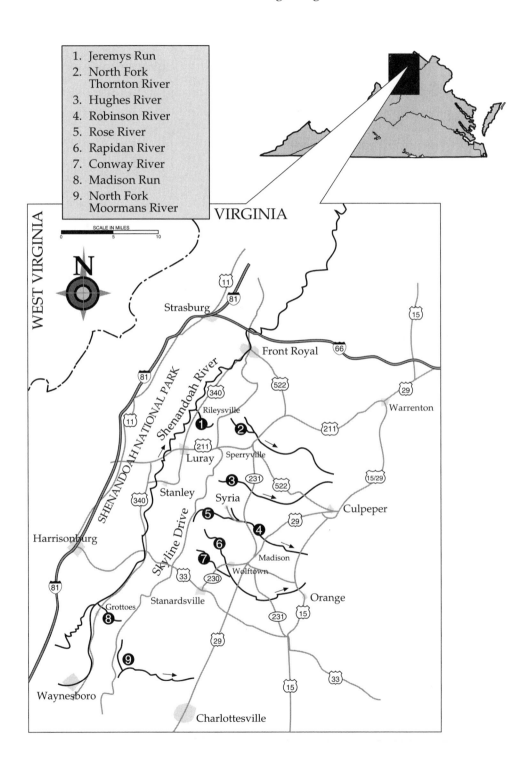

1. Jeremys Run
2. North Fork Thornton River
3. Hughes River
4. Robinson River
5. Rose River
6. Rapidan River
7. Conway River
8. Madison Run
9. North Fork Moormans River

VIRGINIA

WEST VIRGINIA

SCALE IN MILES

N

Strasburg

Front Royal

Rileysville

Luray

Sperryville

Stanley

Syria

Harrisonburg

Madison

Wolftown

Grottoes

Stanardsville

Orange

Waynesboro

Charlottesville

Warrenton

Culpeper

of each pool. Begin by fishing the tail and edges of one pool from the pool below, maintaining a low profile and casting where the fish cannot see you. Then bend over and move stealthily to the banks near the tail of the pool and fish upstream carefully.

In Murray's book, the park superintendent points out a surprising fact: "Park managers are charged with protecting *all* the natural resources in the park; *however, game fish* [including trout] *are the only species of wildlife in the park that visitors are allowed to take out* [emphasis added]." A fine will be imposed on anyone who so much as picks a wildflower or shoots a squirrel, but on many streams there is no penalty for taking home six nine-inch wild brookies.

Regulations

To fish the Shenandoah National Park, you need a Virginia state fishing license. (You do *not* need a Virginia trout license, and you do *not* need a National Forest Stamp.) Licenses may be obtained in advance by contacting the Virginia Department of Game and Inland Fisheries, 4010 W. Broad Street, P.O. Box 11104, Richmond, VA 23230-1104, or calling (804) 367-1000. Licenses may also be purchased at K-Marts and Wal-Marts, as well as at the Panorama, Big Meadows, and Loft Mountain waysides. A list of closed streams, streams designated for harvest, and Catch-and-Release regulated streams can be obtained with the license.

In the mid-nineties, park managers conducted an extensive regulatory review with input from several TU chapters and the Virginia Council of TU. Under the resulting revisions, park authorities have opened streams designated as Open for Harvest or Catch-and-Release to fishing year-round, using single hooks and artificial lures or flies only. (The park used to close October 15.) It is hoped that the Rapidan and the North Fork of the Moormans, upon their recovery, will be regulated as Catch-and-Release-only streams.

On streams allowing harvest, the daily limit will be six trout, of nine-inch minimum length. For more information, call the park office at (540) 999-2243.

Access

Because the scale of this chapter's map is larger, I could not include every road named in the text. In those cases I have referred to DeLorme's *Virginia Atlas and Gazetteer* (VAG). Harry Murray's book (see Statewide Resources in the introduction to this section) provides detailed stream descriptions and directions to all the park streams, both from Skyline Drive and from roads outside the park. Maps (see Resources below) are also an excellent resource for fishing the park. The streams below, listed north to south, are my favorites, but there are many others, and since the advent of 1996 regulations permitting catch-and-release fishing on all open park streams, anglers can explore smaller streams and discover new resources.

Hatches, Flies, and Best Times to Fish

I wish I could count on fishing the park in March, because—when weather permits—fishing the park is a glorious way to begin the angling year. But one has to wait until late April and early May for predictable weather.

Spring (April to May)

The key to finding good spring fishing is water temperature. Because it snows and freezes in the park on spring nights when temperatures in the valley may be balmy, it's not easy to predict stream conditions more than a few days in advance. One way to do so is to watch the TV weather map. When a system passes over the Blue Ridge Mountains with three or four days of sunny skies and temperatures in the high 40s to low 50s, the water temperature in park streams will reach 40 to 45 degrees Fahrenheit. Once the water is 46 degrees Fahrenheit, hatches begin, and trout will feed on the surface, regardless of water level. When the water is high, anglers should hike to headwaters above feeder streams, where water temperature is a little warmer.

The following patterns should work: Quill Gordons, Hendricksons, Blue Quills, Yellow Humpies, Adamses, March Browns, Mr. Rapidan, Ladyslipper, Patriot, Royal Wulff, Royal Coachman—all in sizes #12–#16. Woolly Bugger, squirrel-hair nymphs, Gold-Ribbed Hare's Ear, elk-hair caddis, and grannom are also recommended. Try small minnow and crayfish patterns during periods of high or off-color water.

May to June. Yellow Sally, big black stonefly, Gray Fox, March Brown, sulphur, Light Cahill, green drakes (for those who can find them), cricket, beetle, and ant.

Summer (June 15 to September 30)

If you've never fished here in low water, you may find the park a little sad. Pools are clear and shallow. Cover is sparse. Fish are very, very spooky, and only the little ones are likely to get caught. Sections of many streams dry up completely. (The water runs underground.) Under these extreme conditions, anglers should refrain from fishing to avoid stressing the trout.

Try big black stonefly, Disco Cricket, Letort and Dave's Hoppers, inchworm, beetle, and ants (black and cinnamon).

Autumn (September to October)

Park fishing in fall is magnificent. Falling leaves add moisture to the streams. Insect life increases. The fish grow bolder. If you're on a park stream in October, you may see a female brookie making her redd. This is a moment to remember—witnessing the reproduction of an indigenous American strain that has survived for millennia.

Fish from the banks in October. The redds disappear quickly, but the roe remains invisible in the gravel. If you step on it, you will kill the eggs.

Continue to use terrestrials, but also try Blue-Winged Olives, caddis patterns, and small nymphs, such as Pheasant-tails and Gold-Ribbed Hare's Ears.

JEREMYS RUN

An early-season stream, Jeremys Run receives a lot of pressure, because it is easily accessed from Skyline Drive. It tends to dry up in summer. Jeremys Run Trail runs along the stream. For access, follow Skyline Drive to the Elkwallow picnic grounds, about 7 miles north of Panorama. Follow trail to the stream. (VAG pg. 74, B-1.)

NORTH FORK OF THE THORNTON RIVER

This is another early-season fishery. My diary indicates that one year I caught six brook trout ranging from eight to eleven inches using black Woolly Buggers in high, off-color water. That was a good morning, but many anglers boast twenty-five- and thirty-fish days! Access from Route 612 just north of Sperryville. Follow 612 to the end of the road at the park boundary. Limited parking available. (VAG pg. 74, B-2.)

HUGHES RIVER

This is a good dry-fly stream. Lower access: Take Route 211 to Sperryville, turn left onto 522 south, then right onto Route 231. Continue 8.5 miles to a right turn onto Route 602, after crossing the lower Hughes River (stocked trout water). Stay on this route approximately three miles; the route number will change from 602 to 601 to 707 to 600 in that stretch. Follow Route 600 to the first parking area on the left. Obtain permit (fee charged) and hike less than a mile to Nicholson Hollow Trail. The best fishing is upstream to Corbin Cabin. (VAG pg. 74, D-2.)

ROBINSON RIVER (WHITE OAK CANYON RUN)

Don't be alarmed by the number of parked cars at the lower end. This is an exceptionally pretty stream, popular with hikers. It suffered some flood damage in September 1996, but it should offer lovely early-season fishing soon. Make a cautious approach; use fine tippets and small flies. Access from Skyline Drive or off Route 600. (VAG pg. 74, D-2.)

HOGCAMP BRANCH OF THE ROSE RIVER

This is accessible from Skyline Drive, approximately twenty miles south of Panorama. Hike down the Dark Hollow Falls Trail or the Rose River

Fire Road to the stream. Or, for a less heavily hiked alternative that offers an easy walk, start at Fishers Gap; cross the drive and follow Pine Road to Hogcamp Branch or take immediate left off trail (on horse trail) to Rose River Falls. This stream is a favorite of angler-photographer Douglas Lees of Warrenton, Virginia. Douglas feels fishing the Hogcamp/Upper Rose is what park fishing is all about—small-stream fishing at its best with a hike in from Skyline Drive past lovely deep pools and lots of fish! (VAG pg. 74, D-1.)

ROSE RIVER
To fish the upper section, walk about one and one-half miles from the lower parking area, past the fire road gate until the road bears left, away from stream. Drop down there, and fish up- or downstream. The lower section can be accessed from Route 231 to Route 670 until it ends at a parking lot. The Rose is heavily fished, because many anglers look for holdover browns from the lower (stocked) water. (VAG pg. 74, D-1, and pg. 68, A-1.)

IVY CREEK
This little stream (not shown on map) should only be attempted with a compass and a Shenandoah National Park or Potomac Appalachian Trail Conference map. Off Skyline Drive, the gradient is steep and the trails poor. It's a tough walk in and out but worth it when you get there. Good trout population the length of the stream. (VAG pg. 67, B-5.)

RAPIDAN RIVER
Catch-and-Release regulations apply from Hoover Camp downstream through the Rapidan Wildlife Management Area. This is a fabled stream, but it has recently been damaged by floods in 1995 and 1996. The upper and middle section were not as seriously harmed, and the stream should recover nicely with two or three seasons of "normal" weather.

From Criglersville, take Route 670 to a left turn onto Route 649 to reach the middle and upper sections. Access the downstream sections via Route 662. (VAG pg. 68, A-1.)

CONWAY RIVER
Take Route 33 to Stanardsville, then left on Route 230. Go three miles and turn left on Route 667, which parallels the stream. Drive as far as you can and walk in to the second ford. Fish upstream. (VAG pg. 68, A-1.)

MADISON RUN
Madison Run is on the western slope of the park. I fished it with Jim Finn on a dank April day just before a cold front settled in. We caught only a

few brookies before the rain lowered the water temperature and the fish ceased to feed.

This is a stream to which I will soon return. It is fifteen feet wide with enticing long pools, short riffles, and an easy gradient. For the best fishing, walk in at least fifteen minutes. The water gets bigger, prettier, and more productive as you walk upstream.

Get to Madison Run by taking exit 245 off I-81 onto Route 659 east (Port Republic Road). Make a left on Route 663 to parking lot and stream. (Or, take Route 663 off Route 340 in the town of Grottoes.) (VAG pg. 67, B-5.)

NORTH FORK OF MOORMANS RIVER

Before a flood devastated this river in 1995, it was an extraordinary example of what Catch-and-Release regulations can do to improve a fishery. My first fish on a good morning was a fourteen-inch brown trout! I thought I was caught around some of the deadfall under which the trout lay.

Moormans was closed after a flood in 1995 and had a second major slug of water in 1996, but it will slowly recover from the damage. Ask at a local tackle shop about its current condition and regulations. To reach the Catch-and-Release section, take Route 29 to Route 250 west to Route 240 west to Route 810 north to Route 614. Park at the park's locked gate. Special regulations begin at the gate and continue upstream to the headwaters. (VAG pg. 67, C-6.)

IF YOU GO . . .

From Washington, the northern entrance to Shenandoah National Park is on Skyline Drive, about seventy miles west of Washington via Route 66. To access secondary roads to eastern slope streams, take Route 522 south (off Route 66). An alternate route south is Route 340 to Front Royal, Luray, and points south. From Richmond, take Route 64 west (Charlottesville) to exit 107 (Crozet) or exit 99 (Afton, at the south entrance to park).

Tackle Shops and Guides

The Angler's Lie. Arlington. Large tackle shop. (703) 527-2524.

Blue Ridge Angler. Harrisonburg. William Kingsley and Robert Hill, proprietors. Tackle, guide service, schools. (540) 547-3474.

The Tackle Shop. Charlottesville. Flies, tackle, guides. Also carries spin-fishing and hunting equipment. (804) 978-7112

Mossy Creek Fly Shop. Bridgewater. Jim Finn, proprietor. Orvis outfitter. Excellent selection of flies and tackle. Jim's dry humor contains much wisdom. Classes and guide service. (540) 828-0033.

Murray's Fly Shop. Edinburg. Harry Murray, proprietor. Flies, tackle, schools, guides. Harry wrote the book on Shenandoah Park streams and also specializes in bass on the Shenandoah River. (540) 984-4212.

The Outdoorsman. Henry R. (Hank) Woolman, guide. The Plains. Experienced guide and former president of the Rapidan chapter of TU. (540) 253-5545.

Rhodes Fly Shop. Warrenton. Orvis dealer. (540) 347-4161.

Shenandoah Lodge. Near Luray. Charlie Walsh, proprietor. Orvis dealer. Emphasis on schools and multiday packages. 1-800-866-9958.

Trout & About. Phil Gay, guide. Arlington. Phil fishes park streams, the Jackson River, and many other wild trout waters. (703) 525-7127.

Where to Stay

Graves' Mountain Lodge. Route 670, Syria. Near the Rapidan and the Conway. Rooms, cabins, restaurant. Moderate. (540) 923-4231.

The Hatch. Edinburg. Nice inn in the valley near the Shenandoah River and Harry Murray's Fly Shop. Breakfast, dinner available. Moderate. (540) 984-4212.

Holiday Inn. Afton, at the junction of I-64 and Route 250. Convenient to the southern park streams. Restaurant. Moderate. (540) 942-5201.

Mimslyn Inn. Luray. Large old-fashioned hotel overlooking Luray. Bar, restaurant. Inexpensive to moderate. (540) 743-5105.

The Inn at Sugar Hollow Farm. Thirteen miles west of Charlottesville. Private baths. Expensive. (804) 823-7086.

Skyland and Big Meadows Lodge. Two big family-oriented lodges on Skyline Drive. Moderate. 1-800-999-4714.

Camping

For information on camping in the park, call (540) 999-2282.

Bud-Lea Campground. Madison. (540) 948-4186.

Endless Caverns Campground. New Market. (540) 740-3993.

Where to Eat

The Shenandoah Valley is a rural area with few noteworthy restaurants. Some of the lodgings listed above include dining. For additional eateries, ask at the tackle shops, or visit the Parkhurst Restaurant on Route 211, two miles west of Luray—the Parkhurst has the best food in the area.

Resources

Park information: Shenandoah National Park, Rt. 4, Box 348, Luray, Virginia 22835. (540) 999-2243.

Licenses. Virginia Department of Game and Inland Fisheries. (804) 367-1000.

Virginia Atlas and Gazetteer. DeLorme, P.O. Box 298, Freeport, Maine 04032. (207) 865-4171.

The Potomac Appalachian Trail Club (PATC). 118 Park St., SE, Vienna, Virginia 22180. (703) 242-0693. These maps very good. They are clear, published in color, and show all streams, tributaries, trails, and roads in the park.

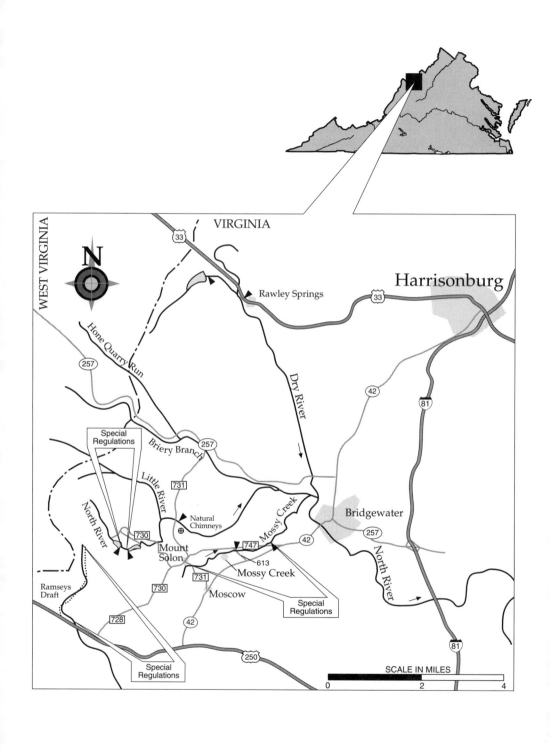

CHAPTER 21

Westcentral Virginia I: Mossy Creek and Streams in the George Washington National Forest—the Dry River, the North River, the Little River, Briery Branch, and Ramseys Draft

MOSSY CREEK

Mossy Creek, near Bridgewater, is one of the best-known trout streams in Virginia. Situated within three hours of Washington, it is a limestone spring creek regulated as a Fly-Fishing-Only, Catch-and-Release fishery. Given these restrictions, the quantity of trout in the stream, and the protection it receives from TU and other conservation groups, it is not surprising that Mossy is popular with anglers from the nation's capital.

Spring creeks are finicky, and Mossy is no exception. One day the trout will be extremely active, and the next—under seemingly identical conditions—the water will appear dead and you won't catch a thing. About twenty feet wide, the creek wanders through open meadows and lightly canopied farmland. There is no wading in Mossy. Anglers must cast from the banks, frequently from a kneeling position, and shoot long, delicate presentations over the tall weeds to the water. The flood of 1995, which devastated many Virginia trout streams, improved Mossy. Unwanted silt was scoured from the bottom, refreshing the streambed.

The premier hatch on Mossy is the Trico. Starting in late May and continuing through the first heavy frost of the fall, Trico spinners attract big browns. Cloudy, overcast days produce the most surface takes, but any summer morning on Mossy Creek is productive. After the early spinner fall, the trout continue to look up, and terrestrials work well. Disco Crickets and beetles, hoppers, and ants will catch fish throughout the day.

Mossy is stocked by the Virginia Fish Commission with fingerling trout each fall. By the time these fish reach twelve inches, they are no longer easy to catch. A twenty-inch fish is a challenge, and there are plenty of them in the water.

Mossy Creek

Regulations
Mossy is regulated as a Trophy Trout Stream, restricted to fly fishing only. There is a creel limit of one fish per day, more than twenty inches long. A free landowner permit is required. Write VDGIF, P.O. Box 996, Verona, Virginia 24478 for a permit. (540) 248-9360.

Access
Mossy Creek is located in Virginia's Shenandoah Valley south of Bridgewater on Route 747. Take exit 240 off I-81 to Bridgewater. Make a left at the light onto Main Street, Route 42. About three miles out of town, Route 42 makes an abrupt ninety-degree turn to the left.
   • Continue *straight* on Route 747 toward Natural Chimneys and you will see a sign for parking at the lower public water.
   • To get to the upstream parking area, continue on Route 747 until you see old Route 613 on the left and Mossy Creek Presbyterian Church. The parking area is on old Route 613 just over the hill past the church.
   All anglers must walk to the water from the parking areas. Do not cross the fields, whether or not there are posted signs. Landowners have made agreements with local conservation and angling groups, and these arrangements must be respected.

Hatches, Flies, and Best Times to Fish
Winter (December to March)
Big streamers (Woolly Buggers, sculpins, Zonkers, #8–#12), Blue-Winged Olives (#18–#20).

Spring (April to May)
Sulphurs (#14), black caddis (#18), yellow drakes (#10), golden drakes (#10–#12), Ginger Quills, Adamses, Light Cahills. Standard attractors like the Royal Coachman, Patriot, and Yellow and Red Humpy patterns also take fish.

Summer (June to September)
Hoppers, beetles, ants, and crickets (Bob Cramer's Disco Cricket works wonders). Sulphurs (#18) and Tricos.

Fall (October to November)
Blue-Winged Olives (*Beatis* patterns, #18–#26). Large streamers will take aggressive, prespawning browns.

GEORGE WASHINGTON NATIONAL FOREST

The George Washington National Forest encompasses 1.2 million acres of gentle mountainous land rising on the west side of the Shenandoah Valley. Jim Finn, owner of Mossy Creek Outfitters, hosted me on an angler's tour of the best trout streams in and out of the park.

Regulations

To fish in the George Washington National Forest, anglers must have a Virginia State Fishing License and a National Forest Stamp. Unless you are fishing stocked trout water (listed in the Trout Stocking Plan in the book of state fishing regulations), you do not need an additional trout license. Anglers fishing Wild Trout waters or special regulations areas *not* listed in the Trout Stocking Plan only need the state fishing license.

DRY RIVER

The Dry River is a long piece of water, a twenty-five-foot-wide river that runs from Brushy Mountain in Rockingham County to its confluence with the North River near Bridgewater. This is a very popular stocked trout stream, and it receives a lot of pressure early in the season.

Despite its name, the Dry River can be fished year-round, except during the worst droughts. It is fishable after Ramseys Draft and the lower North River (see below) have dried up. Switzer Dam Reservoir on Skidmore Fork creates part of the water supply for Bridgewater. The impoundment ensures ample water for three miles downstream of the dam throughout the year.

Regulations

Because it is stocked trout water, a trout license is required to fish the Dry River.

Access

Take Route 33 west from Harrisonburg to Rawley Springs. Catchable-size rainbow and brown trout are stocked at Rawley Springs on Route 33. There are numerous pull-offs on Route 33 west of Rawley Springs.

The Skidmore Fork (not shown on map), below the dam, is not stocked. This is one of Jim Finn's favorite local streams. The water is small but extremely productive, and Finn often takes eleven- to thirteen-inch brook trout. Much of the water below Rawley Springs runs through private land. Ask permission to fish in this area unless you enter where there are signs for public access.

NORTH RIVER

This is a good early-season stream from its headwaters in the George Washington National Forest downstream to Bridgewater. From Natural Chimneys upstream, the water is fifteen to twenty feet wide and shallow in most places. It is stocked in the spring, fall, and winter. Jim Finn first showed me the water at Natural Chimneys in August. The water was low. He recommends this section as a spring fishery. Between March and early June, Hendricksons, Blue Quills, Quill Gordons, and iron blue duns work well.

The special regulations water (upstream) gets very low in the summer, hence the Delayed-Harvest regulations. There is plenty of cool holding water between the two impoundments.

Regulations
The one-and-one-half-mile stretch between the Elkhorn Dam and the Staunton City Reservoir is regulated as a Delayed-Harvest, Catch-and-Release area. From October 1 to May 31, only single barbless hooks and artificial lures or flies may be used, and all fish must be released. From June 1 to September 30, six fish more than nine inches long may be taken. Standard trout regulations apply on the rest of the stream.

Access
• At Natural Chimneys, off Route 730. At the Stokesville Store (north of Route 730), turn left or right to the stream.

• North River Gorge Trail off FR95 west of Stokesville. Hike in five miles to fish for wild brookies and holdover browns. There are campsites along the trail, which is detailed on the USFS Dry River District Map.

• At Staunton Dam—FR95B.

• At Elkhorn Lake Dam—off FR95 and FR96.

Special regulations apply between the Staunton Dam and the Elkhorn Lake Dam.

LITTLE RIVER
The Little River is lovely in April and early May, but it dries up very quickly and most of it traverses private property. The enthusiastic angler can access the water on FR101, north of Stokesville at the concrete bridge that crosses the stream. For about two hundred yards upstream, fishing is public. (VAG pg. 66, A-2.)

BRIERY BRANCH
Briery Branch is stocked with rainbow trout and has wild brookies in its headwaters. It is a good early-season stream. Access it from Route 257 west of Bridgewater.

Hone Quarry Run is a small remote tributary of Briery Branch. It too has wild brook trout in its headwaters and is easily found from Route 257 west of Bridgewater.

RAMSEYS DRAFT
Jim Finn sent me with Vann Knighting, one of his guides, to fish Ramseys Draft, the premier wild trout stream in the George Washington National Forest. Vann, a native of Staunton, Virginia, has fished for trout since he

was five years old. His grandfather, E. J. Knighting, taught him. Knighting was the author of *The Hills of Childhood*, a true story of fourteen children growing up in rural Virginia during the Depression. Seven boys and seven girls learned to hunt and fish to put food on the table. Although he releases his fish, Vann continues the tradition, putting family and angling first. His day job is delivering pharmaceutical supplies between 6:00 A.M. until 2:00 P.M. This schedule leaves late afternoons and evenings free.

The ghost of E. J. Knighting is palpable if you fish Ramseys Draft with Vann. He explained how his grandfather took him and his brother to mountain streams for wild brook trout. They hiked to upland plateaus for native trout like those in Ramseys Draft. Vann has developed an attractor pattern, which he named the Granddad Fly as a tribute to his grandfather. It is a bushy, orange-and-brown dry fly that works magically on brook trout. One of its advantages is that it is an easy fly to see in turbulent spring water. It proved itself convincingly when we fished, taking ten brook trout for Vann and six for me.

Ramseys Draft achieved wild trout status accidentally. It was a popular stocked stream until a major flood destroyed it in 1969. After the disaster, the state ceased stocking the water. A few years later, significant numbers of wild brook trout were counted. Since then, the upper reaches have been declared a federal Wilderness Area, and trout have not been stocked since 1991. No motor-driven, mechanical, or electric tools or vehicles of any kind are allowed in the Ramseys Draft Wilderness.

The Ramseys Draft Wilderness Area is a well-known hiking destination. The lower end of the stream holds good trout, but it is the upper reaches that give the stream its reputation. To reach upper Ramseys Draft, you must cross upland meadows and stands of virgin hemlock. The fishing is difficult, as you must negotiate downed trees and huge boulders. But the wild fish are worth it. Vann caught a sixteen-inch brown on the Granddad Fly in the Wilderness. He says that taking a foot-long brookie here is the technical equivalent of catching a twenty-four-inch brown on Mossy! The stream is at its best at first light in the spring.

Ramseys Draft is not a very large stream. It ranges from thirty feet wide near its mouth on the Calfpasture River to twenty feet in the Wilderness. The lower reaches are easy to wade once the initial spring runoff slacks. Lack of cover and base flow cause the water to get warm and low in summer.

Regulations

Ramseys Draft is regulated as a Wild Trout Stream. Artificial flies or lures only with single barbless hooks are permitted. All trout less than nine inches must be released.

Access
To reach Ramseys Draft from Bridgewater, take Route 42 south to Route 250 at Churchville. Turn right (west on Route 250), drive fifteen miles, and look for the Mountain Home Picnic Area on the right. A footpath follows the water upstream 7.5 miles to the top of the mountain. Walk at least forty minutes to the best trout water, above the land affected by the 1969 flood.

Hatches, Flies, and Best Times to Fish
Not surprisingly, Virginia's mountain trout streams fish best in the spring. They are also productive in October, when falling leaves and increased precipitation augment the water flow.

Spring (March, April, and early May)
Little brown stoneflies, Quill Gordon, March Brown, Gray Fox (#12–#16). Caddis imitations: #18 black and #16 green (grannom). Granddad Fly (#12).
    Mid-May and June: Blue Quill (#14), sulphur (#14–#18), Cahill (#12–#16), elk-hair caddis (#16), Adams Parachute, Granddad Fly (#14).

Summer (June to September)
Imitations of terrestrials: crickets, ants, beetles and, hoppers.

Fall (October to November)
Terrestrials, Blue-Winged Olives (#18–#20), tan caddis (#16–#18).

IF YOU GO . . .
It is about two hours from the Capital Beltway or northern Virginia to Bridgewater (Mossy Creek). Take I-270 or I-70 to Frederick, then go south on Route 340, west on Route 7 to I-81, and south to exit 240 (Bridgewater). Bridgewater and Harrisonburg are also convenient gateways to the George Washington National Forest.

Tackle Shops and Guides
    Blue Ridge Angler. Harrisonburg. Full-service fly shop. Float trips on the Jackson and Shenandoah Rivers. (540) 574-3474.
    Robert Cramer. Guide. Trips on Mossy Creek (private water), the Jackson River, and in the George Washington National Forest. (540) 867-9310.
    Mossy Creek Fly Shop. Route 42 at traffic light on Main Street, Bridgewater. Jim Finn, proprietor. Orvis dealer. Guide service, including private sections of Mossy, Beaver, and Smith Creeks and other streams. (540) 828-0033.

Trout & About. Arlington. Phil Gay, guide and instructor. Guides on Shenandoah Park streams, Mossy Creek, and other waters within two hours of Washington. (703) 525-727.

Where to Stay

Belle Grae Inn. Staunton. Moderate to expensive. (540) 886-5151.

Boxwood B&B. Hinton. Nancy Jones, a local historian, operates this establishment: large rooms, good food, good company. Convenient to George Washington National Forest streams. Moderate. (540) 867-5772.

Holiday Inn. Rockfish Gap, Afton. At the south end of Skyline Drive, the junction of I-64 and Route 250. Moderate. (540) 942-5201.

Village Inn. Route 11 between Harrisonburg and Bridgewater. Take exit 243 off I-81. Go left at the light and the Village Inn will be one and one-half miles on the left. Clean Mennonite establishment. Inexpensive. 1-800-736-7355.

Joshua Wilton House. Harrisonburg. Formal Victorian B&B. Restaurant. Expensive. (540) 434-4464.

Camping

George Washington National Forest Campgrounds. Dry River Ranger District. (703) 962-2214.

Where to Eat

The Blue Stone Restaurant. Lacey Springs. Good food. Moderate.

Joshua Wilton House. Harrisonburg. Formal restaurant with European recipes served in rich sauces. Expensive. (540) 434-4464.

Village Inn. Harrisonburg. Good home cooking by Mennonite owners. Closed Sundays. Very convenient to Mossy Creek. Inexpensive. (540) 434-7355.

There are many fast-food restaurants in Harrisonburg, but good cooked-to-order food is hard to find.

Resources

George Washington National Forest. Maps, information. (703) 962-2214.

CHAPTER 22

Westcentral Virginia II—Bath County: The Cascades, the Jackson River, and Big Back Creek

Bath County is an unspoiled Virginia resort area little known beyond state borders. The county sits next to the Allegheny Mountains in the western part of the state near the West Virginia line. The Homestead, one of the most luxurious resorts in the East, spreads over sixteen thousand acres of Bath County mountains and farmland. There are two golf courses, a ski area, a horseback-riding stable, a trout stream, numerous tennis courts, and several restaurants—in addition to hotel rooms and scattered cottages. Many of the recreational facilities can be used by visitors as well as guests.

In earlier times, waiters at the Homestead were required to balance serving trays on their heads, leaving their hands free to pick up dishes. I remember being taken there for tea as a child. I wondered if those lanky men of Caribbean heritage walked so ramrod straight at home. Today, the town of Hot Springs, where the Homestead is located, still seems like a medieval village, with most of the people working for one employer.

THE CASCADES

A torrent of water has carved a series of forty-foot waterfalls through the gorge full of wild trout, wildflowers, and wildlife known as the Cascades (not on map). This may be my favorite mountain trout stream in the mid-Atlantic. Its flora and fauna offer some of the most beautiful surroundings in the region. Angling just doesn't get much prettier than it is along the banks of the Cascades, particularly in the upper two miles when the wild-flowers are in bloom. On a recent trip, I felt as if I were in an equatorial plant museum, surrounded by orchids, jack-in-the-pulpit, trillium, and exotic daisies.

The Cascades are owned by the Homestead. The lower two miles are stocked, and the upper two miles support streambred rainbow and brook trout. The upper reaches were stocked with rainbows until 1984. By that time, the strain had taken over and displaced the native brookies. Thus streambred 'bows, not brook trout, are the dominant species.

I last fished the Cascades in August. There was plenty of water and the fish were cooperative, if wary. Once I figured out they would take

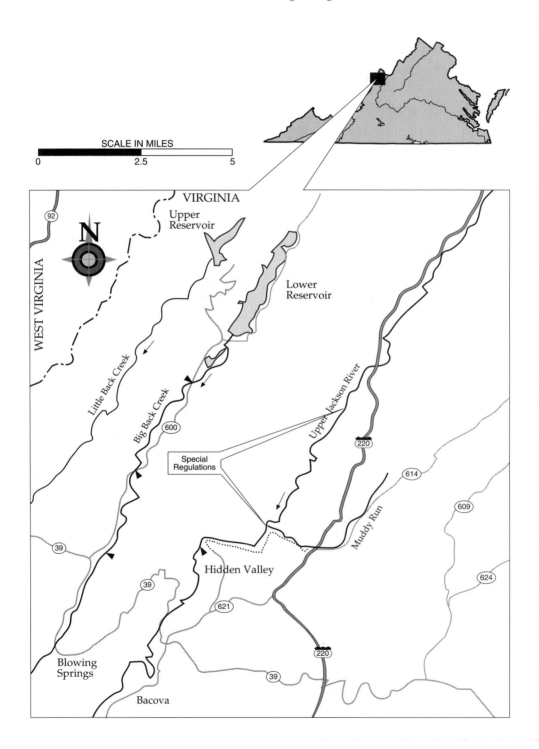

DOUGLAS LEES

The Cascades

Green Weenies as if their final meal, I caught more than a dozen trout in an hour. I approached each pool from the tail, picking up some fish at the outflow and an occasional trout from the depths. Lots of trout held near the top of pools, gulping in the oxygenated water that fell over the rocks from the tail of the preceding water. It is important to maintain a low profile once you have stepped up to a pool. Like mountain trout anywhere, fish in the Cascades are picky and careful after the spring high water recedes.

A $20 fee is required to fish the Cascades. It's not much to pay, given the cost of maintaining access to the water. A wooden scaffold supports a walkway and staircase that is built up and over the rocks and waterfalls. This walk enables hikers and anglers to reach parts of the stream that would otherwise be inaccessible. Every spring, the walkway is overhauled, and after severe winters, it requires major structural repairs.

Regulations
Artificial flies and fly tackle only may be used on the Cascades. All fish must be released.

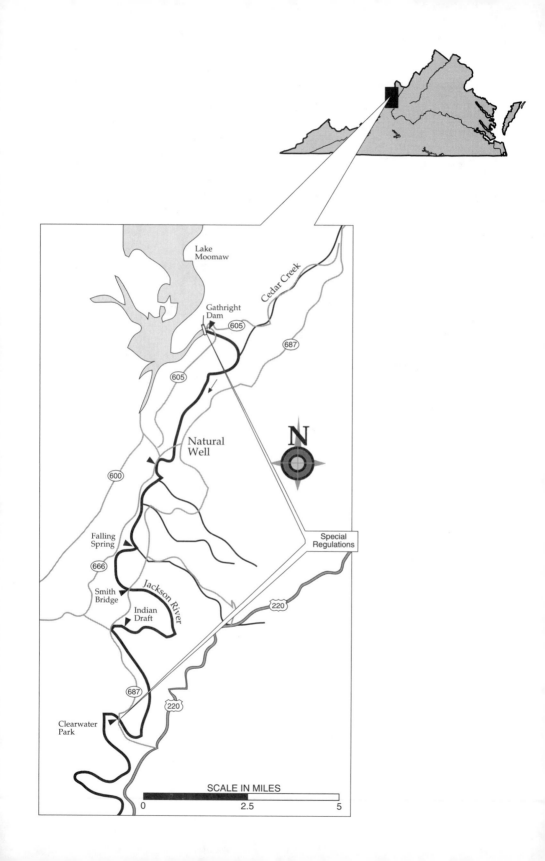

Lake
Moomaw

Cedar Creek

Gathright
Dam

(605)

(687)

(605)

Natural
Well

(600)

Falling
Spring

(666)

Jackson River

Smith
Bridge

Indian
Draft

(687)

(220)

(220)

Clearwater
Park

Special
Regulations

N

SCALE IN MILES

0   2.5   5

Access
To reach the Cascades, take Route 220 to Hot Springs. Look for the Out-post Fly Shop on Cottage Row in the Homestead complex, where you can get a permit to fish the Cascades whether or not you stay at the Homestead.

Hatches, Flies, and Best Times to Fish
The Cascades are spring fed. A year-round water temperature of 55 degrees Fahrenheit makes the stream an option even during the winter. In the spring, torrents course down the mountain, and streamers, Woolly Buggers, and other large patterns will work well.

When the water level drops, standard eastern spring season mayflies emerge. March Browns, Quill Gordons, sulphurs, and green drakes are among the best producers. Attractors such as the Coachman, Patriot, and Ausable Wulff patterns also do well. Remember that water temperatures drop during the night on mountain streams. Except during very hot weather, Cascades trout are not active until midmorning, so don't waste your time with early-morning arrivals.

In August, I had good luck with little brown stoneflies, Pheasant-tail nymphs, caddis, and terrestrials—in addition to the Green Weenie. But the Green Weenie and an elk-hair caddis (#16) took by far the most fish! In the fall, there are *Baetis* hatches—use Blue-Winged Olives (#18–#20). A tip: Do not be without Chuck Kraft's C. K. Nymph on the Cascades.

The list of flies provided with the Jackson River section (below) will serve as a guideline for the Cascades and other streams in Bath County.

THE JACKSON RIVER
Until 1997, Virginia's Jackson was on its way to becoming one of the best trout fisheries in the mid-Atlantic. It is a freestone stream, the lower section of which is a tailwater fueled by cold water released from the bottom of Lake Moomaw through the Gathright Dam. The fishery is active all year.

Fishing the Jackson is really two distinct experiences. There is the nineteen-mile tailwater from Gathright Dam to Clearwater, and there is the freestone upper section above the lake. Below Clearwater and Coving-ton, the Jackson becomes a warm-water fishery.

The Middle Jackson
The stretch of the river below Gathright Dam and above Covington is a sixty- to one-hundred-foot-wide seam of water winding its way through meadows and woodlands, much of which is private property. Although the Jackson is big navigable water, I found the footing stable and the wad-ing unthreatening, with the exception of the section just below the dam. Chest waders and a staff are advised because of the size of the water.

I first fished below the dam with Vann Knighting, a guide from Mossy Creek Outfitters. Vann introduced me to the black fly larva (Simultiidae) "hatch" that is the hallmark of the Jackson below the dam. We arrived at 7:30 A.M. We saw no other vehicles, but we counted hundreds of black fly duns on the water. It was an overcast day; the air temperature was 58 degrees Fahrenheit and the water 55 degrees Fahrenheit. We rigged up, waded out, and began to cast black fly pupae. Although we saw no working fish, we cast with confidence.

After a half hour without a hookup, Vann wondered aloud where the other anglers were. This stretch is noted for crowds of fishermen, fly and spin anglers alike. We covered the water thoroughly for two hours. Vann finally waded to shore after working a twenty-foot stretch of "sure thing" water along the far bank for more than half an hour. He explained that the particular reach had always produced for him in the past and was usually occupied by fly anglers. Neither of us could figure out what the problem was that morning.

I returned the next day, again to an empty parking lot. I didn't bother to fish. My guess is that the unseasonable drop in air temperature put the trout off their feed for a day or two.

Natural Well

As the sun rose higher, Vann and I drove downstream to the access area below Natural Well. I was hoping to catch the tail end of the morning Trico hatch on the middle Jackson that I had heard much about. I was not disappointed. When I leaned over the Natural Well bridge, there were clouds of Tricos hovering above the water. I had not seen this many "trikes" since a remarkable morning some years ago on Pennsylvania's Spring Creek near Bellefonte. We entered the water at the public access, but by the time we reached the Trico water, the hatch was on the wane. I vowed to be in place the next morning.

Vann and I spent the rest of the morning casting to dimpling fish on the midsection of the river. This section of the Jackson looks like a giant spring creek, the way the trout rise across the braided currents of the river. They came up hither and yon, taking the tiniest of midges in seemingly random fashion. After trying a series of small midge patterns, Vann got a hookup using a Griffith's Gnat (#22). We spent the rest of the morning catching twelve- to fourteen-inch browns using midge cluster patterns (Griffith's Gnat and a small Parachute Adams) in a long flat reach of unshaded water.

That same day, I returned to the river farther downstream (at Indian Draft) late in the afternoon, in time to catch fish on sulphurs and terrestrials. The next morning I met the Trico hatch as planned and took six good trout more than a foot long.

Sadly, the middle section of the Jackson is now managed as a Put-and-Take fishery, stocked with rainbow and brown trout. There is natural reproduction in the tributaries.

Regulations

The rights to fish the nineteen miles of the middle Jackson between Gathright Dam and Covington have been under dispute for a number of years. The issue is whether landowners on either side of the river own the bottom of the navigable water (as deeded to them, they say, through a king's grant in colonial times) and whether they can therefore control who fishes there. In May 1997, the case was decided in favor of the landowners, rendering all of the water private. At the same time, the Game Board decided to allow bait fishing in this section of the river. The situation does not bode well for fly anglers or for those who use light spinning tackle and barbless hooks.

Current regulations state that angler access to the water is limited to the public access sites, unless fishermen have express permission to cross landowners' property. Anglers who wish to fish from the banks are required to ask the landowner's permission (and should not be surprised to be turned down). *Anglers wading or floating the river by boat may not fish the water anywhere the banks are posted.*

Access

From the Gathright Dam on Lake Moomaw downstream to Clearwater Park, there are six public access points:
- Parking lot at the dam.
- Public access parking lot off Route 638 (not shown on map) near Natural Well.
- A pull-off on Route 666 at Falling Spring. Posted.
- At Smith Bridge on Route 687 (there is not much parking here and banks are steep). Posted.
- At Indian Draft on Route 687 (this is a big parking lot and boat launch).
- At Clearwater Park on Route 687.

The Upper Jackson (Hidden Valley)

The upper Jackson is classic freestone trout water. The special regulations section can be accessed only by hiking 1.7 miles upstream from Hidden Valley Campground to the swinging bridge. The walk is worth it. It took me forty minutes to walk to the regulated water and another fifteen to find productive water. Once there, I caught lots of fish. My most memorable was a very large brown trout that took a crayfish pattern and fled—

unchecked—upstream! I saw his head and guessed his length overall at eighteen inches.

I caught two ten-inch trout before the big one and later landed three others more than a foot long on a #10 Madame X, the big ugly fly of choice to those trout that August afternoon. I saw yellow drakes *(Potamanthus)*, tan caddis, sulphurs, olives, and a number of midges coming off the water all afternoon. This section of water is about thirty feet wide, with a number of fifty-foot-long pools overhung by ledge rock and evergreens. There are alternating deep runs and riffles—classic trout water. I will return to the upper Jackson frequently, inspired by that big trout that took my Madame X in August.

Regulations
This section is regulated as Trophy Trout water. Single barbless hooks and flies only may be used for a three-and-one-half-mile stretch beginning at the swinging bridge (1.7 miles above Hidden Valley) at the mouth of Muddy Run and extending upstream to the last ford on FS481D. Anglers may keep two trout per day, sixteen inches or more in length. All others must be immediately released.

There are several miles of Put-and-Take water both above and below the special regulations section of the upper Jackson. These reaches are well worth fishing after the spring season, when most bait anglers have put away their rods.

Access
Take Route 220 north to Route 39 west. Go three miles to Route 621, and turn north (right) on Route 621 to the Hidden Valley Recreation Area (on its own road one and one-half miles from Route 621). The Hidden Valley Campground is located here. There is access to the stocked water at the campground. Park at the lot near the Hidden Valley B&B and walk upstream 1.7 miles (follow path across meadow) to the special regulations area. The Trophy Trout waters may also be accessed from upstream via Route 623 below the Poor Farm.

Hatches, Flies, and Best Times to Fish
The Jackson nurtures most eastern mayflies, as well as caddis and stoneflies. The notorious black fly larvae (Simultiidae) (#16–#20) and hellgrammites (#2–#4) can be used throughout the year. Midges also emerge year-round. In deep water, crayfish (#12–#14), Muddlers (#10–#14), Woolly Buggers (#12–#14), and big streamer patterns (#2–#10) take fish.

Winter (February to March)
Below Gathright Dam: black flies *(Simulium vittatum)* (#16–#20); midges (#20–#24).

Early season (March to April)
The farther downstream from the dam one fishes, the more mayflies there are. Early black caddis (#14), green caddis (#16), March Browns (#14).

Spring (May to June)
March Browns, Quill Gordons, Blue-Winged Olives, Cahills, sulphurs (#14–#18), Little Brown Hendrickson *(Serratella deficiens, #16)*, green drakes, spotted sedge *(Hydropsyche caddis, #16)*. Vann Knighting's Grand-dad Fly and other high-floating attractors work wherever mayflies emerge.

Summer (June to September)
Middle section: black caddis (#18), brown drake *(Hexagenia atrocaudata)*, grannom *(Brachycentrus)*, Tricos. Upper section: terrestrials and midges (black, olive, cream midges in #20–#24), giant golden stonefly (#8–#10), large black stonefly (#8–#10), smaller black and/or brown stoneflies (#12–#14), yellow drake *(Potamanthus)*, sulphurs, tan caddis (#16), Blue-Winged Olives (#18–#20).

Fall (October to November)
Tricos until frost. Blue-Winged Olives (#16–#20), midges, ginger caddis, and the autumn mottled sedge *(Neophylax, #16)*.

BIG BACK CREEK
Big Back Creek is an alternative fishery to the Cascades and the Jackson River should these waters be crowded, fishing poorly, or otherwise indisposed. Larger and broader than the Cascades and far less popular than the Jackson, Big Back Creek is a stocked, thirty- to forty-foot-wide freestone stream. It lies one valley west of the Jackson and provides excellent fly fishing. Because it is part of a flood control project, there is an ample supply of water, although in summers of bad drought, the level may become too low to fish.

Big Back Creek has several very long, deep pools. It's a good idea to fish from one side or the other, because there are deep holes separating the banks. In periods of low water, the trout stack up in these big pools, and they should be left alone. Wading is not a problem, because the bottom consists of fist-sized rocks, sand, and pebbles.

Big Back Creek flows through a park and recreation area that includes two man-made bass lakes. The park has rest rooms, parking, a beach, and a playing field.

Regulations
From the bridge over the stream on Route 600 (at the spillway) upstream to the pump house near the bass lake, Catch-and-Release regulations apply.

Access
Take Route 220 to Route 39 west. Drive over Back Creek Mountain into the George Washington National Forest. Turn left at the Blowing Springs Campground sign.
  • To reach the upper end of the special regulations stretch, go right off Route 39 onto Route 600 at Mountain Grove general store, and continue north to the Recreation Area.
  • To reach the center of the mile-long special regulations stretch, park on Route 600 at the spillway. I caught two foot-long trout just above the spillway in the space of an hour late in the season.

Hatches, Flies, and Best Times to Fish
During periods of high water, fish hellgrammite imitations and Pheasant-tail and Red Fox or Squirrel nymphs. Mayfly hatches in the spring include Quill Gordons, Blue Quills, Cahills, sulphurs, and Blue-Winged Olives (sporadic). Caddis emerge all year. Big Back Creek has no large mayflies and no Tricos.

IF YOU GO . . .
Warm Springs is about four hours (210 miles) from Washington and three and one-half hours (155 miles) from Richmond. From Washington and points north, take I-66 west to I-81 south to Route 275 (exit 225) west to Route 250 west, then Route 42 south to Route 39 west to Route 220 south two miles.
　　　From Richmond, take I-64 to I-81 north to Route 250 west. Then take Route 254 out of Staunton to Route 42 and follow the directions above.

Tackle Shops and Guides
　　Ralph A. Cleek. Between Warm Springs and Monerey. Guides on the Jackson. Cleek also rents his private water on the upper Jackson near Bolar. (540) 839-2759.
　　Robert Cramer. Dayton. Orvis-endorsed guide for George Washington National Forest, Mossy Creek, and the Jackson River. (540) 867-9310.
　　Chuck Kraft. Charlottesville. Guide service on the Jackson and small-mouth bass rivers. The best anglers I know say Chuck Kraft is the best guide and angler *they* know! (804) 293-9305.
　　Mossy Creek Fly Shop. Bridgewater. Jim Finn, proprietor. Guiding on Mossy, Jackson, George Washington National Forest streams. Full-service Orvis shop. Vann Knighting guides through this shop. 1-800-646-2168.
　　The Outpost. The Orvis fly shop at the Homestead, Hot Springs. Tackle, guides, instruction, and large selection of flies. Good information on the Jackson and Big Back Creek. Make reservations here for the Cascades. Beaver Shriver, who ran the Outpost for years, still owns the

company but is now with Frontiers. Jason Woods is the angling expert, and Sherrie Pound co-manages the shop.

Where to Stay

Hidden Valley B&B. Hidden Valley. Also known as Warwickton, a property of the United States Forest Service. Four miles from Warm Springs in the George Washington National Park stands this nineteenth-century Greek revival house where *Sommersby* was filmed. The house is leased to Pam Stidham, a fine hostess with an historical understanding, who runs it as a B&B at the lower end of the upper Jackson. Expensive (but not very) and worth it! (540) 839-3178.

The Homestead. Hot Springs. According to a recent rate card, the least expensive rate is $178 for two, plus 15 percent service charge and tax. 1-800-838-1766.

The Inn at Grist Mill Square. Warm Springs. Expensive. (540) 839-2231.

Hillcrest Motel. Hot Springs. Inexpensive. AAA. (540) 839-5316.

Meadow Lane Lodge. On sixteen hundred acres of private land along the upper Jackson. Includes two miles of private stocked water. Expensive. (540) 839-5959.

Old Earlehurst B&B. Beaver Dam Falls, overlooking Sweet Springs in Alleghany County. Roselyn Humphreys, innkeeper. Ask about fishing the private stretch of Sweet Springs Creek. Moderate. (540) 559-3071.

Rip's Natural Well Lodge. Hot Springs. Natural Well, at the junction of Route 687 and Route 638. Mr. and Mrs. E. H. Andrews, owners. Two miles below Gathright Dam on the Jackson River. Two efficiency units with kitchenette, one double and one single bed in each room. No breakfast. Inexpensive to moderate. (540) 965-4749 or 965-4748.

Roseloe Motel. On Route 220 between Warm Springs and Hot Springs. Clean and simple. Rooms with kitchenettes. AAA. Inexpensive. (540) 839-5373.

Three Hills Inn. Route 220, Warm Springs. Three Hills has been an inn since 1917. It has a fantastic view, large guest rooms, and cottages. Ed McArdle, a gourmet chef, operates the Muse restaurant on the premises. Moderate to expensive. (540) 839-5381.

The Bath County Chamber of Commerce (see Resources below) has many additional listings.

Camping

George Washington National Forest. All public campgrounds. (540) 839-2521.

Hidden Valley Recreation Area. On the upper Jackson. (540) 839-2521.

Peaceful River Campground. Private. (540) 996-4256.

Where to Eat

The Inn at Grist Mill Square. Warm Springs. Good atmosphere, average food, slow service. Expensive. (540) 830-2231.

The Muse at Three Hills Inn. Route 220, Warm Springs. Excellent, healthy gourmet meals prepared by chef Ed McArdle. Best food in the area. Expensive. (540) 839-5381.

Sam Snead's Tavern. Hot Springs. A favorite with golfers. Moderate to expensive. (540) 839-7666.

Springs Grill. Warm Springs. On Route 220. Kitchen open late. Moderate. (540) 839-3236.

Warm Springs Inn. Route 220 at Route 39 east. Moderate to expensive. (540) 839-5351.

Resources

Bath County Chamber of Commerce. (703) 839-5409 or 1-800-628-8092.

Highland County Chamber of Commerce. (540) 468-2550.

The Insider's Guide to Virginia's Blue Ridge. 1-800-422-4434.

George Washington National Forest. (703) 962-2214.

West Virginia

OVERVIEW

Some of the wildest country in the mid-Atlantic region is in the Mountain State, one of the last freshwater angling frontiers in the East. This is the land of the black bear and the rattlesnake, the hillbilly and the independent. It is also the state with the largest wilderness acreage east of Montana.

Trout fishing opportunities are little known across state lines, and the sport takes a backseat to turkey and deer hunting locally. But West Virginia's bright waters are very much a part of the local landscape, sparkling through gorges below upland pastures dotted with sheep and rock outcroppings.

If you don't know the territory, exploring for trout in West Virginia will make you run for a compass and a guide. Road maps are inadequate and directions confusing. The roads follow the "hollers," continually switching back and forth to get over the mountains. Often, you can't get there from here in less than an hour or so. For those who enjoy trout fishing for its peaceful surrounds, West Virginia will not disappoint.

Most West Virginia streams are freestone. The length of the trout season depends on adequate rainfall and snowmelt in the spring and continued precipitation in the summer. The former is often severe and the latter frequently insignificant.

During the spring thaw, melting snow gushes off the mountains, carrying a high degree of toxic acid runoff from precipitation into the water. Then, about mid-May, the rain stops and streams recede. Within a week or two, drought sets in. It is as if God's water pitcher has run dry: After pouring and pouring, when He picks up His pitcher in mid-June to sprinkle the grass, nothing comes out. Drought-free years in West Virginia are the exception. Most West Virginia fly anglers take their trout between early May and mid-June—between the tapering of runoff and the onset of the dry summer. By late June, streams can be down to a trickle through bone-dry bare rock—sad to see and impossible to fish. In summers with normal or higher levels rainfall, the streams become productive again by September and can be fished through October.

WEST VIRGINIA TROUT STREAM MANAGEMENT

The challenge to the West Virginia Department of Natural Resources (WVDNR) is to solve problems caused by the extremes of the weather and acid rain that make anything more than a rudimentary Put-and-Take trout program difficult. The fact that the WVDNR has developed innovative progressive approaches is to be commended, especially in a state steeped in the mystique of stringers of trout bound for the dinner table.

The WVDNR, working cooperatively with the U.S. Fish and Wildlife Service, Forest Service, Soil Conservation Service, coal companies, and West Virginia chapters of TU, has undertaken several water-quality and habitat improvement projects over the last few years. The objective is to mitigate problems resulting from acid precipitation and acid mine drainage, thus improving aquatic life in the streams year-round. Under the Blue Ribbon Stream Management Program, trout have been reintroduced into fifty miles of former wild trout water. An additional 150 miles will be complete by the year 2000.

According to Donald Phares, assistant chief of coldwater management for the DNR, most of the work involves adding limestone particles to acidic water (to increase alkalinity) and installing structures to create holding places for fish. The program is a progressive one, assigning priorities to waters targeted for trout. On streams earmarked for Blue Ribbon treatment, water quality is improved by releasing limestone chips into headwaters to decrease acidity and sweeten the watershed. Limestone projects are opening a way to increase alkalinity on a number of streams at relatively modest expense.

Habitat is improved by putting structure in the water. Large enough to withstand raging spring floods, boulders ranging from one to five cubic feet are dropped midstream. These provide shelter for trout during periods of heavy runoff. Jack dams, current deflectors, and other in-stream current constrictors have also been installed to create safe lies.

In the Monongahela National Forest, where much of the state's coldwater resource is located, the once-renowned Cranberry River is making a comeback. A large water-powered mill adds limestone slurry (crushed stone and milky water) to the North Fork of the Cranberry just above its junction with the main stem (see chapter 26).

Charles Heartwell, a former staff member at the WVDNR and long-time proponent of wild trout management, believes the fisheries show increasing promise. He thinks the Blue Ribbon program could result in the reclamation of the historically prominent West Virginia streams of the last century: the Cranberry River, Blackwater River, and Shavers Fork of the Cheat. These all have Blue Ribbon designation and all have received limestone treatment.

If West Virginia continues to increase the number of stream miles managed under the Blue Ribbon program and Catch-and-Release regulations, and *if* the DNR can mitigate the negative effects of precipitation (and lack thereof) and acidic runoff, in-stream trout reproduction will be common in a few years.

Several years ago, the WVDNR took the state's native brook trout streams off the stocking list, allowing the fish to establish a wild population. In other streams with exceptional water quality, the department has taken a put-and-grow approach—only fingerling trout are stocked and these only in order to strengthen and supplement the wild fish.

I dream of a time when I fish for wild trout in West Virginia in water as good as what now exists in Maryland and Pennsylvania! For the moment, the angler must be content to scout for wild trout and to cast to stocked and holdover trout in some of the most untamed water in the region.

HATCHES, FLIES, AND BEST TIMES TO FISH

Plan a West Virginia trip for early in the year—after mud season and before summer. Late April, May, and early June are ideal. There is very little angling pressure on designated trout streams after spring stockings, so late spring and early summer are good times to catch fish and avoid crowded water. When streams in the lower reaches of the watershed dry up, it is worthwhile hiking to remote wild trout tributaries.

Two notes of caution: First, get off West Virginia rivers quickly if a storm approaches. Rivers such as Dry Fork, Shavers Fork, Elk River, and the South Branch of the North Fork of the Potomac can become raging torrents within minutes. Call (304) 637-0245 for current stream conditions. Second, there are rattlesnakes in West Virginia, although I've not encountered any thus far. Watch where you put your hands when climbing in the rocks on sunny days.

The following list of effective flies for West Virginia was prepared by Charles Heartwell, who owns Charlie's Charmers Fly Tying. Hatches in West Virginia are as sensitive to weather and temperature as anywhere in the region. The times of emergences vary from year to year. This list can be used for all the streams mentioned in this section.

Early-season (March to mid-April)
Little black stonefly (mid-March, #18), streamers (Muddler Minnows, Black-Nosed Dace, sculpins).

Spring (mid-April to mid-May)

Early brown stonefly (#14), little Blue-Winged Olive (#18), Blue Quill (#16–#18), Quill Gordon (#12–#14), Hendrickson (#12–#14), grannom, green caddis (#12–#16).

Mid-May to mid-June: Gray Fox (#12–#14), March Brown (#10–#12), green drake (#8–#10), sulphur (#12–#18), Blue-Winged Olive (#12–#16), Yellow Sally (stonefly, #12–#14); caddis imitations: green (#12–#14), tan (spotted sedge, #14).

Late May: sulphur (#12–#14), little sulphur dun (#16–#18), Blue-Winged Olive (#12–#16), little tan caddis (#14–#16), chocolate caddis (#12), gray caddis (#12–#14).

Summer (mid-June to July)

Light Cahill, (#12–#14), Cream Variant (#10 at dusk), Pale Evening Dun (#14–#16), yellow drake *(Potamanthus distinctus,* #10–#12), Dark Blue Quill (#16–#18). Terrestrials: ant, beetle, grasshopper, inchworm, cricket, and caterpillar imitations.

June to September: Sulphur, Blue-Winged Olive, Cahill, stonefly, and caddis imitations will continue to work through the summer. Terrestrials (beetles, ants, hoppers, and crickets) are on the water from late June until frost.

Fall (September to October)

Little white-winged black fly (#22–#28), Blue-Winged Olive, terrestrials.

STATEWIDE RESOURCES

West Virginia Tourist Office. 1-800-CALL-WVA. This agency provides all kinds of tourist information.

West Virginia Department of Natural Resources. Box 67, Elkins, West Virginia 26241. (304) 637-0245. This agency gives out information about stream conditions and sells fishing licenses. It's a good idea to get your license by mail from the DNR before your trip, because they are hard to find locally.

West Virginia Trout Fishing Guide. A list of trout streams and their regulations. Available from the WVDNR (above).

Maps for Monongahela National Forest, Cranberry Wilderness Area, Seneca Creek Wilderness Area. (304) 636-1800.

Hiking Guide to Monongahela National Forest. 60 maps. 164 trails. $11.45. Available from the USDA Forest Service, 200 Sycamore Street, Elkins, West Virginia 26241.

West Virginia Highlands Conservancy. P.O. Box 306, Charleston, West Virginia 25321.

West Virginia Atlas and Gazetteer. DeLorme, P.O. Box 298, Freeport, Maine 04032. (207) 865-4171.

CHAPTER 23

Eastcentral West Virginia I:
Dry Fork, Gandy Creek, Glady Fork, Laurel Fork, and the Blackwater River

A few years ago, I spent a day with Clarksburg TU member Jim Martin taking an extensive tour of the tributaries of the Cheat and Potomac Rivers. As a boy, Jim used to hike and camp throughout the Monongahela National Forest, where much of the state's best trout water lies. He was able to whisk me from pull-off to pull-off of inviting trout water.

West Virginia streams are not easy to locate. The state seems to specialize in names like the Left Fork of the North Fork of the West Branch of the Such-and-So River. When I was exploring the state, I had to purchase county road maps or national forest maps to find the secondary and tertiary roads near the water. (A detailed map of all the streams in the state omitted the roads.) Now, *fortunately*, DeLorme has come out with the *West Virginia Atlas and Gazetteer*, which I highly recommend consulting before you strike out for trout.

Had I not met with Charles Heartwell at the DNR office the day after my drive with Martin, I would never have been able to reconstruct the way to all the water Jim showed me. Even so, I recommend going with a guide or a friend familiar with the area if you are fishing West Virginia for the first time.

For the purposes of directions in chapters 23 and 24, I use Elkins as a starting point for directions to access points. Numbered routes designated FR are Forest System Roads; FT identifies Forest System Trails.

DRY FORK

Larger than most West Virginia trout streams, Dry Fork is one of the state's most popular fisheries, frequented by bait and spin fishermen as well as fly anglers. It is about forty feet wide and can run very high and strong early in the season. Casting is easy, but a wading staff and felt soles are recommended.

Route 72 follows the stream between Hendricks and Red Creek, and this (the bigger) water is most popular with the bait and spin fishermen. Dry Fork contains holdover brown trout as well as spring stocks and is heavily fished early in the season. Ready access from the road is the enticement from Opening Day through May.

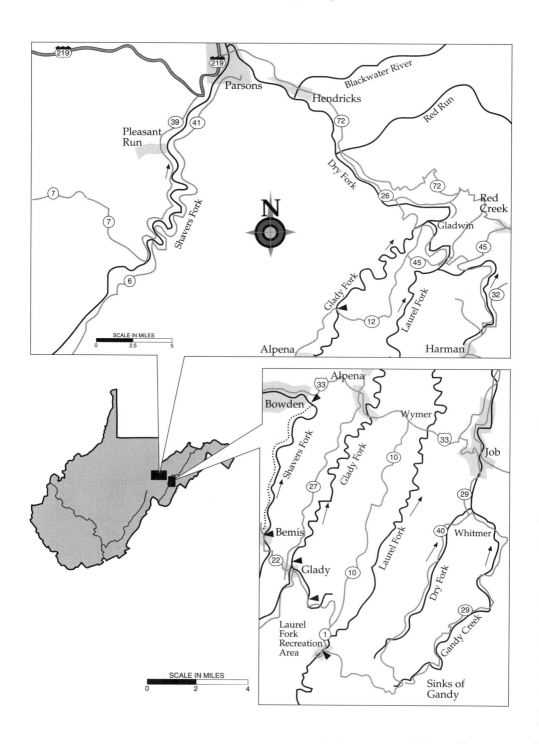

Access

Dry Fork is stocked from the Route 33 bridge at Harman to Red Run (near Hendricks). There many pull-offs along Route 72 east of Hendricks, in Gladwin, and along Route 29 between Harman and Whitmer.

To reach the river, take Route 219 from Elkins to Parsons. Then take Route 72 east to Hendricks. Dry Fork makes an abrupt ninety-degree turn to the south near the junction of Route 32 and Route 72 at Red Creek.

GANDY CREEK

This stream is one of my favorites. A small mountain tributary of Dry Fork, Gandy Creek is no more than twenty-five feet wide. It falls gently from the Sinks of Gandy to the river. Casting and wading are no problem, but there is a lot of open water, and the trout are spooky.

Gandy is stocked from Lower Two Springs upstream to Grant's Branch, near the old Civilian Conservation Corps camp (not shown on map). This reach of Gandy used to support native brook and brown trout and it still has a bona fide population of wild browns and brookies near the headwaters. In the lower reaches, four- to five-pound holdover brown trout are taken annually.

Because of its good water quality, Gandy has been placed in the Blue Ribbon program. Boulders have been placed midstream and in shallow channels to increase holding water and otherwise improve the trout habitat.

Access

Gandy's drawback is that it is very accessible and therefore gets a lot of angling pressure. Take Route 33 east from Elkins. Between Harman and Job, turn right on Route 29, which parallels the water upstream past Whitmer to the Sinks of Gandy.

GLADY FORK

I have not had a chance to do more than look at Glady Fork, but many West Virginians claim its upper reaches provide some of the best trout fishing in the state. Its lower reaches lack cover and warm up during periods of low flow in summer. The stream is stocked from Route 33 east of Alpena downstream eleven miles to Kuntzville.

In spring, native brookies come out of the upper tributaries into the main stem, providing excellent opportunities to catch wild mountain trout. Glady is small but sufficiently open so that casting is easy and wading is not a problem.

Access

To reach Glady, take Route 33 east from Elkins to Alpena. The Alpena Restaurant and Lodge will be on the left. Turn left (north) at the lodge on Route 12 and go approximately five miles. The road will cross the stream in roughly the middle of the nine miles of stocked water.

To get away from angling pressure and fish for some wild trout, turn left onto FR162 before you cross the stream. Drive two miles to a locked gate, park, and walk in another two or three miles. Fish back to the gate.

LAUREL FORK

The Laurel Fork of Dry Fork flows from south to north beginning on Middle Mountain just south of Spruce Knob. From its origin on private land, it flows into federal land—the Laurel Fork South Wilderness Area. The entire stream is as picturesque as any in the state. There are high mountain meadows with beaver ponds and wild brookies.

David Thorne, an angler who has fished in West Virginia for many years, likes to fish the Laurel Fork as it begins to descend the mountain. There are deep pools, undercut banks, logjams, and rootholds, all providing cover for wild and holdover trout. The WVDNR and the West Virginia council of TU both stock fingerlings in Laurel. The stocking is the occasion of their annual fall council meeting at Shot Sherry Cabin on Spruce Knob.

The Laurel Fork Wildernesses are bisected by FR423 and Laurel Fork Campground, a USFS facility. The campground access area is stocked by the WVDNR in spring and fall. Downstream from the campground are larger pools holding big browns. Thorne's personal best was sixteen inches, but before it broke him off on a roothold, he hooked and got a glance at one more than twenty inches long. Laurel Fork is slippery, so felt soles are advised.

Access

* Take Route 33 to Wymer and turn south on CR10 (also called FR14) for ten miles to FR423. Go left on FR423 one and one-half miles to Laurel Fork Campground. Fish up- or downstream.
* Trout fishing is good downstream to Route 33. Below Route 33, there are large brown trout, smallmouth bass, kayakers, and canoeists.

THE BLACKWATER RIVER

The WVDNR has established a major reclamation project on the Blackwater River in the canyon section from Davis upstream past the mouth of the North Fork. The rehabilitation project includes the Blackwater above and below the falls, in the gorge. (This area is not shown on map.)

In 1996, brown trout were stocked in this section for the first time. According to Ray Menendez, the WVDNR fisheries biologist, anglers who fished the water that season were pleased with the fish they caught in the fall. Charlie Heartwell predicts that by the year 2000, the Blackwater will again have the great hatch of green drakes for which it was famous fifty years ago!

Currently, the Blackwater is regulated as a Catch-and-Release stream from the Route 29/1 bridge in Blackwater State Park downstream three and one-half miles to its mouth on the North Fork of the Potomac.

Access

Getting into the gorge to fish is tough going. It requires walking on top of (or falling through) mountain laurel and rhododendron. The best way in is to enter below the falls and walk downstream. The route is not for the faint-hearted or those with bad knees!

Contact the WVDNR directly for updates on stream reclamation and advice about access. There are tentative plans for trails into the area.

To reach Blackwater Falls State Park, take Route 33 to Harman. Turn left onto Route 32 to Davis. At Davis, take CR29 and follow signs to the park.

IF YOU GO . . .

Baltimore is about 250 miles from Elkins, West Virginia. Take I-70 west to Hancock, Maryland, then take I-68 west to Keysers Ridge, Maryland. Go south on Route 219 to Elkins. Washington, D.C., is 200 miles from Elkins. Take I-66 west to I-81 south to Route 55 to Seneca Rocks, then west on Routes 55/33 to Elkins. Pittsburgh is about 160 miles. Take I-79 south to Route 33 east to Elkins.

Tackle Shops and Guides

Evergreen Fly Fishing Company. Clarksburg. Frank Oliverio, guide. (304) 623-3564.

Fastwater Flyfishing School. Harman. On the Dry Fork at the junction of Route 33 and Route 32. Michael and Enoch Snyder, proprietors. (304) 227-4565.

Upstream Anglers. Morgantown. Paul Kurincak, proprietor. (304) 599-4998.

Mike Cumashot. Valley Head. Experienced angler and guide. (304) 572-3416.

Canyon Rim Outfitters. Davis. Especially knowledgeable about the Blackwater Canyon area. (304) 259-2236.

Paul Fowler. Guide. P.O. Box 435, Thomas, West Virginia 26292.

Where to Stay

Alpine Lodge. Alpena, near Bowden. Centrally located to many trout streams: fifteen minutes to Glady, Laurel, Seneca, and Dry Fork. Restaurant and coffee shop. Private baths. Inexpensive. (304) 636-1470.

Blackwater Falls State Park. Big public lodge catering to families. Rooms, cabins, and campsites. Call (304) 259-5216.

Brookside Inn. Route 50 (George Washington Highway), Aurora. Breakfast and dinner included (optional). Wondrous food for the discriminating, healthy palate. Moderate. (304) 735-6344.

Cheat River Lodge. Near Elkins. Inexpensive. Also available: private cottages with hot tubs. (304) 636-2301.

Tunnel Mountain B&B. On the lower slope of Cheat Mountain, four miles east of Elkins. Paul and Ann Beardslee, proprietors. Caters to anglers. Inexpensive to moderate. (304) 636-1684.

The Econo Lodge, Days Inn, Best Western, and Super 8 chains are all represented in Elkins. 1-800-CALL-WVA.

Camping

Blackwater Falls State Park. Cabins. (304) 259-5216.

Judy Springs Campground. Seneca Creek Wilderness Area. Call the District Ranger. (304) 257-4488.

For additional campgrounds: 1-800-CALL-WVA.

For information on camping in the Otter Creek or the Seneca Rocks National Recreation Area, call the U.S. Forest Service in Elkins. (304) 636-1800.

Where to Eat

Cheat River Lodge. Near Elkins. Restaurant and bar overlooking the lower Cheat. Good food. Inexpensive. (304) 636-2301.

C. J. Maggie's American Grill. Elkins. Inexpensive. (304) 636-1730.

The Front Porch Restaurant (and Country Store). Seneca Rocks. A fine place for a lunch break while fishing the North Branch of the Potomac. Inexpensive. (304) 567-2555.

The Sunken Garden. Elkins, in the Days Inn. Chinese food in the Mountain State. Inexpensive. (304) 637-7315.

There are numerous eateries in Elkins, and local general stores have good sandwiches.

Resources

Elkins-Randolph County Chamber of Commerce and Randolph County Convention and Visitors' Bureau. (304) 636-2717.

West Virginia Department of Natural Resources. Elkins. Stream conditions and licenses. (304) 636-1800.

All tourist inquiries: 1-800-CALL-WVA.

CHAPTER 24

Eastcentral West Virginia II: Shavers Fork of the Cheat River and Its Wild Trout Tributaries, Seneca Creek, and the North Fork of the South Branch of the Potomac River

SHAVERS FORK OF THE CHEAT RIVER

One year, my first trout of the season was a fat fourteen-inch rainbow taken from the Cheat River. I was fishing the upper Shavers Fork in front of the Cheat Mountain Club, a one-hundred-year-old private lodge turned rustic resort. Henry Ford, Thomas Edison, and Harvey Firestone were among its guests in the 1920s. The setting could not have been more ideal: a stretch of sparkling water at the foot of a terraced lawn shaded by old sweeping pine trees. I imagined a butler standing on the bottom step of the terrace, taking an old gent's rod with one hand and extending a julep with the other.

The Shavers Fork originates on the north side of Snowshoe Mountain (Cheat Mountain). It is joined by Second Fork, which flows off Bald Knob, the second highest point in the state. Above Cheat Bridge, the stream is usually referred to as upper Shavers. It lies in a high drainage basin bordered on the west by Cheat Mountain ridge and Back Mountain to the east.

From Cheat Bridge downstream to Route 33 at Bowden (not shown on map), the Shavers Fork is well stocked and heavily fished. The most popular area is near Bemis.

By the time the river reaches Bowden, it is often referred to as the Cheat, but in reality it is the lower Shavers Fork. The Cheat proper begins at Parsons (in Tucker County) at the confluence of Shavers Fork and the Black Fork. (The Blackwater River and Dry Fork join to form the Black Fork.) From there, the Cheat flows north into the Lake Lynn Dam impoundment in Point Marion, Pennsylvania, creating Cheat Lake near Morgantown. Just downstream of the lake, the Cheat empties into the Monongahela River, flowing north to Pittsburgh.

The upper Shavers Fork has had problems resulting from acid precipitation and acid mine drainage. However, the mines are now closed, and the WVDNR is reclaiming fifty miles of Shavers Fork from Old Spruce to

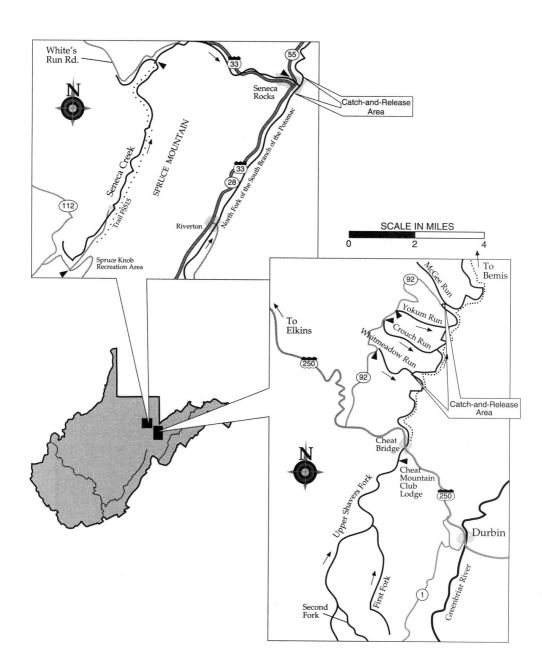

the Stuart recreational area. Several tributaries have been treated with limestone to correct the pH level and sweeten the water.

Situated in the Monongahela National Forest, the water at Cheat Bridge is about fifty feet wide. The streambed is slick, and a wading staff and cleats are advised during spring runoff. You can reach the water at the bridge. Wild rainbows and brown trout can be found above the bridge.

A five-and-one-half-mile stretch of the upper Shavers Fork is stocked and regulated as Catch-and-Release ("Fish-for-Fun" in West Virginia). The stretch begins at Whitmeadow Run and continues downstream to the mouth of McGee Run. According to West Virginia outdoor writer John McCoy, this water nourishes a stupendous green drake hatch late in May. McCoy says the spinner fall has to be seen to be believed.

The tributaries of upper Shavers were the first in the state to benefit from limestone treatment under the Blue Ribbon Program. For a number of years before 1986, the WVDNR found no trout in these little streams. A year after they were treated with limestone, fingerling trout were stocked. Within another year, the trout population had taken hold and was reproducing. According to fisheries biologist Ray Menendez, by 1990 a full-scale trout fishery was in place.

Access
  • Native wild trout tributaries and Catch-and-Release area. Take Route 250 south from Elkins thirty miles to the top of Cheat Mountain. Turn left on FR92. The streams are listed with mileage on signs at the turnoff onto FR92: Whitmeadow—5, Crouch—7, Yokum—8, McGee Run—10. These roads provide access to the Shavers Fork River in the Catch-and-Release area. This is the most accessible wild trout water in West Virginia. The little streams produce numerous brook trout early in the season and remain cool in summer. July and August fishing can be very productive—a rare opportunity in West Virginia.
  • Cheat Mountain Club Lodge. Continue past FR92 and cross the Cheat River Bridge. Turn right at the sign for the Cheat Mountain Club Lodge and ask permission to fish. The lodge owners control a two-mile stretch of private water managed for Catch-and-Release and allow fly anglers access.
  • Stocked section near Bemis. Take Route 33 east from Elkins and turn right (south) onto Route 27 to the village of Glady. At Glady, the road forks; bear right on Route 22 to Bemis, the nonvillage that Jim Martin calls "the definitive end of the road in a state full of dead ends!"

The river is stocked with browns and rainbows for twenty miles from Bemis downstream to Stuart Park. There are no roads between the two points. A railroad bed provides a good hiking trail for anglers. Drop down to the water at the mouths of the tributaries. Anglers should not be surprised to see something round and woolly in their peripheral vision— this area has one of the largest black bear populations in the East!

SENECA CREEK

Seneca is said to be the best wild trout stream in West Virginia. It is never stocked, and it holds wild rainbows and trophy brookies. As might be expected, it is not easy to reach and therefore not heavily fished. Like Laurel, Seneca is in a wilderness area. It requires a long hike to reach the stream. The Seneca experience fulfills the trout angling image: stillness, remote beauty, and lots of birds and other wildlife. The mouth of Seneca is on the North Branch of the South Fork of the Potomac River.

Access

• Take Route 33 east from Elkins, cross the bridge over Dry Fork, and stay on Route 33 for twelve miles to White's Run Road. Turn right on White's Run Road. The stream runs along the road for two miles.

• To fish a more remote area, take White's Run Road to FT515, called the Horton Trail. Hike south on the trail to the creek. It is about three miles from the forest service gate at Seneca (at the mouth of White's Run) to good fishing. The quality of fish and the falls of Seneca will make the hike worthwhile. I did best below the falls.

• From the south, enterprising anglers can hike in to the remote Judy Springs campsite on Seneca Creek. To do so, continue up Gandy Creek on Route 29, turn left on FR1 and left again on FR112. Go about one mile on FR112, and look for parking on the left and a sign pointing to Judy Springs Campground three miles down the trail. Walk down this trail, called the Seneca Creek Trail or FT533, to Judy Springs Campground.

THE NORTH FORK OF THE SOUTH BRANCH OF THE POTOMAC RIVER

More than a decade ago, the U.S. Soil and Conservation Service provided the WVDNR with $50,000 to improve habitat on a long stretch of the North Fork that had been decimated by a flood in 1985. Channels were created, and boulders were put into the water. Stream deflectors were built. The results were new hiding places and holding water for trout. According to the DNR, the fishery has now fully recovered.

The three-quarter-mile Catch-and-Release stretch of the North Branch is part of this restoration effort. The reach is behind the Seneca Rocks Visitors Center and is at its most productive at the mouth of Seneca Creek. If the trout aren't cooperating, you can amuse yourself watching the climbers hanging from Seneca Rocks several hundred feet overhead.

Access
From Elkins, take Route 33 east to its intersection with Route 28 at Seneca Rocks. Park at the Visitors Center to fish the Catch-and-Release stretch. The entire river—from Riverton downstream to one-half mile above the confluence of South Branch near Cabins—is stocked. This water can be reached by parking along Route 28, which follows the river.

IF YOU GO . . .
Elkins is about 250 miles from Baltimore, 200 miles from Washington, and 160 miles from Pittsburgh. From Baltimore, take I-70 west to Hancock, then use I-68 west to Keyser's Ridge. Go south on Route 219 to Elkins. From Washington, take I-66 west to I-81 south to Route 55 southwest to Seneca Rocks, then west on Route 55/33 to Elkins. From Pittsburgh, take I-79 south to Route 33 east to Route 219 south to Elkins.

Tackle Shops and Guides
Mike Cumashot. Valley Head. Experienced angler and guide. (304) 572-3416.

Evergreen Fly Fishing Company. Clarksburg. Frank Oliverio, guide. (304) 623-3564.

Elk River Trout Ranch. Monterville, at the headwaters of the Elk River. Tackle, fee fishing for kids (and for trout to take home), and year-round cabin rentals. (304) 339-6455.

Where to Stay
Cheat Mountain Club Lodge. Near Durbin. Very attractive old hunting lodge atmosphere. Private rooms and baths. Moderate to expensive. (304) 456-4627.

Richard's Inn. Route 219/250, Huttonsville (between Elkins and Valley Head). This old-fashioned Victorian country inn is a winner in all respects. It serves two meals a day (plus a picnic lunch), has a good wine list, and rents nicely furnished, spacious rooms with private baths. Moderate to expensive. 1-800-636-7434.

Yokum's Motel. Seneca Rocks. Adjacent to the North Fork of the South Branch of the Potomac. Inexpensive. (304) 567-2351.

Also use the list of lodging and restaurants in chapter 23.

Camping
  Tygart Valley Campground. Huttonsville. (304) 335-2997.
  For additional campgrounds: 1-800-CALL-WVA.

Where to Eat
  Cheat Mountain Club Lodge. Near Durbin. Good food and wine in an atmospheric setting. Moderate to expensive. (304) 456-4627.
  Richard's Inn. Route 219/250, Huttonsville (between Elkins and Valley Head). Excellent service, food, wine list. Moderate. 1-800-636-7434.

CHAPTER 25

Central West Virginia I:
The Elk River, Slaty Fork of the Elk River,
and the Back Fork of the Elk River

Many forward-thinking West Virginians see fishing, skiing, and other tourist attractions as the best solution to the state's economic problems. Others maintain a take-it-or-leave-it (and we'd rather you left) attitude, determined to their bone marrow to keep the state unspoiled by tourists. These traditionalists encourage recreation, but of the home-grown variety.

In Webster Springs, the nearest town to the Elk River, the biggest event of the year is the Annual Webster County Woodchopping Festival, a celebration of the timbering heritage of the Webster County hills. Competitors come from as far away as Australia, England, Oregon, and New Zealand. Side attractions include muzzle loading, horse pulling, ax throwing, tobacco spitting, sheep shearing, and horseshoe pitching. The State Turkey Calling Championship is held here, and the Paul Bunyun [sic] Pedal Tour Bike Race has recently been added to the roster. The festival takes place over Memorial Day weekend, creating a gridlock of vehicles worthy of wide berth.

The Friday before the holiday weekend, Keith Comstock, owner of Cranberry Wilderness Outfitters, drove me on a day-long tour of trout streams in the Gauley and Elk River watersheds. We had lunch at Myrl's Dinner Bell in Webster Springs and then took Bergoo Road (Route 26) out of Cherry Falls to the hamlet of Bergoo. In Bergoo, I was introduced to Carol, an enterprising woman with a cottage industry. Carol's shop is in the back room of a badly lit, sparsely stocked store. There she handsews custom Gore-Tex fishing and hunting clothes. Vests can be ordered in bright orange for anglers who fish during hunting season or in a variety of camouflaged patterns. The hunting coats are exceptionally warm and sturdy.

Carol's order spike is filled with so many slips that I guessed it would be two seasons before an order could be filled. Carol said not so; she has a number of seamstresses on her payroll. The establishment is known as Carol's Variety Store. It also carries flies from Charlie's Charmers and Woodie's! Carol will rent you a log cabin at a very reasonable price. I often meet people like Carol in West Virginia. It's why I go back a lot.

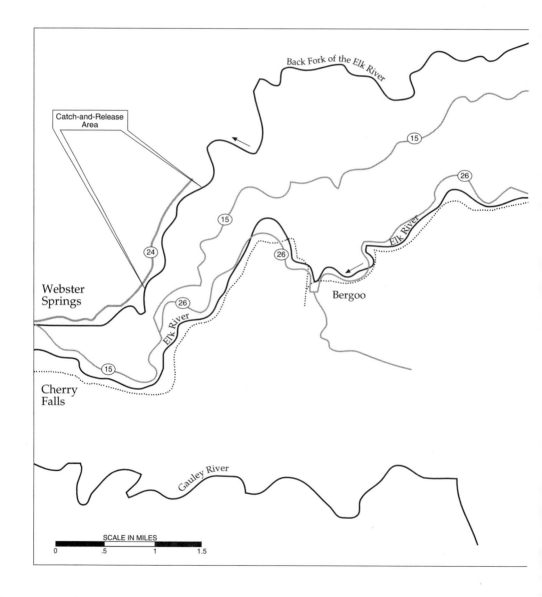

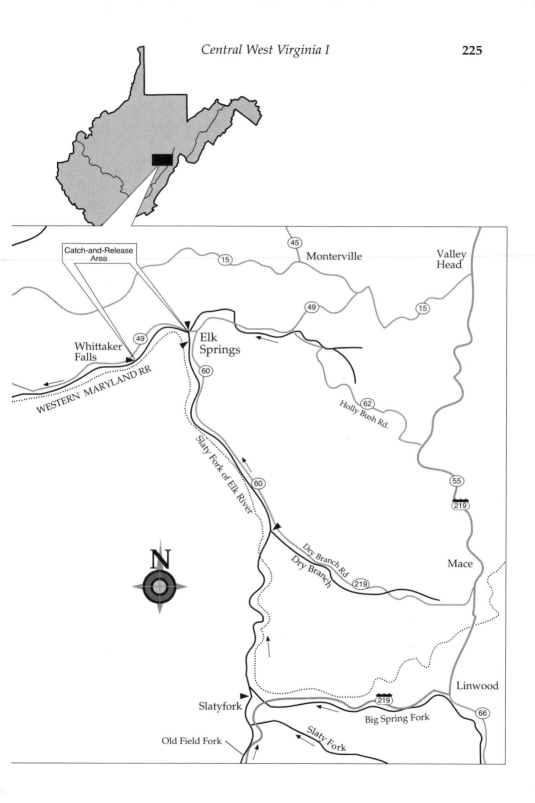

THE ELK RIVER AND THE SLATY FORK OF THE ELK RIVER

Many West Virginia trout anglers agree that the Elk River is currently the best trout stream in the state. Its sizable water flows through limestone and is rich with a variety of hatches, it fishes well year-round, and has withstood floods and other catastrophic events over critical periods of time. Because it is fed by cold springs at Elk Springs, the water remains pleasant all summer, and there is significant natural trout reproduction in good years.

I fished the Elk one Sunday in May with David Keene, a Washingtonian who spends weekends at his house on top of Point Mountain. Keene used to frequent the special regulations section of the Back Fork of the Elk, but now, he says, the Elk main stem fishes so well and receives so much less pressure that he prefers to fish it.

It was a humid, damp afternoon—the kind where I ooze sweat after walking twenty-five feet in waders and constantly have to wipe fogged eyeglasses. We fished the water below the railroad bridge at the coal yard near Elk Springs. We cast diligently for some time without a hookup. Casting was not a problem, but I couldn't find a fly in my arsenal to interest a fish. The river simply wasn't fishing well on this occasion, we concluded, but David (and many others) have very good days on this water. He catches large browns on a regular basis, preferring to walk well beyond the bridge past easily accessible water.

The upper reaches of the Elk, usually called Slaty Fork, result from the confluence of three primary tributaries (Big Spring Fork, Slaty Fork, Old Field Fork) at the hamlet of Slatyfork. These streams are fed by high-quality limestone aquifers in Pocahontas County. The Slaty Fork proper begins downstream of Beckwith's Lumber in Slatyfork.

There are five miles of quality wild trout water below Slatyfork that hold brook, brown, and rainbow trout. The only access to the water is along a railroad track that more or less follows the course of the stream. There are currently no regulations on this water.

The final mile of this stretch dries up during the summer. However, the water continues underground for several miles through limestone caverns, reemerging at Elk Springs as the clear, cold, nutrient-rich stream now called the Elk River.

A two-and-one-half-mile Catch-and-Release section begins at Elk Springs (below the Elk River Trout Ranch) and continues to the Rose Run Bridge just above Whittaker Falls. This stretch has all kinds of productive trout water: deep runs, riffles, pocket water, and pools. The water quickly develops into a sixty-foot-wide river that runs strong after heavy rains. Pull off near the railroad tracks and look for riffles emptying into slow pools. This is the area I fished with David Keene. Use a wading staff when the water is high; otherwise, the footing is good.

DOUGLAS LEES

Slaty Fork of the Elk River

Local TU members, landowners, and the WVDNR work to provide quality year-round angling on Elk. Good fishing is not limited to the Catch-and-Release areas. Wild and holdover fish can be found as far downstream as Webster Springs. This unregulated water is a resource for fly anglers after the spring stockings, when put-and-take anglers end their season.

Access
* To reach Slaty Fork (upper Elk), take Route 219 south from Elkins to Slatyfork. Proceed another mile to Beckwith Lumber Company and take a secondary road to the right (beside the lumber company) to a sign that reads, "Do Not Go Beyond." Beckwith Lumber leaves room for a few cars to park at the tip of its access road. Anglers should walk down the railroad tracks to fish.
* To reach the Elk main stem, take Route 15 east from Webster Springs three miles and turn right onto Route 26, Bergoo Road. After about five and one-half miles, you will come to the K&N Campground. Continue along the road, and the Elk River will be on the right. Park where you can find access to the water. This section is regulated as Put-and-Take, but it provides good sport after the spring stockings.

- To reach the Catch-and-Release section, take Route 15 west from Valley Head about three miles. Then take Route 49 (Valley Fork Road) off Route 15 east of Monterville. Go to the junction of Valley Fork Road and Elk River Road at Elk Springs. If you go right you will come into a big rail yard for a coal company. Although it looks like a dead end, continue on and park at the railroad bridge fifty yards beyond the coal yard.

Or, take Route 219 south to Mace and turn right on Dry Branch Road to its junction with Elk River Road.

THE BACK FORK OF THE ELK RIVER

The Back Fork is a beautiful stretch of water. Once I saw it, I understood why local fly fishers and the WVDNR chose this water for special regulations. The stream is shaded by pines and hemlocks. The water is about thirty feet wide, spilling over huge boulders into dark green pools. It's one of those scenes in which photographers use long exposures to make the whitewater look like cotton candy. This is big pocket water interrupted by long deep runs and riffles.

The stream can be very slippery, so use a wading staff and cleats or felt soles early in the season. So frequently do local fly anglers come here that some maintain semipermanent parking places reserved by stools on the banks!

Access

To reach the Catch-and-Release section, take Route 219 south from Elkins to Route 15 west (just north of Valley Head). Take Route 15 west to Webster Springs, and then take a right on Back Fork Road (CR24). The Fish-for-Fun area begins two miles upstream from Webster Springs at the Bennett Avenue bridge and extends another four miles upstream. There is a deeply rutted road that branches off Back Fork Road near the lower end of the stretch and parallels the stream to its upper end. Four-wheel-drive vehicles with high clearance are advised.

From the south (Richwood), take Route 20/55 to Webster Springs and follow directions above.

The Back Fork is also stocked from Webster Springs upstream one-half mile immediately below the Catch-and-Release area and again in a half-mile stretch below Sugar Creek. In these reaches, Put-and-Take regulations apply.

IF YOU GO . . .

From Washington or Baltimore, the trip takes about four and one-half to five hours.

From Washington, take Route 50 (or Route 66) west. Then pick up either Route 55 off I-81 south of Strasburg or Route 28/220—off Route 50 at Junction. Then take Route 55 west until it becomes Route 33 into Elkins.

From Baltimore, take I-70 to Frederick, then take Route 340 south to Route 7 west (near Winchester) to Route 50 west. Turn south on Route 28/220 at Junction to Route 55. Follow Route 55 west until it becomes Route 33 to Elkins. Alternate route: Take I-70 to Hancock, Maryland. Then take I-68 west to Route 219 south to Elkins.

Take Route 219 south from Elkins to Huttonsvile and Valley Head. Turn right on Route 15 west to Webster Springs.

From Pittsburgh, the trip is also about four and one-half hours. Take I-79 south. Turn east on Route 33 at Buckhannon to go to Elkins, or turn east on Route 15 to Webster Springs.

Elkins is 60 miles north of Webster Springs.

Tackle Shops and Guides

Appalachian Outfitters. Mill Creek. Sam Knotts, co-proprietor. Off Route 219 in Mill Creek. (304) 924-5855,

Carol's Variety Store. Bergoo. Flies from Charlie's Charmers and Woodie's. Custom-made fishing vests and hunting coats. A must-see stop-off! (304) 949-3437.

Mike Cumashot. Experienced angler and guide. (304) 572-3416.

Elk River Trout Ranch. Monterville, at headwaters of the Elk River. Fee fishing for Idaho rainbows. Cabins for rent. (304) 339-6455.

Elk Mountain Outfitters. Slatyfork, at Big Springs Corner (Routes 219 and 66). This is primarily a ski outfitter (for Snowshoe Mountain) and sportswear store. It has some fly-fishing tackle and flies. Casting lessons and equipment rental. (304) 572-3000.

Evergreen Fly Fishing Company. Frank Oliverio, guide. Clarksburg. (304) 623-3564.

Where to Stay

Webster Springs, Slatyfork, and Huttonsville are all convenient for anglers fishing the Elk River.

Cardinal Inn B&B. Route 219, Huttonsville. Moderate. (304) 335-6149.

Elk River Touring Center. Slatyfork. Caters more to skiers than fly fishers. Moderate. (304) 572-3771.

Hutton House. Huttonsville. Twenty-six miles from Snowshoe Mountain. Lauretta Murray, proprietor. Six rooms with private baths. Moderate. (304) 335-7601.

The Inn at Snowshoe. Slatyfork, at junction of Routes 219 and 66. Moderate. (304) 572-2900.

Richard's Inn. Route 219/250, Huttonsville. Twenty-two miles south of Elkins and twenty miles north of Snowshoe Mountain—about midway between Route 15 (the turnoff to Webster Springs) and Elkins. This restored Victorian house has thirteen guest rooms (and suites) with private baths. Restaurant, wine list. Moderate to expensive. 1-800-636-7434.

Slatyfork Farm. Slatyfork. B&B, campground, cabin rentals. Very nice restored farmhouse in a mountain valley. Moderate. (304) 572-3900.

Valley View Motel. Mill Creek. At the junction of Routes 250 and 219. Inexpensive. (304) 335-6226.

Mineral Springs Motel. Webster Springs. On the banks of the Elk River. Inexpensive. (304) 847-5305.

Nakiska Chalet. On a mountainside near Valley Head. Moderate. (304) 339-6309.

Camping

Elk Springs Campground. Elk Springs. Call the Elk Springs Country Store & Trout Ranch. (304) 339-2474.

For information on state campgrounds, call 1-800-CALL-WVA.

Where to Eat

Elk River Touring Center. Slatyfork. Moderate. (304) 572-3771.

Richard's Inn. Route 219/250, Huttonsville. This Victorian country inn serves breakfast and dinner and can provide a picnic lunch. Caters late dinner for anglers. Moderate. 1-800-636-7434.

Hamricks. Webster Springs. Country cooking. Inexpensive. No reservations.

Myrl's Dinner Bell. Webster Springs. Country cooking. Inexpensive. No reservations.

The Restaurant at Elk River. Route 219, Slatyfork. Moderate to expensive. (304) 572-3771.

CHAPTER 26

Central West Virginia II: The Cranberry River (including Dogway Fork and the North and South Forks), the Williams River, and the North and South Forks of the Cherry River

In a state that could win a national championship for its unusual place names, the Nicholas-Webster County area near Richwood and Webster Springs would take the gold. There are hamlets named Carl, Mace, Mingo, Muddlety, Pickle Street, and Camden-on-Gauley. Not to mention streams like Dogway, Houselog, Birch Log, Lick, and Big Beechy and people called Oakey, Ova, Hickle, Beulah, and Myrl. In West Virginia, these monikers ring true as the sap in their roots. Ask anyone local—there's always history in the name.

Richwood, the biggest town in the Cranberry River area, also has the distinction of being the ramp capital of the world. Ramps are wild leeks found in the West Virginia mountains in the spring. Because Richwood ramps are among the best, the Feast of the Ramson is celebrated every year in early April. The event is a modern version of the old Ramp Feeds of frontier days.

Keith Comstock, owner of Cranberry Wilderness Outfitters, was my host on the Cranberry River and other streams in the Gauley River District. Keith is the nephew of James Comstock, the noted West Virginia humorist and publisher of the *West Virginia Hillbilly,* one of the finest weeklies in the mid-Atlantic, until his death in May 1996. The Comstocks have owned land in West Virginia since 1800, when Keith's great-great-great-grandfather, William Comstock, stopped and stayed instead of continuing to the Ohio frontier.

According to Comstock, the Gauley River watershed, which includes the Gauley River, the Elk, the Cherry, the Cranberry, and the Williams Rivers, has some of the best-quality waters in the state. There is very little acid mine drainage, but some of the rivers, notably the Cranberry, have been impacted by acid precipitation. In the 1950s, there were fifty-four species of aquatic life in the Cranberry. By the 1980s, pollution in the form of acid rain had reduced the number to four. By the mid-1990s, it had recovered enough to hold sixty-five species.

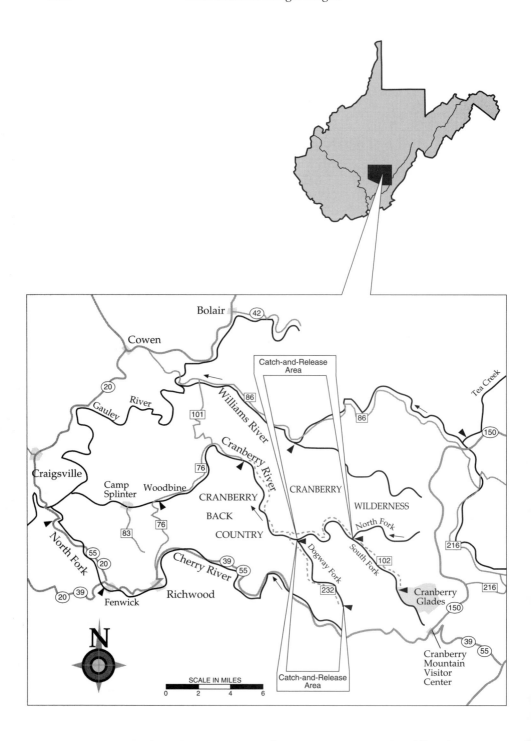

THE CRANBERRY RIVER (INCLUDING THE DOGWAY AND THE NORTH AND SOUTH FORKS)

The Cranberry was exceptionally renowned and productive from the 1940s until the late 1950s, when acid precipitation degraded the water quality. Between the late 1950s and 1991, the Cranberry was barren—sterile, beautiful, and sad.

Still a gem to behold, the river is as clear as a spring and a little bit yellow. The streambed is lined with rocks and pebbles tinted the color of butterscotch candy. In late May, I could see to the bottom of the water throughout the upper section. Its grade is very gentle, and casting and wading are easy. There are plenty of trees to cast shade over the water. You can easily walk to the water from the wide dirt track that runs the length of the upper section. Many anglers use mountain bikes to reach their favorite sections, because no motorized vehicles are allowed in this backcountry area.

My brother Dick McIntosh and I had the good fortune to travel the upper Cranberry by mule taxi. Our mule, a pony-sized bay named Jack, pulled four of us in a bright-green-and-yellow buckboard the sixteen-mile length of the upper section. The total load must have been nearly five hundred pounds, but it never fazed Jack.

Jack's best pace was a brisk trot, and he maintained it down the track, his long, bunny-like ears upright and forward. When the mule was called by name, one ear dropped slightly and turned around, listening for more. After about twenty minutes, Jack began to get anxious, whinnying and neighing, looking for his customary companion mule. We discovered this was Jack's inaugural solo trip. He tried to slip his traces at one point but was quickly corrected by driver Jeromy Rose, now the mayor of Richwood. (Jack's behavior has since reformed, and he travels willingly by himself. At the time, Rose was mid-campaign, with little time for mule training.) A striking young man with olive skin and a long jet black ponytail, Rose made trout a political issue. One of few who believe that tourism and planned growth will *not* wipe out rugged pride and individualism in the Mountain State, Rose is intent on stream reclamation and wild trout projects. He is a champion of limestone efforts and Catch-and-Release regulations. He believes that the trout fishing will provide Richwood with a much-needed source of income from appropriate tourism.

A few miles from the trailhead, Jack the mule was halted so that we could examine what Comstock calls "the Giant Rolaid," the large limestone mill near the mouth of the North Fork of the Cranberry. A substantial trough diverts acidic water from the North Fork through limestone slurry and returns sweetened water (at a higher pH level) to the river. This is the largest of the DNR's limestone plants.

Our first angling stop was the South Fork of the Cranberry, a small stocked stream that also holds a population of wild trout. Casting is limited on the South Fork, except near its mouth. But I was never challenged because Oakey, one of our guides, had unwittingly bicycled off with my rod when he left to prepare lunch. I watched my brother land a couple of small fish.

After a picnic at the Tumbling Rock Creek shelter, I spent several hours fishing alone on the upper Catch-and-Release water. I caught a few small browns, but I didn't see as many fish as I had hoped for. A few sulphur duns appeared now and then, but there was no significant hatch activity. When I stopped to turn over stones, their undersides were as clean as their tops. No nymphs!

Fisheries biologist Ray Menendez explained that the increase in the number of acid-sensitive insects (mayflies and caddis—bugs that do not tolerate acidic water well) has been slow on the Cranberry. However, each year, samples are more encouraging, and the river now contains a number of holdover trout. The first trout old enough to spawn in the river did so in 1996. Menendez believes the upper Cranberry has a good chance of developing a population of streambred trout, but doubts the lower end, which is recovering as a smallmouth bass stream, will ever do so.

Menendez reported extraordinarily good fishing on the Cranberry in August 1996. He camped out late in the month and took a large number of seven- to fourteen-inch trout using a small Parachute Adams fly in the mornings and an elk-hair caddis during the day. While he was fishing, a black bear stole his afternoon snack—a cantaloupe—from his camp and came back the next evening looking for a second.

The main stem of the Cranberry is stocked from its mouth (at the Gauley River) upstream twenty-two miles to the confluence of the North and South Forks. Except for the Catch-and-Release areas, it is regulated as a Put-and-Take fishery.

THE DOGWAY FORK

Menendez is pleasantly surprised at the tremendous response of the Dogway Fork to limestone treatment. He explains that the stream, where a few acid-tolerant brook trout used to be collected in summer, has shifted to alkaline pH levels, and trout now reproduce here. The insect population is also more plentiful than ever. Forty- and fifty-fish days are not unusual on Dogway.

Dogway Fork has one of only three Fly-Fishing-Only regulated areas in West Virginia. From its mouth at the Cranberry for its entire length, Fly-Fishing-Only regulations apply. Access is on foot only. Take FR232 from the mouth of the stream on FR76, or from the trailhead near Cranberry Glades.

THE NORTH AND SOUTH FORKS

The North Fork of the Cranberry is sterile until one-quarter mile above its junction with the South Fork at the beginning of the main stem. This final quarter mile benefits from the limestone mill and is regulated as a Catch-and-Release area.

The South Fork of the Cranberry is managed as a Put-and-Take fishery and is stocked from the main stem upstream two and one-half miles to Little Red Run. Access the South Fork by foot from the Cranberry Glades parking area or by using FR102 into the Back Country Area. The stream is rich with bugs and fish. Do not ignore it in the face of its more glamorous cousins (such as Dogway).

Access and Regulations

The sixteen-mile dirt road through the upper section of the Cranberry forms the border between the Cranberry Back Country and the Cranberry Wilderness Areas. No motorized vehicles or equipment are permitted in either area, and no camps or fires are allowed in the Wilderness Area. Access is on foot, bicycle, or by the Cranberry Wilderness Outfitters' mule taxi.

On the main stem of the Cranberry River, Catch-and-Release regulations apply from:

- The confluence of the North and South Forks of the Cranberry downstream 4.3 miles to the bridge at Dogway Fork. Access is by foot on FR102 from the Cranberry Glades Parking area or from FR76 (above Richwood).
- In Nicholas County, from the Woodbine Recreation Area downstream 1.2 miles to Camp Splinter (at Jakeman Run). Access this section from FR76.

THE WILLIAMS RIVER

The Williams River is managed as a Put-and-Take fishery. It joins the Gauley near Cowen. The main stem picks up its flow from Tea Creek (above FR86 in the northeastern part of the district), from the Middle Fork (which originates near FT271 and FT272 west of the Highland Scenic Highway [Route 150]), and from the Little Fork.

The Williams is a bigger river than the Cranberry and is more difficult to wade early in the year. The water runs very high in the spring, making it unruly to fish when other waters are at their prime. It increases in width —from thirty to fifty feet—after the Middle Fork enters at FR231 and FR86, and big pools make good fishing into the summer.

Menendez says that water quality on the Williams is decent, and there is a good population of brown trout above Day Run Campground. The best fishing on the Williams is often in July and August, when the terrestrials are very popular with the trout and the stream is pleasant for anglers to negotiate.

Recently, a Catch-and-Release regulated section has been added to the Williams. It extends two miles downstream from the mouth of Tea Creek. This stretch can be accessed from FR86. There is good pocket water here, as well as deep shoots and pools. Try it in the summer when fish are looking for terrestrials.

The Williams is stocked from Coal Tipple (below Laurel Run) upstream twenty-two miles to the low water bridge above Day Run Campground.

Access
• The upper reaches of the Williams can be reached through the Handley Public Hunting and Fishing Area off FR216 and FR86. Turn off Route 219 at Edray onto CR17 west, and follow it to FR86 and the water. This is small water but good fishing—mostly for browns that reproduce in the upper Williams.

• FR86 can also be accessed from Route 150 (the Highland Scenic Highway) about one mile above Tea Creek. Tea Creek is somewhat acidic (hence its name) but nonetheless has a population of wild brown trout.

THE CHERRY RIVER
The Cherry runs through the town of Richwood. It can be accessed from a number of pull-offs along Route 20/55 west of Fenwick. This is friendly water, only about thirty feet wide above Richwood and no problem to fish or wade.

The primary threats to the Cherry are the common West Virginia foes: acid rain, acid mine drainage, and clearcutting. Also, it is heavily fished, because it is stocked along Route 20 from Richwood seven miles downstream to its mouth at the Gauley River. The main stem of the Cherry can also be fished conveniently from behind the Methodist Church or the post office in Fenwick (a hamlet outside of Richwood). Fish are taken there all summer long, and smallmouth bass come up to spawn.

The lower Cherry (upstream from Craigsville) fishes well in the summer. Try standard terrestrials (especially grasshoppers), and attempt to seduce one of the large holdover browns that lie there.

The Cherry River TU chapter is working to reclaim the river; however, habitat and water quality need more improvement before in-stream reproduction can take place and Catch-and-Return regulations are appropriate.

The North Fork of the Cherry
This stream lies in its own intact watershed. The trees are seventy or more years old, because the area hasn't been logged since the 1920s. There are

no houses along the North Fork and there is no development. The only deterrent to quality water is acid rain in the runoff from Bear Run, a good-sized tributary. The Cherry River chapter of TU is working to install limestone tumblers and correct the pH in the tributary, thus enhancing the water quality. The WVDNR has this stream high on its list of those to next receive limestone treatment.

The North Fork is stocked from one mile above Richwood upstream ten miles along Route 39 to the bridge at Carpenter Run. It can be found from any one of a number of pull-offs along the road.

The South Fork of the Cherry

This stream has had little negative impact from mining. It runs behind the town of Richwood along a dirt road that can be found—if you know the area—behind the Richwood Junior High School football field. Comstock says there are wild browns here.

The South Fork is stocked from one mile above Richwood upstream nine miles to Cold Knob Fork. I advise a visiting angler to accompany a local friend or guide. There are private properties where the landowners are not only unfriendly, but just plain hostile. I was advised not to fish from Weaver City to Handlefactory Hollow—a hillbilly stronghold of the most predictable kind.

The stream fishes well through July. In rainy and stormy periods, it rises soon but recedes as quickly.

Laurel Creek, another tributary of the Cherry, is worth fishing in the Saxman's Hollow area. This little stream holds wild brown trout. Take the first left after the bridge in Fenwick on Laurel Creek Road (CR39) and stop and fish wherever you like.

IF YOU GO . . .

From Washington or Baltimore, the trip takes about five and one-half hours. Take I-81 south to I-64 west. Exit at Sam Black Church and take Route 60 northwest to Charmco. There, turn north on Route 20, which joins Route 39 east at Nettie. Take Route 39 east to Richwood, or turn north on Route 20/55 to reach Webster Springs. From Pittsburgh, the trip is about five hours. Take I-79 south to Route 19 south. Then take Route 55 east at Muddlety to Richwood.

Nonanglers will find much to do in the Richwood area. The Highland Scenic Highway (Route 150) leads from Richwood to Route 219 on Elk Mountain (about forty-five miles). The Cranberry Glades botanical area is one and one-half miles off Route 39/55—one-half mile west of the Visitors Center. This fascinating 750-acre cranberry bog and tundra is worth a short walk along a handicapped-accessible boardwalk before hiking (or mule taxiing) down FR102 to fish the Cranberry River.

You can visit Hillsboro, Pearl Buck's birthplace, or the Falls at Hills Creek (twenty miles east of Richwood off Route 39/55). These are the second highest falls in West Virginia. But in my opinion, the next best thing to fishing is hiking the trails in the Cranberry Back Country and Wilderness Areas.

Tackle Shops and Guides

Cranberry Wilderness Outfitters. Richwood. Keith Comstock, proprietor. Destination fly shop, mule buckboard taxi, and fly-fishing trips on the Cranberry River. Guided wade trips on the Elk, Williams, Cherry. 1-800-848-8390.

Mike Cumashot. Experienced angler and guide.

Elk Mountain Outfitters. Slatyfork, at Big Springs Corner (Routes 219 and 66). (304) 572-3000.

Where to Stay

Four Seasons Lodge. Richwood, on the Cherry River. Inexpensive. (304) 872-7400.

The Watergate Inn. Richwood. A favorite of truck drivers. Will do in a pinch. Inexpensive. (304) 846-2632.

The town of Summersville is located twenty-five miles west of Richwood. Numerous motel chains are represented there, and there are also B&Bs and restaurants. For more information, call the Summersville Area Chamber of Commerce at (304) 872-1588.

Camping

Holly River State Park. Near the Williams River. Cabins. (304) 493-6353.

Cranberry backcountry camping. Elkins. U.S. Forest Service. (304) 636-1800. There are a limited number of campsites along the Cranberry and the Williams Rivers that can be reserved for no charge on a first-come, first-served basis.

There are numerous other camping opportunities in the area: Summit Lake Campground, Camp Splinter, Tea Creek Campground, and Cranberry Campground. Call 1-800-CALL-WVA for more information.

Where to Eat

Barrenshees Restaurant and Tavern. Just outside of Richwood. Good steaks and sandwiches. Caters to anglers. Moderate. (304) 846-2808.

C&S Restaurant. 46 Oakford Avenue, Richwood. Family restaurant. Good for breakfast or lunch. Inexpensive. No reservations.

Richards Inn. Route 219/250, Huttonsville. This Victorian country inn serves breakfast and dinner and can provide a picnic lunch. Caters late dinner for anglers. Moderate. 1-800-636-7434.

Hamricks. Webster Springs. Country cooking. Inexpensive. No reservations.

Myrl's Dinner Bell. Webster Springs. Country cooking. Inexpensive. No reservations.

The Restaurant at Elk River. Route 219, Slatyfork. Moderate to expensive. (304) 572-3771.

Resources

Richwood Chamber of Commerce. (304) 846-6790.

Gauley District Ranger Station. Monongahela National Forest. (304) 846-2695.

West Virginia Tourist Office. 1-800-CALL-WVA.

Index